SAP
NATION
3.0

Manifest Destiny

VINNIE
MIRCHANDANI
author, *Silicon Collar*

SAP Nation 3.0

For information about this title or to order bulk copies and/or electronic media, and for SAP and other IT advisory services, contact:

Deal Architect, Inc.
P.O. Box 262262, Tampa, FL 33685
www.dealarchitect.typepad.com
vm@dealarchitect.com
1-813-884-4908

ISBN: 978-0-9909296-9-7   eBook
        978-0-578-44619-6   Paperback

Printed in the United States of America
Cover and Interior Design: 1106 Design
Editing: Mark Baven and Margaret Newman

This book is dedicated to buyers of enterprise technology. They are the unsung stakeholders who pay the big bills and still do the bulk of the work delivering measurable outcomes.

Table of Contents

ACKNOWLEDGMENTS

Even though the title of the book is SAP-centric, I interviewed a wide range of customers, who talked in addition about many other vendors. The customers are listed in Section 0 and their profiles spread through Ch.3, 5, 6 and 7. All were brutally honest about what they did or did not like on their projects. Vendors will cringe when they read some of those comments, but other customers should benefit from their candid feedback. A point worth making is that vendors are likely to home in on the negatives in comments about their competitors. Trust me, all of them have similar warts.

Next, I want to thank Stacey Fish at SAP. While many others at SAP were helpful, she was my go-to contact and arranged for me to talk with several SAP customers and executives. In a world where software vendors only want to publicize positives, she allowed me "unfiltered access" to these executives. I told her to help SAP put its "best foot forward." What I expected was plenty of marketing; what I also got was plenty of conversation and candor.

Similarly, I want to thank Geoff Scott and Tom Wailgum of ASUG. Scott contributed the foreword and Wailgum helped facilitate several customer conversations. I also want to thank numerous SAP observers, including competitors and industry influencers, for their feedback.

Some readers will find the conversations a bit long. Here's the reality — we only ended up using 15–20% of what was in the transcripts. Customers, in particular, like to hear from their peers — the executives who spoke to me at length did so for their benefit.

With every book, I try to leverage evolving publishing technology. This time, Zoom conferencing helped me record conversations, and the Voicea transcription bot, Eva, tried to keep up with all the tech industry jargon. I came to rely heavily on Tina Pham of My Office Owl to provide the human translation. She had to work through multiple accents and acronyms. She was my inspiration for Section 0 called "Do you speak SAPese?" which summarizes some of the burgeoning TLAs common in SAP world and the broader tech sector.

Next, there is the editing and design team. Mark Baven has edited my last several books and did the same admirably for this book. He is a technology editor and thus has an advantage over my wife Margaret Newman, who does a readability review on all my books. Their job was to simplify, as much as possible, complex conversations. The graphics also helped simplify some of the conversations thanks to Brenda Lewis of Lewis Creative Services. Friends like Tom Chimera crawled through drafts of the book. It takes a village to edit a book. As with software, the more scrubbing a book gets, the better is the end result.

This book has many unique nuances. We find few readers eye the front materials, or click through to the footnotes. We ended up dropping the Preface and doing a "mini Preface" in Chapter 1. In my first book, I had over 600 footnotes. This one has fewer than 100. Most attributions are provided in-text.

As usual, Michele DeFilippo, Ronda Rawlins and their team at 1106 Design helped with the cover and book design.

Finally, much to my delight, Amazon continues to push the frontiers of digital publishing. However, over half my books still sell in print format, so thanks to Corporate Graphics Commercial for their contribution on that front.

My style of writing is case study and third-party heavy. I try to keep my own voice to under 15% of every book. As an analyst, I have plenty of opinions but I try to keep them muted in my books. Still, you should blame me for any typos and sections that displease you.

A book is by definition a snapshot in time. Given the change I describe at SAP and the tech industry, I expect to post frequent updates on my blogs.

Westward Ho!

Foreword

∿→

I have the honor to be the CEO of the Americas' SAP Users' Group (ASUG), the world's largest independent group of SAP customers. Vinnie, in his role as industry analyst, and I talk on a regular basis where we share what we are hearing in the SAP universe — and there's always something to talk about. For this book, I introduced him to several of the customers (who are ASUG members) profiled in the following pages. He asked me if I could describe my perceptions of how SAP has changed in the eyes of its customers during the last five years. I joined ASUG in January 2014, and the timing coincided with Vinnie writing the first volume of *SAP Nation*.

In offering my view on SAP's evolution and the ASUG-SAP relationship, it would have been easy to fall into familiar platitudes about the importance of relationship building. Earning trust. Talking openly. Spending quality time with each other.

While those are, in fact, accurate representations of several of the elements used to advance the relationship since I joined ASUG in January 2014, that's not the whole story.

The whole story, actually, starts back in the late 1980s. At the time, this special type of German business software, called SAP, was starting to come ashore at North American companies. And so it went for four businesses in North America, and four people at their respective companies: Shelley Hart, Richard Lloyd, Gregory Horne and Reid Andrews. Their individual tasks were roughly the same: Figure out how to implement and use this SAP software their companies had purchased. These four, one could say, were the modern-day, digital version of the early pioneers.

They hatched a plan to start a user group and met for the first time, in 1991, at the Embassy Suites Hotel in Philadelphia. They were shocked to see 150 people show up. Necessity had once again bred invention, and ASUG was born. By design, the co-founders wrapped their early plans around three pillars — education, networking and influence. And those pillars remain as the bedrock of the organization today.

So when I think about the progression of the relationship between SAP and ASUG, I often liken it to the evolution of enterprise software: We've moved from the siloed, green-screen GUIs of the 1980s to the consumer-grade, interconnected user experiences of the cloud systems today.

Now, I realize there's a monumental gulf between those two user experiences. And the journey we've traveled was not unlike the transition that many of our thousands of members have been on with their SAP systems. This quote by Art Williams is apropos: "I'm not telling you it's going to be easy — I'm telling you it's going to be worth it."

So how have we changed the relationship? As I look back, it all started with basic communication: getting two parties in a room to discuss each of our respective organizational motivations and missions, and customer-centric goals. Ultimately, though, it always came back to the ways in which we both could serve our respective communities, which as you might expect, are nearly one in the same.

We represent SAP customers — they place their trust in us — and we view our role as the independent voice of the SAP customer as paramount. Every conversation at ASUG starts with: How does this help our customer base? If it doesn't help any of them to be successful on their SAP journeys, then there's likely no good reason to move forward. I should say that that's a key message we share with SAP all the time. And it resonates with their leadership.

I believe that the customer relationship with enterprise software is fundamentally different than with other, more tactile products. This software is complex because the organizations that operate it are complex. They operate across vast geographic boundaries among different languages, cultures, practices, processes and regulations — things that are moving, shifting and reshaping all the time. In order for all of this to work, there has to be continuous dialogue and engagement. This is not a motor or a widget that gets installed once and is expected to operate for years. The day this software is implemented it begs to be modified, changed and retooled. That is just the nature of the beast.

As SAP has changed to become more cloud-centric, ASUG has changed, too. We invested in new ways of learning and connecting like-minded SAP customers and partners, and we launched new programs and services all with the goal of helping our customers maximize the return on their SAP investments.

The process has taken time and energy, and key to it has been the involvement of our members, including our 12-person

Board of Directors and more than 300 volunteers. Which leads me to an example from 2017–2018, one that is emblematic of how much the relationship has changed and how it's benefited SAP customers. The topic? SAP licensing and indirect access (IA) of SAP software.

For many years, licensing was a "third rail" topic: look at it, discuss it among yourselves but don't ever collectively — as a customer contingent — touch it. That all changed in 2017, when SAP customer anxiety peaked due to several high-profile lawsuits against SAP customers over IA. ASUG's involvement started with a proactive letter from the global user groups, led by ASUG, to SAP's Executive Board. What followed next was a series of intense but productive discussions — real back-and-forth between SAP customers, user group leaders and SAP executives that soon expanded to customer concerns around sales and audit practices. There were many trips to Walldorf and meetings in Newtown Square. There were weekly conference calls, exchanges of working documents and redefining of long-standing licensing definitions.

Again, it wasn't easy, but the work was worth it. As expected with a topic as complex and ever-changing as software licensing, there's still more to be done. But this engagement exemplifies the new relationship between SAP and ASUG. One that relies on open, customer-centric dialogue and the desire to find mutually beneficial results.

The journey is ongoing, and change is near constant — business demands on technology are ever increasing. There's no doubt ASUG's relationship with SAP will continue to evolve, progress and be tested at times. But we remain steadfast in our belief in the collective power of the network of ASUG members and optimistic about the future for all SAP customers.

As you read this book, you will recognize many of your peers who Vinnie has interviewed. I am encouraged they have shared their candid opinions on a variety of SAP products, practices and partners. I hope their strategies help you shape your own journeys.

And as always, customer stories are the very best way that we as a network learn and progress. I encourage you to share yours — both the good and bad. It's not always easy to do, but it really is important.

— Geoff Scott, CEO, Americas' SAP Users' Group

Tom Sawyer's Fence

⌁⟶

I had expected Hasso Plattner, co-founder of SAP, to be tired. In fact, I suggested we postpone the meeting, but from 25 years of similar meetings, I knew he looked forward to the banter with analysts. For me, the payback usually came from watching public relations jaws drop at something he would say during such meetings. Usually there would be an admonition after the session of "Don't you dare use that!"

This meeting was safe enough — talk of multitenancy, quantum computing, blockchain and microservices. But then he started talking about Tom Sawyer and Peter Pan, two characters who have brought him much joy throughout his life.

He did his best Mark Twain impression in describing how young Tom Sawyer had turned whitewashing a picket fence — a punishment for skipping school — into a group activity. He had conned his friends into thinking it was fun and required a unique skill — "Only one in a thousand, maybe two thousand can do it." He was so convincing that his friends paid him for the privilege of doing that tedious task in the hot sun.

Over the decades, the tale has clearly helped Dr. Plattner motivate customers and employees even when he is making a radical proposal. As he told us in that meeting:

> "Ten years ago, I had an idea which really worked: streamline ERP applications to basically record only transactions. And everything else is then an algorithm to exploit the data. Facebook doesn't know what aggregates are. Why do we have aggregates?
>
> That worked. Many people didn't believe that this could work, especially inside SAP. This freed us completely. Today [with S/4], it's all on-demand. On-demand is much quicker because people are not permanently rolling up and looking at rolled-up data. If they want to change it, it's instant.
>
> That is really gratifying."

The reason I had expected him to be exhausted was because he had led a two-hour keynote on the main stage prior to our meeting. Anyone who has done public speaking knows how much energy that requires. He then had done a one-hour press conference. Sensing his fatigue, I had asked him a softball question on sports technology and he joked about how I always asked him tough questions.

But here was the old warrior, now, talking about more people to cajole and win over. Even if it takes a decade. Even when there is still plenty of cynicism about HANA.

That's when it hit me: Don't write off Dr. Plattner or SAP yet. There's plenty of fight left in this old dog.

Someday soon, I hope to ask him exactly how Peter Pan has helped him through his career.

SECTION 0

Do You Speak SAPese?

I know, I know...

Yes, the ancient Romans did not have a numeral for zero and Wikipedia lists hundreds of languages by country and SAPese is not one of them. And yet …

… trust me, you will likely read this section more than any other. Just scan it for now. It has three resources you should find indispensable:

1) A listing of customer case studies.
2) A sampling of strategies covered in the case studies.
3) A partial list of SAP-related product names and acronyms you will see early and often.

A Tapestry of Customers

The following is a listing of entities profiled in the book. They are presented in detail in Chs. 3, 5, 6 and 7.

I personally interviewed the majority of executives who are quoted. They spent countless hours talking to me, reviewing their audio transcripts and their book profiles. For a handful of other customers, I extracted the text from videos of their presentations at SAP and other events or from their quotes in articles.

Entity	HQ Country	Vertical Focus	Ch.
Accuride	U.S.	Automotive Wheels & Motion Solutions	7
Bombardier	Canada	Aerospace and Railways	5
Bruce Power	Canada	Utilities	7
Carpenter Technologies	U.S.	Manufacturing, Industrial Alloys	6
Cintas	U.S.	Corporate Uniforms	6
CLP Power	China	Utilities	7
Costco	U.S.	Retail, Membership Warehouses	3
EBSCO	U.S.	Information Services	7
Endeavour Energy	Australia	Utilities	5
GEBHARDT	Germany	Internal Logistics	5
Graham Construction	Canada	Construction Services	6
Hoerbiger	Switzerland	Manufacturing, Industrial Valves	5
Johnsonville Sausage	U.S.	Food Processing	6
Kaeser Kompressoren	Germany	Manufacturing, Industrial Compressors	5
Louisiana-Pacific	U.S.	Construction Materials	3
Lufthansa	Germany	Aviation	3

Entity	HQ Country	Vertical Focus	Ch.
Motus Integrated Tech	U.S.	Automotive Accessories	7
Munich Re	Germany	Reinsurance	5
Naturipe Farms	U.S.	Agricultural Produce	6
NETZSCH	Germany	Industrial Manufacturing	6
New England Biolabs	U.S.	Life Sciences, Enzymes	6
Old World Industries	U.S.	Auto Supplies	6
PBF Energy	U.S.	Petroleum Refining	7
Pregis	U.S.	Industrial Packaging	3
Queensland OSR	Australia	Government	5
Rainforest Connection	U.S.	Nonprofit Technology	3
RemIQz	The Netherlands	Sports and Entertainment	5
Roche	Switzerland	Medical Devices, Pharma	5
San Francisco 49ers	U.S.	Sports and Entertainment	5
Sanofi	France	Life Sciences	7
Terumo BCT	U.S.	Life Sciences, Blood-Related	6
Under Armour	U.S.	Apparel and Footwear	7
Unilever	U.K.	Consumer Packaged Goods	7
Waterwatch Cooperative	The Netherlands	Nonprofit	5

A Plethora of Strategies

In the first volume of *SAP Nation,* we had described several strategies that customers were trying out to optimize their SAP investments. They included HP "ring-fencing" SAP with cloud solutions from other vendors, Embraer moving to TPM, AstraZeneca changing its talent model and insourcing more tasks, British Gas adopting more open source and commodity technology, and Microsoft implementing a two-tier ERP model.

In this book, we have classified SAP customers into four broad groups — Risk-Takers, Modernizers, Diversifiers and Bystanders. Across them you will see, in the five years since, that many of those strategies have gone mainstream. So you will see names like Plex, Rimini Street, Salesforce and Workday at many of the customers. In addition, now we see a wide variety of new strategies. Here is a sampling:

- Ring-fencing ECC with many of SAP's own cloud properties, as with SuccessFactors at Terumo BCT and components of C/4 at Pregis.

- Two-tier deployments with SAP ByD and S/4 in their subsidiaries.

- Migration from ECC to S/4 on-premise at Johnsonville Sausage.

- New implementations in the S/4 Public Cloud as at a restaurant chain.

- New implementations of the SAP Analytics Cloud as at the Executive Huddle at the San Francisco 49ers.

- Trying out relatively new on-premise, but impactful SAP functionality like IBP at Louisiana-Pacific.

- Trying out Leonardo ML pilot projects as at Costco and Queensland OSR.

- Developing new ISV functionality on SCP as Vertex has done with their indirect tax app.

- Moving to new licensing and hosting models like Bombardier with IBM.

We also are seeing blends from this growing toolbox of strategies. So, we are seeing companies migrate to newer SAP products and simultaneously shifting to TPM vendors for support of legacy SAP products. GEBHARDT has been implementing a variety of SAP cloud products around its ECC on-prem implementation. Additionally, it has developed a customer portal and set of predictive maintenance services using Leonardo IoT and AIN capabilities.

Given the wide proliferation of products and terminology in SAP World, my firm, Deal Architect, recommends (and often facilitates for clients) an intense offsite meeting to help customers take a fresh look at SAP and the broader market. That confab should cover and assess the fit of many of the strategies above, while also evaluating internal and external talent and fit with emerging technology trends.

Product names and Acronyms

One of the toughest jobs for the team that helped craft this book was keeping up with the relentless flow of product names and acronyms that SAP, Gartner and people like me unleash on the linguistic world. My poor transcriptionist had the challenge of interpreting these terms from interviews in American, Australian, British, Canadian, Dutch, French, German, Indian, South African and other accents. SAP has a longer list, for internal use, of these acronyms. ASUG and other user groups have published their own, shorter versions.

Here is a partial cup of alphabet soup you will encounter in the book:

AFS	Apparel and Footwear Solution	CPG	Consumer Packaged Goods
AI	Artificial Intelligence	CPQ	Configure, Price, Quote
AIN	Asset Intelligence Network	CPU	Central Processing Unit
AMS	Application Management Services	CRM	Customer Relationship Management
AP	Accounts Payable	CX	Customer Experience
API	Application Programming Interface	DMO	Database Migration Option
APO	Advanced Planning and Optimization	DMS	Document Management System
AR	Accounts Receivable	DSAG	Deutsche SAP Anwender Gruppe—German-speaking User Group
ASUG	America's SAP User Group		
AWS	Amazon Web Services	EAM	Enterprise Asset Management
B2B	Business to Business	EC	Employee Central
BOM	Bill of Materials	ECC	ERP Central Component— also conflated with R/3 and Business Suite
BPC	Business Planning and Consolidation	EIM	Enterprise Information Management
BW	Business Warehouse	EPM	Enterprise Performance Management
ByD	Business ByDesign	ERP	Enterprise Resource Planning
C/4HANA	Customer Cloud for HANA, shortened to C/4	ETL	Extraction, Transformation, Loading
C4C	Cloud for Customer		
CAD	Computer Aided Design	GDPR	General Data Protection Regulation—EU legislation
CIO	Chief Information Officer		
CMM	Capability Maturity Model		
CMO	Chief Marketing Officer		

GEF	Geographical Enablement Framework	NBA	Next Best Action
GIS	Geographic Information System	NFV	Network Function Virtualization
GL	General Ledger	PaaS	Platform-as-a-Service
GRC	Governance, Risk and Compliance	PLM	Product Lifecycle Management
GUI	Graphical User Interface	PO	Process Orchestration
		PSA	Professional Services Automation
HCM	Human Capital Management		
HEC	HANA Enterprise Cloud	PUE	Power Usage Effectiveness
HpaPaaS	High-productivity application PaaS		
		R&D	Research and Development
HRIS	Human Resources Information Management— also referred to as HCM	RPA	Robotic Process Automation
		S/4HANA	SAP Business Suite for HANA, shortened to S/4
IA	Indirect Access	SaaS	Software-as-a-Service
IaaS	Infrastructure-as-a-Service	SAC	SAP Analytics Cloud
IBP	Integrated Business Planning	SCM	Supply Chain Management
IDM	Identity Management	SCP	SAP Cloud Platform
IO	Inventory Optimization	SD	Sales and Distribution
IoT	Internet of Things	SI	Systems Integrator
IPaaS	Integration PaaS	SME	Small and Midsized Enterprises
IS-U	Industry Solution—Utilities		
ISV	Independent Software Vendor	S&OP	Sales and operations planning
		SSO	Single Sign-On
KPI	Key Performance Indicator		
		TCO	Total Cost of Ownership
LMS	Learning Management System	TPM	Third-Party-Maintenance and Support—also 3PM
LOB	Line of Business		
MES	Manufacturing Execution System	UI	User Interface
		UX	User Experience
ML	Machine Learning		
MM	Materials Management		

A Tale of Two Continents

CHAPTER 1

The North American
Continent in the 1800s

⌁→

Welcome to the third volume of the continually unfolding saga at the world's largest application software company. When I wrote the first volume of *SAP Nation*, five years ago, SAP looked vulnerable. Besides the runaway costs and massive project failures experienced by some customers, SAP appeared preoccupied with its HANA database and almost bored with enterprise applications. Much more concerning, a wide range of competitors were circling around. Indeed, right after S/4 was launched in early 2015, Dr. Plattner was quoted as saying, "If this doesn't work, we're dead. Flat-out dead. It's that simple."

As this book will show, Dr. Plattner's worst worries have not materialized. S/4 has not been a runaway success but SAP's competition has not exactly gone for the jugular either. SAP's product portfolio and customer base have grown significantly and the stage is set for the next few chapters.

The setting today is similar to that of when the young U.S. nation acquired Louisiana from France in 1803. The real estate doubled but the population was mostly concentrated around the Atlantic Coast. SAP's product real estate has similarly grown, but the majority of its over 400,000 customers are clinging to their previous "homes." Migrating this customer base is SAP's first big opportunity. In addition, an even bigger opportunity awaits. The U.S., energized by a Manifest Destiny call, expanded all the way to the Pacific Ocean.

To understand SAP's bigger opportunity, you have to look back to 2000 when enterprise tech vendors — especially ERP/CRM vendors led by SAP, their systems integrators and other partners — were set to dominate the corporate technology landscape. They had emerged very strongly from the Y2K crisis, and the launch of the EU's common currency promised another bonanza. Instead, their share of the enterprise steadily declined over the ensuing two decades. They missed out on the contract manufacturing of smart products, digital marketing, cloud infrastructure, industrial internet, process automation and several other trillion-dollar markets. Two decades ago, not many of us had heard of Accenture Interactive or Foxconn. Few of us considered Amazon or GE or Alibaba as tech vendors. Few of us would have speculated that Apple, near dead, or Google, not born yet, would have many times SAP's annual revenue. The market is fragmented — waiting for fast followers who missed out on the first wave of opportunities. Could that be SAP? Sea to shining sea awaits across the continent of enterprise computing. Is SAP willing to lead with a similar Manifest Destiny call to motivate customers? Like many historical "empires," SAP's world continues to shift and morph as it racks up "conquests" and "defeats."

Let's first start with a brief history of the North American continent in the 1800s. Let's catalog how a "start-up," the U.S., achieved its radical expansion.

The North American continent in the 1800s

In 1800, the United States, then the original 13 colonies, was a young, skinny country. Two-thirds of the population lived within 50 miles of the Atlantic Ocean. You could have placed bets on who would win the race for North America — would it be the Americans, the Spanish, the British, the French, or maybe even the Russians or the Dutch? Over the next few decades, Americans had the biggest market share.

In 1801, when Thomas Jefferson became the third President of the United States, the majority of the country's population lived between Boston and Washington, DC. Under previous British rule, the Royal Proclamation of 1763 had declared the boundaries of the 13 colonies as the Appalachian Mountains. Any travel or settlement beyond the mountains was considered illegal.

In his inaugural address, Jefferson talked about a nation "with room enough for our descendants to the hundredth and thousandth generation". Free from the British (somewhat — battles would continue for decades after), the Mississippi River now represented the western boundary for the country. Given the strategic importance of the river — and especially that of the port of New Orleans, which was a major distribution node for U.S. products — the U.S. was keen to purchase at least the port from the French. Its previous owners, the Spanish, had revoked some of the free access. The U.S. was offered something much larger. Napoleon's plans to re-establish France in the New World were failing, and in 1803 he offered to sell the entire Territory of Louisiana (not just today's state), totaling 827,000 square miles, for a mere US$15 million.

The U.S., then a fledgling nation, could not afford even that good a deal. It had to borrow money and repay it over the next 20 years. As former Massachusetts Congressman Fisher Ames wrote, "We are to give money of which we have too little for land of which we already have too much."[1] Many thought Jefferson did not have the constitutional authority to execute the treaty. The boundaries agreed upon were vague, and for years afterwards would lead to conflicts with the Spanish and the British.

But Jefferson proceeded with the deal, and the Louisiana Purchase doubled the land mass of the nation. He then sponsored a Corps of Discovery to explore the West. He did not want to lose the race for the fabled Northwest Passage that would connect Europe to Asia. A quarter century earlier, Britain had offered a £20,000 prize for explorers to discover this route.

Meriwether Lewis and William Clark were the leaders on the epic trek of over 8,000 miles, lasting two-and-a-half years, taken by the Corps of Discovery. Jefferson had instructed them:

"The object of your mission is to explore the Missouri River, and such principal stream of it, as, by its course and communications with the waters of the Pacific

[1] https://www.history.com/news/8-things-you-may-not-know-about-the-louisiana-purchase

Ocean, may offer the most direct and practicable water communication across this continent ... Those who come after us will ... fill up the canvas we begin."[2]

That canvas revealed over the next couple of decades a series of battles with the British which could have ended the burgeoning democracy, especially after the British burned down the White House in 1814. It also showed a gradually expanding Union. Indiana became the 19th state in 1816; Missouri the 24th in 1821.

Later U.S. presidents kept adding to the country's real estate. President James K. Polk oversaw in the 1840s the greatest territorial expansion of the United States, including Texas, California and the Pacific Northwest. Polk had to also fight plenty of cynicism about the cost of such expansion, and the political cost of not resolving the slavery issue before taking on more real estate. In 1867, Secretary of State William H. Seward negotiated the purchase of Alaska from Russia. At roughly two cents an acre, it was a steal — given the mining, petroleum and tourism bonanza since then. At that time, however, with the country struggling under debts from the Civil War, it was derided as "Seward's Folly."

The complexity and danger of the Lewis and Clark expedition made it a 19th-century moon shot. Their maps and commentary on various native tribes along the way opened up routes. Wave after wave of pioneers followed west. Many went on the Oregon Trail as mountain men and missionaries, others with the Mormon migration to Utah and the California

---

[2] https://www.pbs.org/weta/thewest/program/episodes/one/corpsof.htm

Gold Rush of 1849. The westward floodgates opened up with the completion of the transcontinental railroad in 1869.

While American leadership arranged for the real estate deals, it took grit and plenty of sacrifice for the population to move west. Wagon trails averaged only 15 miles a day. Covered wagons were too bumpy and dusty, and so most pioneers actually *walked* the hundreds of miles west. They suffered through high winds in the Great Plains, the extremes of the Rockies and hostility from natives. Those who went by steamboat did only slightly better, facing risks of boiler explosions and water hazards.

And yet, there was a westward pull, with a sense that "It's written down somewhere — it's got to be." If people could not see it in the stars, hear it in political speeches or imagine it in their holy books, they did find a pungent coinage in what John L. O'Sullivan wrote in the July–August 1845 issue of the *Democratic Review*:

> "It is our manifest destiny to overspread the continent allotted by Providence for the free development of our yearly multiplying millions."

Jefferson may have thought in terms of hundreds (or thousands) of generations, but he clearly underestimated how quickly the country's people would move west. Within five generations, by the end of that century, the country's citizens were dwelling from "sea to shining sea."

Today, the term "Manifest Destiny" has a checkered image. It evokes confident expansionism but also brings to mind the mistreatment of Native Americans, Black slaves, Mexicans,

Mormons and even Chinese workers who helped build the railroad. It reminds us of the many hardships faced by women, the horror of the Civil War and the near-extermination of the American bison. Many paid a heavy price to make the Manifest Destiny a reality.

However, the 19th century also saw the U.S. transformed into a major granary for the world, and an industrial power. It led to massive creation of wealth — culminating in what Mark Twain called the Gilded Age. Naturalists like John Muir and avid outdoorsmen like Theodore Roosevelt (later president) created a national parks system which is even today the envy of the world. The century also featured the construction of the Erie Canal and the transcontinental railroad — and a vibrant, driven stream of immigrants.

A century after Jefferson, Theodore Roosevelt would become the 29th president of the U.S. In his inaugural address, he pointed to new challenges the country faced. He also summarized the amazing previous century that Jefferson had ushered in and helped the country dream into being:

> "Such growth in wealth, in population, and in power as this nation has seen during the century and a quarter of its national life is inevitably accompanied by a like growth in the problems which are ever before every nation that rises to greatness. Power invariably means both responsibility and danger. Our forefathers faced certain perils which we have outgrown."

In contrast to what Jefferson faced in 1801, the major enterprise tech vendors like SAP, Oracle, IBM and HP were on top of the "continent" of enterprise computing in 2001. Market leadership was theirs to lose, and in many ways that is exactly what they have done: We see a fragmented market, and an opportunity for someone to step up, acquire massive chunks of "real estate" and similarly motivate customers to move "west."

CHAPTER 2

The Enterprise Computing "Continent" in the 2000s

~~→

Most people, even technology veterans, have a hazy notion about what a Gartner analyst does on a day-to-day basis. I certainly did not know what my task list would look like when I joined the analyst firm in 1995. Contrary to myth, analysts actually do not spend much time throwing darts to place tech vendors in Magic Quadrants. Rather, they listen to vendor briefings, they do research, they develop and deliver presentations on market trends. In actuality, they spend most of their time on client queries. Gartner had an elaborate call tracking and scheduling system called GAMEC (a somewhat contrived acronym for Gartner Automated Management of Electronic Contacts) to facilitate 30-to-60-minute consultations with clients.

Erik Keller, a former analyst, who we used to call the "Godfather of ERP," reminisced:

"When I joined Gartner in 1988, a good GAMEC yearly metric for an analyst was between 400–500 inquiries — with only a couple of studs who handled nearly 1,000 inquiries. In the mid-1990s, at a retreat, a dozen or so analysts were awarded a plaque for having over 1,000 inquiries and were teased by most analysts as being in the "needing to get a life" club. Within two years, the new normal was 1,000 inquiries yearly, with our group having the largest load."

By Keller's definition, I did not have a life for the entire time I was at Gartner. Having come from Price Waterhouse where I ran a software intelligence group, I handled many of the ERP software queries around SAP, Oracle, PeopleSoft, JD Edwards and other client/server vendors. Having done multiple implementations, I also handled many of the ERP systems integration queries around Deloitte, IBM and other SIs. In my five years at Gartner, I fielded nearly 7,500 such client calls and meetings. To call the market hot would be a gross understatement.

Beyond providing Y2K relief and preparing companies for the EU common currency, we observed how ERP was allowing companies to replace dozens of departmental applications. We could see how enterprise data and processes were starting to homogenize across the globe. Through most of the 1980s, I had spent many a frustrating hour convincing clients to buy packages, and not write custom code. Now, it was satisfying to see the buy-versus-build pendulum swing decisively to the buy side.

Enterprise tech was flying high. SAP and its peers with their hardware, database and implementation partners had an amazing few years. Yes, business slowed down a bit after the Y2K crisis passed, but enterprises liked many of the results they had seen in their first wave of ERP implementations, and "westward expansion" appeared certain for these vendors.

Yet at Gartner, we were starting to raise red flags. For all the talk of "enterprise-wide coverage" that ERP promised, we had started to identify plenty of areas like CRM, SCM, MES and EPM where specialist vendors like Siebel, i2 Technologies and Hyperion had deeper functionality. In fact, at Gartner we had a field day coming up with new three-letter acronyms. The SIs that implemented those ERP packages made the customer project scope even narrower. They were most comfortable with white-collar accounting, HCM and other corporate areas. They helped very few customers implement functionality on the shop floor, the warehouse, the R&D lab and other operational areas. When you left the manufacturing sector, ERP functionality was particularly shallow. Try supporting utility billing, insurance claims processing, retail merchandising, pricing/promotions in CPG, size and color complexities in apparel and footwear, patient records in healthcare and hundreds of other industry-specific applications.

Few customers understood that ERP was like buying a plane that has a life span of 20 to 30 years and needed constant tuning and refurbishment. Customers had to learn to adjust to waves of "post-live" projects and staffing. There were frequent upgrades, hosting and network investments, and application management contracts. SIs, in turn, were siloed — some could do implementations, but many were not interested in upgrades or infrastructure hosting. Indian providers were better at post-implementation services, could apply CMM Level 5 and Six Sigma continuous improvement mindsets, but they had to learn how to apply that expertise to packages. Their heritage was primarily supporting custom-built systems.

The stage was set for what I described in the first volume of *SAP Nation*: an out-of-control ecosystem and poor quality projects. As the book's back cover summarized:

> "From its humble beginnings in Germany, SAP sky-rocketed to become a global powerhouse and the technology backbone for tens of thousands of enterprises. The economy around it grew even faster, and "SAP Nation" now approaches the GDP of Ireland in size. This book documents both trajectories, based on decades of research and interviews of hundreds of customers, market analysts and competitors. SAP's influence has declined in the last decade, as enterprises invest in cloud, social, analytical, mobile technologies and in custom development of "systems of advantage" in their products, channels and business models. Yet, shockingly, customer spending in SAP Nation remains stubbornly high. The model in the book estimates post-recession investment at more than one trillion dollars (yes!). This book brings out loudly the voice of SAP customers as they cope with this runaway economy."

The Ups and Downs of the Last Five Years

SAP looked vulnerable when I wrote the first volume of this book series, five years ago. Besides the runaway costs and massive project failures at some customers, even more concerning was the fact that the competition was circling around.

Oracle had a decade's lead with its Fusion cloud applications over what SAP was working on — S/4. Microsoft had already invested billions in its Azure cloud data centers, and could have used them to significant advantage in business applications.

Infor had a new management team that was focused on vertical applications for many industries.

Customers were using Workday, Ultimate Software and Salesforce to "ring-fence" SAP, and were deploying lighter cloud applications, like NetSuite, in global, two-tier ERP settings. Those SaaS vendors had introduced the efficiencies of multitenancy to the overpriced enterprise applications market. They bundled software, application management, hosting and upgrades into one contract, which was priced as a per-user service.

TPM vendors like Rimini Street, Spinnaker Support and Support Revolution, with their cut-rate pricing and, especially, their support for customizations, threatened to hollow out SAP's highly profitable ECC maintenance revenue stream.

S/4 has not been a runaway success, but SAP's competition has not exactly gone for the kill either.

Oracle continues to dominate the database market. By many measures, Oracle should also by now be the undisputed leader in enterprise applications. When Computer Associates was on a buying spree in the 1990s, Oracle founder Larry Ellison had commented something along the lines of "every ecosystem needs a scavenger." Starting with the PeopleSoft acquisition in 2004, Oracle went on its own binge, claiming it was time for "industry consolidation." They made significant acquisitions: PeopleSoft for US$10.3 billion, NetSuite for US$9.3 billion, Siebel for US$5.6 billion, Micros for US$5.3 billion and Hyperion for US$3.3 billion. Other investments like i-flex, Portal, Primavera and Retek brought them banking, telecom, complex project and retail functionality, respectively. By 2006, they were loudly celebrating that they were "halfway there" in developing their own next-gen Fusion cloud applications.

For all that, Oracle has done just OK. It has seemed more intent in going after Amazon for the cloud infrastructure and platform markets (in turn, Amazon is going after Oracle's database dominance and claims to have migrated more than 100,000 databases to AWS[3] and also plans to rip out Oracle from the infrastructure than runs its massive retail business). Oracle's cloud infrastructure has yet to pay off; the top four cloud infrastructure players — Amazon, Microsoft, Google and Alibaba — have nearly three-quarters of that segment sewn up. Around business applications, Oracle has focused more on Workday and Salesforce with HCM and CRM functionality, and not so much in manufacturing or other verticals where SAP has greater presence. Its NetSuite acquisition, while helping it increase traction with SMEs, has also led to some brand confusion around its own Fusion product line. While it has launched an exciting autonomous version of its database — which it calls "self-driving" — it has not brought a similar level of automation to enterprise applications.

Microsoft reclaimed the title of world's most valuable company, unseating Apple, in late 2018.[4] However, that was driven primarily by growth in its Azure infrastructure and its productivity products, and not enterprise applications. Bob Evans, who writes the *Cloud Wars* blog, commented how he feels "strongly that it is Microsoft and not Amazon that rules the roost in the cloud."[5] Looking back, it certainly had the opportunity to be a dominant application vendor. In 2000, Microsoft acquired Great Plains (they could not have anticipated this book's westward

---

[3] https://aws.amazon.com/dms/
[4] https://www.wsj.com/articles/how-microsoft-quietly-became-the-worlds-most-valuable-company-1543665600
[5] https://cloudwars.co/worlds-top-5-cloud-vendors-cloud-wars/

theme, and changed the branding of that product to Dynamics GP), which was then a leading mid-market ERP vendor, though primarily in the U.S. In 2002, it acquired Navision, which was a leading ERP vendor in Europe. Both of these companies had made their own acquisitions, and Microsoft found itself with four ERP products — Great Plains, Navision, Axapta and Solomon. In 2003, Microsoft began working on an effort that was code-named Project NextGen, which later morphed into Project Green to rationalize this portfolio. Four years later, Mary Jo Foley, one of the best-known Microsoft media followers, summed it up: "Microsoft must rue the day a few years back that the company hatched the 'Project Green' idea."[6]

Microsoft has largely focused on the CRM segment of the application market, which included making a sizable investment in LinkedIn. Their One Microsoft initiative has allowed them to showcase a wide range of assets to large customers. However, they have executed inconsistently around business applications, depending more on resellers for SME opportunities.

Infor had once been called an "ERP graveyard," as it had accumulated a wide portfolio of ERP brands including Baan, Lawson, MAPICS, SSA Global Technologies and Systems Union. Those in turn had made acquisitions of their own (such as Lawson buying Intentia). Since they arrived in late 2010, Infor CEO Charles Phillips and his team have been reinvigorating the company. Phillips called Infor "the world's largest start-up." The differentiation Infor promised was CloudSuite for 15 verticals (such as automotive, fashion, and food and beverage) and three horizontals (including corporate and human capital management).

---

[6] http://www.zdnet.com/article/microsofts-project-green-still-alive-and-kicking/

Since then, in spite of sizable investments from Koch Industries and others, Infor has not delivered on its promise of vertical functionality. Larry Ellison famously derided dot-com start-ups as "features, not products" in the early 2000s. Infor, similarly, has features for a number of industries but has not delivered operational "books of record" such as merchandising for Retail or electronic patient records for Healthcare. In fairness, neither has Ellison's Oracle delivered cloud-based vertical functionality. Readers can find more detail on the Oracle Fusion, Microsoft Project Green and Infor CloudSuite projects in Chapter 4 of SAP Nation 2.0.

Salesforce has become an 800-pound gorilla in the CRM sector, but could have additionally turbocharged its Force.com platform to bring a more vibrant ecosystem with industry functionality to its customers. Even after a decade, the platform has had limited success, especially when you compare it to the vibrancy of platforms like the Apple iOS store or Fulfillment by Amazon, which were started around the same time. There are now 20 million Apple developers creating apps and in another big milestone, Apple has since paid out over US$100 billion in revenue to those developers.[7] As much as 90% of certain product categories, such as patio furniture, sold on Amazon come from third parties.

Workday has been very disciplined about concentrating on accounting, planning and human-capital functionality. Many customers would like it to expand both geographically and into industry functionality. Instead of building vertical functionality (like it started to for the higher education market), Workday is

---

[7] https://9to5mac.com/2018/06/04/apple-hits-500-million-weekly-app-store-visitors-100b-payouts/

encouraging customers to stay with legacy systems and reach into vertical data with its Prism Analytics tool. In the past, that has required customer investment in data geeks and ETL and other data manipulation tools. Workday is simplifying the effort to allow end users to handle it themselves. It is also rolling out its own platform to allow customers and partners to develop their own vertical and other extensions. It is also investing in promising start-ups through its US$250 million Workday Ventures fund.

"Wait a minute," you may say. As of early December 2018, Salesforce and SAP were almost equal in market capitalization. From a Wall Street perspective, it is hard to not bet on Salesforce, Workday or ServiceNow — and other pure-play cloud contenders, which have been growing robustly within their niches. Indeed, Aneel Bhusri, CEO of Workday, told me in 2017:

> "We have a lot of HR in front of us; we have a lot of finance in front of us … In our previous company [PeopleSoft] at our size, the market was beginning to slow down and consolidate. In this case, it feels like the market is actually accelerating."

But from a customer perspective, you cannot run your enterprise without order entry, billing, manufacturing, logistics and industry-specific functionality. There is only so much you can do with Salesforce, Workday or ServiceNow. You can do even less if you are outside the U.S.

It is a bit like the aviation sector. Southwest is one of my favorite airlines. I love it because it flies nonstop to over 30 cities from my home airport in Tampa, FL. But flights on its 737s average only two hours, and that cannot take me on global treks. If I lived in Germany, Singapore or Rio, it would be even less interesting because Southwest has chosen to stay focused on the North American market.

Partly because SAP's competitors did not target it aggressively enough, and partly because its own cloud acquisitions and developed products afforded it a shield, the company has come through the threat of the last five years relatively unscathed. In fact, when you look at the mob of strong competitors that it had to fend off, it has done remarkably well. In those five years, SAP's customer count has actually increased by 50%. Wall Street has not been as generous to SAP as it has to cloud vendors, but the existential threat that SAP faced has passed.

Can't See the Forest for the Trees?

Anshu Sharma, formerly of Oracle and Salesforce, is now chairman and co-founder of Clearedin. He is also an investor in several start-ups like Workato and Nutanix. He describes the dramatic change in the definition and expectations of "software":

"If I look back 20 years when I got into the software industry, we were very focused. Companies like IBM, Sun and Dell shipped computers and companies like Microsoft and Oracle basically shipped shrink-wrapped software and their job was done. Then, someone like Accenture or Infosys would come in and basically help implement and maintain the software.

Very clear. Very simple. When we look back at that past now from the outside, there weren't too many complications.

When I switch forward and I look at today's Silicon Valley, I would argue more than half of the people I know amongst my peer group are not in what we would have called the "software industry." These are people who work at Airbnb, which is basically a hotel company disguised as a software company. You could argue Salesforce and Cornerstone resemble "old" software like Oracle, because they are still selling "software" as a service.

You look at a company like Pluralsight which is a learning management company that went public last year. Are they a content company selling education or are they a software platform? Is Twilio a telco masquerading as a software company because, at the end of the day, that's what they do, they enable me to call people? If you look inside the company, they're largely an asset-less or telco-less telco, just like Uber is a cab-less cab company. They don't own any telco infrastructure. What they really do is put an API in front of their solution and make it super easy for any of us, tomorrow, to turn on 50 phone lines and start taking or making calls.

If you think about companies like WhatsApp or services like Telegram, Signal, and even iMessage from Apple, you don't really need a centralized company doing all of the work. A lot of the work is often done device-to-device. In fact, WhatsApp was famous for having only 15 people when it got acquired for over US$10 billion. Then you can include companies like Tesla where something as basic as your regenerative braking system is actually a software job. What we've done is expand the definition of what a software engineer is allowed to do.

Today software engineers are applying their skills to solve bigger and bigger problems ranging from healthcare to space to self-driving cars. I would say we exceeded my wildest dreams of what a software engineer could attempt and I'm a pretty optimistic person."

In the meantime, SAP and its competitors, who mostly focused on each other while trying to one-up each other and impress Wall Street, have missed out on large opportunities emerging around them.

After I left Gartner, I did not focus just on ERP or related SIs. I had a front row seat on many of the new, emerging markets. In 2003, after a failed attempt at a dot.com, I started an advisory firm — and also started to blog about technology trends. My Deal Architect blog focuses on enterprise tech — so I could see what SAP, Oracle, Salesforce, Workday, etc. were doing. My *New Florence* blog, on the other hand, had a broader STEM focus and covered innovations in health tech, clean tech, consumer tech and other emerging markets. In 15 years, it has catalogued over 6,000 posts. It also gave me the ammunition to write a number of books that profiled hundreds of case studies. This contrast between the two blogs allowed me to see several trillion-dollar markets emerge — markets that SAP and its cohorts have mostly ignored. The following eight subsections will describe those missed opportunities:

Smarter Products

At the 2011 Consumer Electronics Show in Vegas I noticed Walgreens, the pharmacy chain, show off its mobile refill application. Whirlpool demonstrated its Duet washer/dryers with LCD screens and various laundry apps. Nike introduced its GPS-enabled Sportwatch developed in collaboration with the navigation vendor TomTom. Ingersoll Rand showed off features around its Schlage home security and Trane thermostat products.

Ford chose to unveil its all-electric Focus Electric at CES rather than at the traditional car launch showplace, the Detroit Auto Show, which was scheduled only a week later.

This "aha!" experience became the nugget for *The New Technology Elite* (Wiley, 2011), based on my asking, "What's going on here? These companies live far from Silicon Valley and are known as retailers and auto companies. Why are they competing for booth space and geek attention at CES with technology vendors?"

The book showcased an exciting new generation of smart products and services which leveraged sensors, software and satellites. The new rock stars were product designers like Jony Ive at Apple and Yves Behar at fuseproject. Contract manufacturers like Foxconn, Jabil and Flex and design firms like IDEO benefited from this massive new market. But SAP, Oracle or even Indian outsourcers? Not so much. In fact, based on the attractive design increasingly prevalent in consumer markets, enterprise vendors started to be scrutinized for their own poor UX. I have heard Mark Hurd, co-CEO of Oracle, quantify these trends in his presentations. He says consumer spend on technology has caught up to enterprise spend — annually about $1 trillion each — and is growing faster. Even more dramatically, over 80% of enterprise tech is spent on keeping the lights on, not innovation. In contrast, the consumer is getting almost pure innovation for her dollar. What Hurd does not point out is that because of Oracle or at his previous company, HP, or peers like IBM, software maintenance, EDS outsourcing and other charges have been large contributors to the enterprise tech stagnation. They have delivered nowhere near the price/performance improvements or innovation that consumer tech has seen. It should be no wonder then that the tech the consumer gets at home on Sunday night or in her car is so much better than what she finds at work on Monday morning.

Similarly, IT outsourcing started to be benchmarked against contract manufacturing. Apple has stayed loyal to Foxconn through multiple releases of iPods, iPhones and iPads. This continued in spite of sweatshop accusations, employee suicides and explosions in its Chinese facilities. Most companies like to balance sourcing between company-owned and outsourced plants, and certainly across different geographies. Apple has been willing to take the risk of putting its eggs in the Foxconn basket. Why? Because Foxconn has delivered billions of high-quality Apple devices under intense delivery and secrecy pressures. The BOM for their products changes every few weeks. Even in a country like China which has to encourage labor-intensive models with its large population, Foxconn has been rolling out robotics and precision equipment. Why should IT outsourcers not step up to similar quality, speed and cost benchmarks?

CX — Customer Experience

The definition of the CRM market has grown in scope to include sales force automation, customer and field service, digital marketing, e-commerce and other customer-facing activities. Salesforce has become the 800-pound gorilla in this segment, but Microsoft, Adobe, Oracle, ServiceNow, Zoho, Hubspot and many other specialists offer a rich array of choices in the market. When SAP launched C/4HANA in 2018, it made this increased scope one of its biggest priorities.

CRM vendors are increasingly focused on the entire customer experience and CX is the new byword for this sector. And yet, most of these vendors (with exceptions like the Adobe Advertising Cloud and Salesforce's Datorama acquisition) have

missed out on some of the biggest budgets in the CX segment —
digital advertising. In the last two decades, digital advertising
has grown from near zero to over US$200 billion a year. Eons
ago, digital advertising had already outrun print advertising.
Now it has overtaken TV advertising. Marketers have moved to
programmatic advertising, where machines, more than humans
buy advertising. Google, Facebook and increasingly Amazon
are the big beneficiaries of this shift in marketing dollars.

With the massive growth in digital advertising, Accenture
Interactive has aggressively acquired digital agencies, making
it now the biggest agency in the world. It would be fair to say
it is influencing CX trends as much, if not more, than the early-
generation CRM software vendors did. Accenture Interactive has
little in common with its traditional IT outsourcing brethren.
Accenture's IT outsourcing group does plenty with ERP and
CRM software vendors. Interactive does fine on its own and
includes as clients the chief marketing officers (CMOs) of over
three-quarters of the Fortune 100. It does not need to chase
after Salesforce or SAP.

Industrial Internet

In 2012, I saw Jeff Immelt, then CEO of GE, on stage, dwarfed
by one of his GEnx aircraft engines, which power many of the
newer Boeing 787 Dreamliners. It was an effective way to present
the fact that the engine is a massive data source and generates
over a terabyte of flight data a day. He was introducing GE's
vision of the Industrial Internet. At the same event, I saw a
panel of executives describing opportunities in what has since
become more commonly known as IoT, or the Internet of Things.
Present were Deborah Butler, then CIO of Norfolk Southern,
who described fuel efficiencies from smarter locomotives and

preventative maintenance supported by track-side sensors. Michael Niggli, then President and COO of San Diego Gas and Electric, described smart meters and transformers. Gary Beck, Alaska Airlines' VP Flight Operations, described how the massive data that aircraft already create — performance feedback, G-forces related to turbulence and other airspace data — could be shared across the friendly skies rather than being summarized via air traffic controllers.

GE had talked about the "power of 1%": 1% in fuel savings for aviation and utilities, 1% of productivity improvement in healthcare, 1% reduction in oil and gas cap-ex, etc. The payback they described was in the hundreds of billions. You hear similar claims from IT vendors, but somehow the tiny 1% factor made it much more believable.

GE has since had a meltdown over issues related to its capital and power business units. But the presentation I saw back in 2012 woke up executives in every industry to the power of listening to machines. And it has led to a batch of smaller vendors like C3 and Uptake as well as other industrial asset companies like Siemens and Schneider Electric that are helping companies realize that 1% payback. GE had invested in Pivotal, a unit of Dell, as part of its Industrial Internet efforts, leaving SAP, IBM and other enterprise vendors to play catch-up.

Cloud Infrastructure

In *The New Polymath* (Wiley 2010), I described Amazon's service-oriented architecture journey as follows: "Having invested in these services and found a much cheaper and scalable Linux-based infrastructure, Amazon decided to 'externalize' the Web services starting in 2002." For that book, I had also interviewed Mike Manos, then with Microsoft, about the "pyramids of the 21st century." These were massive Microsoft Azure data centers that would drive the emerging world of cloud computing. The book was written in 2010, but the investments had started much earlier.

In *The New Technology Elite*, I profiled Facebook's pioneering Prineville, OR, data center that opened in 2011. It delivered 38% energy efficiency and 24% lower costs compared to contemporary facilities. It had a PUE of 1.07 — one of the best in the industry. Even more impressively, in a secretive, competitive industry, Facebook shared specifications and mechanical designs of the data center in what has since blossomed into the Open Compute Project community.[8]

In the first volume of *SAP Nation*, I had interviewed Andre Blumberg, CIO at CLP Group, which is the leading investor-operator in the Asia-Pacific electric power sector. I caught up with him for this book to discuss recent trends in his sector and his booming region. Here is what he had to say about the public cloud infrastructure market:

> "We've seen very strong and strict data and cyber security regulations in China, so you've got to move everything back to operate within China if you want to stay compliant, especially for critical infrastructure industries like energy and utilities. So, I can't work with a company that only has a data center in Singapore and Melbourne, right? So, I need to have facilities in China mainland, in Australia, in Hong Kong, and Vietnam, and so forth. That requires a provider being focused, and I don't see, in Asia Pacific, anyone other than AWS and Microsoft at this stage plus local players like Alibaba and Tencent.

---

[8]   https://www.opencompute.org/

Google is coming, but cautiously and on the back of strained relationships with the region, especially in China … I don't see SAP or Oracle anywhere. Oracle has built some facilities in Australia, but with nothing on the roadmap for greater China. So I think it's just a complete waste of investment for these software companies to invest in public cloud infrastructure … just give that up and don't go into this very capital intensive data center play that's just going to consolidate more. Instead leverage the existing hyper-scale public cloud providers."

I hear similar comments from CIOs around the world: Facebook, Amazon and Microsoft — who expected them to be so innovative with data centers and networks? This was a technology infrastructure market where IBM, HP with EDS, Oracle with Sun and large telcos around the globe had dominated. They should have been leading this market in investment and innovation, but for years chose not to do so. Now they are playing catch-up, and others should give up as Blumberg suggests.

Vertical Markets

Consultants still glibly invoke Borders and Blockbusters as examples of companies that did not survive market turbulence, but the reality is you can find examples in most industries. Most sectors have gone through massive changes since the turn of the century. For example, utility billing today has to account for net metering, as consumers and farms supply power back to the grid from their solar panels and wind turbines. Utilities have also moved from scheduled to predictive maintenance, as their large assets now generate operational data. Even their assets and service crews reflect the shift away from coal plants to wind farms. Retailers cannot survive without e-commerce and related reverse-logistics. Shop floors and warehouses are now dotted with robotics, 3-D printers, wearables and sensors.

SAP started off the new century well by investing in various verticals. It launched industry-specific functionality for utilities, oil and gas, apparel, footwear and many other sectors. But it was also losing interest in business applications. Massive investments in platforms like NetWeaver, tools like HANA and analytics acquisitions like BusinessObjects opened new revenue streams, but also distracted it from a business applications focus, especially in industry-specific functionality.

Other enterprise vendors have similarly struggled to keep up with these industry changes. This has led to opportunities for new players. For example, the fintech sector is fragmented with many promising start-ups and offerings from large institutions like Goldman Sachs, but little from the major application vendors. In China, mobile apps like Ant Financial's Alipay and Tencent's WeChat now enable half-a-billion Chinese people to access a dizzying array of financial services to make payments, get loans, monitor investments and credit ratings, pay for taxis and book travel.

Among SAP's competitors, Infor looked most promising as it leveraged Amazon's cloud infrastructure and invested the savings into vertical solutions for healthcare, retail, hospitality and other industries. A decade later, it can boast an improved look and integration among its large portfolio of products, but it has not delivered "books of record" for industry sectors. Infor has announced plans to go IPO in the near future, and perhaps it will use that additional funding to verticalize. Similarly, Oracle has not moved many of its industry-specific offerings like Retek for the retail sector to the cloud. Interestingly, Oracle had engaged

SAP and won a bidding war for Retek in 2005 in a signal that industry applications would be a focus going forward.

While most industries have seen little investment from enterprise vendors, some others have seen a bit too much focus. This uneven investment is highlighted by Dave Hofferberth, an analyst at Service Performance Insight, who told me that over the last couple of decades he has seen over 100 vendors offer PSA functionality to services firms. In fairness, even product companies were growing services arms and were a new market for that functionality, but that is still quite a concentration of investment dollars when much larger sectors are getting very little in funding. It makes you wonder if technology vendors don't have MBAs or access to strategy consulting firms who can help them do white-space analysis on underserved versus oversaturated market niches.

In October 2018, Oracle co-CEO Hurd predicted that 80% of business applications would be in the cloud by 2025.[9] Today, even after two decades of cloud computing, industry and geographic coverage is spotty — by my estimate, less than 20%. For Hurd's prediction to prove accurate, it will take massive new investments in upgrading industry functionality.

If anything, outsourcers like IBM and Capgemini are better positioned to architect next-generation vertical solutions. They support legacy applications and process outsourcing in a wide range of healthcare, financial services and other markets. And they have started to invest in software solutions — Cognizant has Trizetto for healthcare administration, Infosys has a core banking solution, Finacle, TCS offers BaNCS for insurance markets among

---

[9]   https://dealarchitect.typepad.com/deal_architect/2018/10/oracle-openworld-thoughts-from-afar.html

others. Historically, though, they have been more comfortable selling talent versus packaged software. Vishal Sikka, formerly CTO at SAP tried for 3 years as CEO of Infosys to change that culture with limited success. However, with so much vertical white space outsourcers could easily become tomorrow's competitors.

Digital Transformations

In 2014, I narrated *The Digital Enterprise*[10] for Karl-Heinz Streibich, then CEO of Software AG. In the preface, he wrote: "Throughout the book you will encounter the vision of 'Industrie 4.0' that is driving innovation across a wide spectrum of industries around the globe. You will read about GE's vision of the Industrial Internet and how it will bring massive efficiencies to aviation, utilities, and many other industries. You will discover how banks and insurance companies and oil companies and museums and casinos are innovating using a wide range of other technologies."

Most of the multinational customers we profiled in the book were also customers of SAP, IBM and other large enterprise tech vendors. However, in one chapter after another you read about digital transformations in supply chains, product engineering and various customer-facing areas that were done *without* the help of those vendors.

Most vendors claim to be "digital transformation platforms." But if you do not have product engineering, customer-facing operational capabilities, new business model functionality, etc. then you are likely not facilitating "substantive" transformation.

This was another missed market — customers undergoing transformative digital change.

---

[10] https://www.amazon.com/Digital-Enterprise-Karl-Heinz-Streibich-ebook/dp/B07B75S8TG/ref=sr_1_2?ie=UTF8&qid=1547736660&sr=8-2&keywords=the+digital+enterprise

Changing Man-Machine Mix

In 2016, I described the emerging world of automation in the book *Silicon Collar*. I described how robots, drones, self-driving autos, kiosks, machine learning, 3-D printing, wearables, bots and exoskeletons were changing the nature of work in many jobs in every industry. The pioneering projects I described in the book are being done by customers like Amazon, BP, Disney, UPS and others. Enterprise vendors should have been all over this market as such automation is reshaping logistics, customer service, manufacturing and practically every corporate process.

Most enterprise vendors are now talking about AI and ML, but not automation on the shop floor, in logistics or in the oil patch. Also, if you peel their ML onion, you realize many are merely leveraging voice or image recognition technology from Amazon, Google or Microsoft. When you look at the massive amount of image and vocal-accent data their machines had to be trained on, you wonder where enterprise vendors will get their own training data, given that most of it is squirreled away in on-premise customer data centers. They have been creative with branding — Salesforce with Einstein, IBM with Watson and Infor with Coleman (as in Katherine Coleman Goble Johnson, the NASA mathematician profiled in the movie *Hidden Figures*) — but with limited enterprise impact. Indeed, when Salesforce and IBM announced Einstein and Watson would work together, IBM CEO Ginni Rometty chuckled in an interview with *Fortune* that "It's good comedy."[11]

Outsourcers like IBM with an early lead with Watson and Accenture with SynOps, what is calls a "human-machine

---

[11] http://fortune.com/2017/03/06/ibm-salesforce-partnership-ai/

operating engine", a category of RPA vendors and other robotic, drone, wearable vendors are poised to compete more vigorously for this market where business processes historically defined around human workers will now have to increasingly factor machines.

Open Source Software

Holger Mueller, analyst at *Constellation Research*, has written "Why Open Source has won and will keep … winning."[12] In that post, he explained:

> "Somewhere in the early 2000s, Oracle dropped its multi-year, 1000+ FTE effort of an application server to use Apache going forward. That was my first eye opener, and I was a product developer. The next one came in 2013, in my analyst role, when IBM's Danny Sabbah shared that IBM was basing its next generation PaaS — BlueMix, on CloudFoundry. When enterprise software giants cannot afford to out-innovate open source platforms, it was clear that open source was winning. As of today, there is no 1000+ people engineering effort for platform software that has started (and made public), built in house and proprietary, by any vendor. The largest in house projects that are happening now in enterprises, the NFV projects at the Telcos, are all based on Open Source.
>
> And there certainly is commercial success. IBM bought RedHat for US$32B. Early innovators — (one can

---

[12] http://enswmu.blogspot.com/2019/01/musings-why-open-source-has-won-and.html

argue Open Source started with Hadoop) Cloudera and Hortonworks have just joined forces, and other players are seeing record market valuations (e.g., MongoDB at US$4B+) or exits (e.g., MuleSoft by Salesforce for US$6B). And the next cohort of successful Open Source vendors are in the making — look at Confluent, HashiCorp, Kong to just name a few."

Frank Scavo, who runs an IT research firm, Computer Economics, agrees about the massive impact of open source on enterprise computing. In an email thread, he told me:

"Yes, the large tech vendors, such as Google, Microsoft, IBM, etc., have benefited enormously from open source, but they also contribute enormously to open source projects, because it is in their best interest to do so. You know that IBM contributed key IP from its decades-old work in virtualization. Microsoft open sourced Visual Studios Code, and it is now one of the most widely-adopted development environments. Oracle, IBM and others contribute to Linux because it ensures that it runs on and is optimized for their hardware. They all contribute because it is in their self-interest to do so. Moreover, senior open-source developers, especially those who have commit-privileges, are in high demand and are often hired by these same large tech companies. So the whole open source movement has become a virtuous ecosystem where everyone benefits."

However, the impact of open source has been more pronounced in IT infrastructure and platform markets. As Scavo pointed out in a blog post, open source has had limited impact on enterprise applications. He wrote:

> "Since the early 2000s, I have been hoping that open source would catch on as an alternative to the major enterprise apps vendors such as SAP, Oracle, Microsoft, Infor, and others. I would like to see open source as a counterweight to the major vendors, putting more market power on the side of buyers."[13]

In his post, Scavo asks " Where is the Linux of ERP?" Yes, open source has tried and failed in the past with application vendors like Compiere and Odoo, but their opportunity remains with so much white space in vertical and geographic coverage.

The Inconvenient Truth

Enterprise vendors, who were sitting so pretty at the turn of the century, have lagged in many new markets, as profiled in the last bunch of subsections. While many of them still say "the suite always wins" as they woo customers, you could argue they are mostly selling "credential inflation." Vendors who can only support accounting and other back-office functionality feel no qualms calling themselves ERP vendors. SIs who have never set foot on a factory floor call themselves ERP consultants.

More alarmingly, we are starting to see customers get tired of waiting for vendors and go back to building their own replacement systems. With microservices, open source and

---

[13] https://fscavo.blogspot.com/2019/01/why-is-open-source-not-more-successful.html

other options, we are seeing the pendulum swing away from buy back to build. That's a stunning reversal from the 1990s.

Even the one bright spot in enterprise computing — software-as-a-service (SaaS) from the likes of Salesforce, Workday and NetSuite — now increasingly looks like an underachiever.

Even after two decades of the SaaS concept (NetSuite was founded in 1998, Salesforce in 1999), when you overlay their vertical and geographic requirements, many enterprises find that only 20 to 25% of their application needs are supported in the cloud. SaaS vendors' revenues have been growing nicely, at 30 to 40% a year, but they could easily be growing at 100%. They originally gained traction based on attractive pricing compared to on-premise vendors, but now they can themselves be accused of overpricing. Compare them to a vendor like Zoho which uses plenty of open-source code and resources in India. It offers more than 40 of its ERP, CRM and productivity application modules for US$30 an employee or US$75 a user per month. CEO Sridhar Vembu told me over a decade ago he wanted to invert the traditional software model — which typically only invests 10 to 15% of revenues in product and, in contrast, 50 to 70% on sales and marketing. He wrote in a guest column:[14]

> "Personal computers made computing ubiquitous in the developed world. Mobile revolution has swept the globe, with hundreds of millions in developing countries making their first phone call in the last decade .... Yet, in the world of corporate IT, the low-cost revolution is very much unfinished business ... most of what enterprises

---

[14] https://dealarchitect.typepad.com/deal_architect/2006/10/the_real_deal_s.html

pay for software goes towards funding the marketing budgets of vendors. This seems like a universal law that is applicable regardless of whether the vendors have open source or proprietary models, and even extends to on-demand business models."

Vembu wrote that back in 2006, and has been executing to that philosophy.

Salesforce likes to brag, "Lightning strikes twice. For the second year in a row, Salesforce has been recognized by Gartner as a leader in Enterprise hpaPaaS." What exactly *is* hpaPaaS (or huh-PAP-ass, as one analyst snarkily pronounces it)? It is no-code, Agile development. Or, in Gartner's official mouthful, it is high-productivity application-platform-as-a-service. Salesforce brags some more, courtesy of IDC,[15] that the "ecosystem of customers and partners will drive the creation of 3.3 million new jobs and more than US$859 billion in new business revenues worldwide by 2022." The irony appears to be lost — that no-code should cost customers much less, not require millions of new jobs.

Rapidly Changing Expectations

Brad Keywell is the serial entrepreneur who co-founded Groupon, Echo Global Logistics, Mediaocean, Drivin and the venture capital firm Lightbank. With his new company, Uptake, he has had a chance to look at the world of enterprise software, and he commented to me:

"Through learning how and why the enterprise software world got to where it is today, I very clearly see the

---

[15] https://www.salesforce.com/content/dam/web/en_us/www/documents/white-papers/idc-study-salesforce-economy.pdf

foundational flaws that have led to incredibly low customer satisfaction scores for the legacy enterprise software leaders. There is a lack of accountability, given that there's been a divorcing of software from system integration, which is then decoupled from implementation. And, often, that's decoupled from optimization over time.

Most troubling, the customer is left taking all of the risk, outlaying all of the money and then holding the bag if the implementation is a failure. The legacy risk-reward model is out of whack. Legacy software vendors ask for money but then avoid accountability for outcomes. The customer takes all of the risk, and too often is forced to write off a huge investment.

When I started Uptake, I posed some simple questions: 'Why shouldn't enterprise software customers expect a reliable outcome? Why shouldn't enterprise software customers expect applications that work — why would they be satisfied with anything less? Why shouldn't software delivered to the enterprise look just as good as consumer software?' The answers came back loud and clear, and just as simple. Enterprise software needs to deliver outcomes, needs to work on a self-contained basis in delivery of outcomes, and needs to be beautiful and designed with empathy towards users. As simple and clear as that proposition is, too few legacy enterprise software vendors are capable of delivering on that simplicity."

Vembu of Zoho has a similar perspective. The Zoho team is preparing for the day when Amazon decides to become an enterprise software vendor not just an infrastructure player.

The Bezos motto of "your margin is my opportunity" puts the margin rich software industry at risk. Software margins remain very high but the industry is not efficient. Says Vembu:

> "Fifty percent of their revenue is spent on sales and marketing; 50% is now considered just normal. And 70% is not uncommon at all now. If you look at the whole SaaS cloud revolution, it was supposed to deliver us from this exact problem: focus more on software and not so much on the facility of it.
>
> We are spending tens of millions of dollars in cloud infrastructure, all of these storage servers. We know how the costs have come down. There is substantial software in all of these, like in networking.
>
> Yet, ask yourself, why is it that somehow enterprise software prices only go up? Somehow, all of those industries are subject to one kind of economics. But when you come to enterprise software, the economics seems to change."

An example of that thinking comes from Zoho One, a bundle of their applications priced at $30 a month an employee, or $75 a month on per-user basis. It was launched in 2017 with 35 applications; it now has over 40. More apps will soon join the bundle. A dollar a day per employee is a compelling value proposition, when the functionality keeps growing exponentially.

Vendors like SAP, Oracle and IBM also have a branding challenge. How do they attract someone as talented as Nick Hortovanyi? Hortovanyi certainly fits their candidate profile, given that he has spent years as a DBA and IT consultant to Australian multinationals and government departments, and also as a reseller of IBM, Oracle, Sun and Apple products. He is also a talented developer. When he was 14, he created a version of a lunar lander, where the user had to navigate an asteroid field before landing the craft:

> "No two games were the same. It used basic physics related to gravity and force, to control the lander. It was these types of programs where I had an environment, and I had objects interacting in it, that drove my curiosity in computing. I didn't just want to play computer games; I wanted to understand how they worked."

After his experience with corporate IT and vendors, he has a dim view of the field:

> "The majority of computing activities are about entering data to be stored for future reporting of some type. Few projects involved having computers interacting with the real world. A lot of the programming was boiler plate code, that once learnt, lost its appeal. I'd gotten bogged down meeting the requirements of the various programs, sitting for sales and technical certifications. I noticed that the people I was interacting with didn't know about the technology. They didn't have a software background and it was more about sales and marketing with utilizing experts from elsewhere to supplement when required."

Hortovanyi had reached a fork in the road:

> "I applied for the Udacity Self Driving Car Engineer Nanodegree, and was accepted. I learnt so much from

the leaders in ML with deep learning, plus I reacquired some of the math skills that I had lost in the enterprise world. Some of the projects were so rewarding, and they reminded me of what had drawn me to computing when I was younger — that interaction of an agent with its environment. After graduation in late 2017 with the first cohort, I have also completed the Udacity Robotics Software Engineer and Deep Reinforcement Learning Nanodegrees. As of early 2019, I'm working in stealth mode on a new start-up [http://sdcar.ai] where we are focused on deep learning simulators for self-driving vehicles. It's still early days, but using sensors to capture an environment is more interesting to me then building another website or iPhone app.

The old guard aren't the main players. ML is really statistics. Been around for ages. Nvidia, Google and Facebook are the main players in deep learning with tools like Tensorflow and PyTorch leveraging Jupyter notebooks with Python and some C++ ... I really don't hear SAP, IBM, Oracle mentioned at all."

You get that message even louder when you hear Kai-Fu Lee, who has been called the "Oracle of AI" and has funded nearly 150 AI start-ups, mostly in China, which is attracting half of all AI capital in the world. Many of his investments are already valued at over US$1 billion each. He told the TV show *60 Minutes*:

"Silicon Valley has been the single epicenter of the world technology innovation when it comes to computers, internet, mobile and AI. But in the recent five years, we are seeing that Chinese AI is getting to be almost as good as Silicon Valley AI. And I think Silicon Valley is not quite aware of it yet. China's advantage is in the amount of data it collects. The more data, the better the AI. Just like the more you know, the smarter you are. China has four times more people than the United States who are doing nearly everything online."[16]

Back to my earlier reference to Southwest Airlines. Gary Kelly, CEO of Southwest, runs a very disciplined company. I have praised the organization on many occasions. I also spend a lot of money with them. When I go to Europe and have to fly Ryanair or to Asia and fly AirAsia, I wish Southwest was also in those markets so I could enjoy my perks the airline bestows on me.

Similarly, Marc Benioff and Aneel Bhusri have created impressive companies at Salesforce and Workday, respectively. They don't meet Keywell's standards of delivering to outcomes, but they have evolved the enterprise software economic model compared to on-premise models. As a result, many a CIO has asked each vendor to move into other parts of the enterprise. Though the vendors have chosen not to, Wall Street continues to reward them handsomely. It is fair to point out that Wall Street analysts do not worry that Salesforce or Workday cannot process customer orders or run the shop floor or the warehouse. Customers do have to worry about those details — and they know that promises of "no-code" come with a hefty price tag.

Most of these vendors have brilliant technology visionaries: SAP has Dr. Plattner; Oracle has Larry Ellison and Thomas

---

[16] https://www.cbsnews.com/news/60-minutes-ai-facial-and-emotional-recognition-how-one-man-is-advancing-artificial-intelligence/

Kurian (till he moved to Google); Salesforce has Parker Harris; Workday has Stan Swete. The list is long. However, they don't have enough process visionaries who can dream up next-gen shop floors, emergency rooms or warehouses. So you see the industry continue to invest in infrastructure, platforms and tools.

Let us pull in an analogy from the food sector. You go to a restaurant you really like and the chef says she has changed the business model. She is only serving semi-cooked meals now. Enjoy the meal at home. Or come on in, but be aware she is now offering grills. You bring your own ingredients and cook your own. That's a bit of what SaaS vendors are doing with investing so much in PaaS and not extending application functionality. Customers pay them to deliver cooked meals in the form of world-leading business applications; instead, they keep perfecting cooking appliances and grills.

As of 2000, few of us had heard of Alibaba, Amazon, Google, Foxconn and Siemens, at least not as technology vendors. The share of SAP and its cohorts in the enterprise has actually been declining, even as their economics have become less attractive.

Opportunity in the Fragmentation

Actually, the market fragmentation gives SAP a chance to flourish once again.

Over the last few years, SAP has regained some of its application focus. Through acquisitions like SuccessFactors and Ariba it can compete in the cloud back office applications space. With acquisitions like hybris and Callidus, it can compete in some of the cloud front office markets. With S/4, it has shown it still has the application DNA and can still develop complex applications.

SAP continues to bank on its biggest asset — its rich range of customers around the globe and across all kinds of industries.

A SAP executive asked me how they could work with many of the innovative customers profiled in my books. I responded: "Most are already your customers. You don't always associate with the innovators at those companies."

First Mover or Fast Follower?

It is a common debate in business schools: Should one be a "first mover" or a "fast follower"? There are clear advantages to both strategies. First movers get to define markets on their terms. But fast followers often take advantage of the market opportunity created by first movers. They can scale up opportunities after they have been "de-risked."

In technology, we tend to celebrate first movers and innovators. Certainly in enterprise technology, with its sky-high margins, the expectations of leadership are justifiably high.

But does one have to choose? Can you be both a first mover *and* a fast follower? That is the opportunity for SAP. It can reclaim its first mover position in its large, incumbent customer base. Simultaneously, it can become a fast follower in many of the markets it missed out in the last couple of decades.

By 1820, Americans were well ahead in the race against other global powers like the British and Spanish in the effort to dominate the North American continent. Five years ago, it seemed improbable, but by 2020 SAP will have a similar opportunity to lead the enterprise technology "continent." It is building momentum, and has been going through massive changes.

It's not your Dad's SAP, as we will see in the next section.

SECTION II

Not your Dad's SAP

CHAPTER 3

"You Did What?!"

∿→

When I was writing the first volume of *SAP Nation,*
I blurted out "You did what?!" at Dave Smoley, then CIO of
Flextronics (since renamed Flex). His IT council had given him
the green light in early 2008 for a major global SAP project to
consolidate 80 different HCM systems around the world. His
team had spent months evaluating options, systems integrators, budgets and business cases. I reacted that way when he
told me, "I thanked them for approving such a large project,
and then I surprised them. I told them I may come back to
them in the next month with a "better, faster, cheaper" option.
But we have a "fail faster" culture here at Flextronics, so they
were more intrigued with what I may come back with than
surprised." The option he referred to was Workday. At that
point, Workday could not show benchmarks that it could scale
above 5,000 employees, whereas Flextronics had over 160,000
employees at the end of 2008.

In writing this book, I had a similar "You did what?!" moment when Denis Sacré of Sanofi, the global pharma company (described further in a subsequent section) told me:

> "Modestly, at our level, we have got a little bit of a similar story. We were the first company with more than 100,000 employees to have signed with Workday on continental Europe. Even the people at Workday France, long after I signed with them, told me 'We felt that you guys (that's my boss, the HR director and myself) had some real guts.'"

Actually, in writing this book I had plenty of "You did what?!" moments — but in reverse. Companies are reversing decisions and going back to SAP. Others are looking at SAP not just for out-of-the-box ERP solutions, and several of them did not fit SAP's historical industry or business process strengths. Here are five examples:

Costco

ᄿᄿᠵ

Jeff Lyons has a long career in the grocery industry, but not in technology. As he says, AI to him translates to something other than artificial intelligence. (Google "AI and cattle breeding," and you will chuckle at what his AI stands for.) He is, however, a problem solver who called his CIO and asked if he could get an introduction to Mr. Watson. He meant the Watson whose AI and machine learning (ML) prowess he had heard about via IBM's TV commercials.

Instead, his CIO suggested he start with SAP. Costco was already a SAP ERP customer.

Lyons is a Senior VP at Costco Wholesale, the global chain of membership-only warehouse clubs. While known as a wide-ranging retailer, its strongest profit centers are in beef, organic foods, rotisserie chicken, prepared meals and wine. It is in this food area that Lyons had a problem to solve, as he explained:

"For us, wasted product is a big deal. Our rotisserie chickens are not kept on hot trays longer than two hours, and pizza in the food court is similarly rotated out if it has been available for more than an hour. If you overproduce, there's wasted hours that it took to produce the product that you're then throwing away. By identifying waste, you're solving several problems. Firstly, you reduce wasted labor. Second, you avoid waste in packaging. Finally, you don't waste as much product.

We have lots of data — seven years of sales data, MVMs [multi-vendor mailers], IRCs [instant redeemable coupons] and in-store demo data. We also have forecasting tools, and we are pretty good at forecasting from historical data. That usually needs manual massaging — for instance, if a holiday is on a Tuesday, and that had also occurred four years ago, you have to go back, do the references, and that takes a lot of work and estimation. Many times it is misleading, because four years ago the economy was very different than it is today.

As a company, we are driven by what are called the six rights of merchandising, with the top three being the right item, the right quality, at the right price. Being accurate in everything we do is a goal. But, in reality we weren't accurate enough. So where could we get some more help with better forecasting?

We wanted to overlay weather impact on historical sales data. If you're in the Pacific Northwest where I live and it's raining, you shop all day long. If the sun comes out, you stay home and do yard work. In the San Francisco Bay area, they can't drive in the rain, it's too scary. So they stay home. We also wanted to overlay sporting events. In Seattle, we have the Mariners and the Seahawks. We have a location downtown near their stadiums. We wanted to know, when there was a game — did sales pick up or slow down before, during and after the game? In the future, we could nuance that information to see if the home team winning or losing makes a difference in store traffic. We also wanted to look at other drivers. We believe that gas purchases at Costco could be a big component in the machine learning model. How often do our members shop with us after getting gas at our pump?"

SAP started them on a "design-thinking exercise." As Lyons joked, "These people like colored Post-it notes. Let me just warn you — they put them all over the room and make you go through that touchy, feely stuff."

To grapple with the wastage issue, the company launched a ML pilot at one of their San Jose, CA, stores, focused on the bakery division where wastage was an especially serious problem. Starting at 5 a.m., employees would enter damaged, destroyed and on-hand items on a tablet, and SAP generated a production run for them. Lyons described the scenario:

"Anthony Sapien is the bakery manager at this location. He was a big part of the pilot and success of the project because he really adapted to it and didn't shy away from it. We told him only ignore the model if it's totally wrong or it's obvious that it's 100% off. One day, the model called for two batches of croissants. He had only planned on making one, but he decided to follow the model's guidance. He made two batches — that is, 360-some-odd units.

The morning after, they only showed nine units left. So two batches was exactly the right thing to do. He wouldn't have done that on his own. We are encouraged by the experience of a qualified bakery manager like Anthony. At Costco, we are big on tribal knowledge. We have people stay with our company for long periods of time, people that are very good at their jobs, but eventually they may change positions or get promoted. Or maybe they retire. We lose all that tribal knowledge they had on how to run their business, when to grow their sales or grow their inventory and when to cut back. We want the system to help us do that when there are changes at a location. A new manager coming into a location is more likely to be successful because the system is going to say, here's what you need to produce.

The model includes how long it takes for an item to go from the back of the house to the front. So if it has to go through the [bakery] proof box for 45 minutes, get baked up for 30 minutes or go to the decorating table for 10 minutes, all that's calculated. For instance, it might take five hours for a bagel to go from the back of the house to the front, and so if you know it takes five hours and we're totally out of bagels then you better start work on the bagels by 5 a.m. to be out by 10 a.m. So we hope that it will do this for us: set an order of production, suggest quantity of production, and also allow the bakery manager the opportunity to teach his or her people on how to produce the right quality and quantities on a daily basis. If we do that right, then we've reduced some of our shrink, labor hours and our waste. That saves us money, which means we can keep prices lower, pay our people more and, at the end of the day, that's a success in our business."

The pilot concept, which took only about three months to implement, was a rousing success, as Costco reduced labor hours and product waste. Costco is estimated to have saved approximately US$8 million if all locations in this single region had experienced the same success. Costco now plans to roll out the SAP model to an additional 500 bakeries across the United States. Lyons said other areas in Costco's fresh food division could easily benefit from the same concept and derive similar efficiencies:

"We could apply it to our food courts where we sell — among other things — our very popular hot dog and soda. [Case studies have been written about how and why Costco has held constant the US$1.50 price of the combo of a quarter-pound, all-beef sausage, condiments and 20-ounce soda since it was introduced back in 1984.] In the food courts, we have the one-hour-hold rule, so we don't make anything and let it sit in the hot case more than an hour. We need to be pretty good at predicting how many hot dogs, pizzas, etc. we're going to sell.

The food court will be more challenging than the bakery because there is little history to go by as we are upgrading some of our products. So our smoothies will be all fruit, will have no high-fructose corn syrup and no added sugar. We have developed an organic hamburger with two patties and organic cheese for $4.99. The early reception has been great. However, what happens to other items when you introduce a new one? For example, will it shift members from buying a hot dog to a hamburger?"

What about other parts of Costco?

"There is interest, but most of them are waiting for our IT group to deliver it to them. We're just being a little bit more proactive because we have a business need. My areas have cost departments, so labor, productivity and shrink all play a role in our final numbers. When you look at what we call non-foods hard lines and soft lines; products such as appliances, furniture and sundries. They don't have to worry about labor in the same fashion and can focus on driving sales. But for those of us in cost departments, there will be a greater interest. I would think optical, gasoline and pharmacy could benefit. They're also getting some exposure as we talk about our project, so hopefully they'll pick up on it.

As it gets developed even further, we should be able to factor a multi-vendor mailer in three weeks that we didn't have last year. The system should tell us whether we're going to increase warehouse or build traffic. And if we increase traffic, we're going to sell more of this, this and this — because historically, that's what happened. Then we can develop a good game plan; we can bring staff in for the appropriate hours, and we can make sure we produce the right items."

Pregis

∿➤

Pregis is a leading manufacturer and provider of innovative packaging and protective products. Its CIO, Jeff Mueller, described the business model changes that are sweeping through the packaging industry:

"In our industry, the growth business is e-commerce. You loan machines to customers, then sell consumables through those machines. The value or the revenue increases, obviously, with machine uptime. It's the stickiness of being able to keep machines running that keeps us in big distribution centers.

That ties to the Internet of Things. Instead of service techs going out to handle a simple alert, we can do three things. One, route the alerts or have someone contact the customer to keep a machine running when it just needs some small care. Two, have our tech service people be ready to have a one-stop repair if that's needed. Three, and this is the biggest use case, more in the future, to monitor consumption and eventually turn that into value for our distribution partners.

Our distribution partners have lots of manual labor due to people managing inventories for big e-commerce distributors. Being able to monitor consumption, capture, and eventually automate that whole value chain of consumption to order, then to delivery and fulfillment is where we're headed. In an ideal world, we'll move toward packaging-as-a-service and work with our distribution partners to be able to monetize and put in a different model. Instead of product sales, they should offer to bundle services and have everything rolled into one."

He had me thinking "You did what?!" when he told me how he allowed SAP to turn around an IoT opportunity with Pregis they had previously missed a couple of years ago:

"We have two technology stacks — SAP and Microsoft. We have been consolidating around those two stacks. SAP has always been this strong ERP transactional player. So, for example, we moved our Salesforce functionality over to SAP. When it came to the whole Internet of Things and connecting our packaging systems back to the backend SAP transaction processing system, we originally thought that Microsoft was a stronger player.

My team is small but technically very sharp. They were comfortable dabbling with Azure, and Microsoft had done a good job making it affordable for us to start slowly and figure things out. We had put together a solid solution. Our SAP account exec's regular follow-up led to their interest. He had talked to my architecture director and that was the start of the snowball of getting SAP involved.

About three years ago, our Chief Innovation Officer had seen Leonardo at Sapphire. At that time, we thought that it was not mature enough. By 2017, things were different. We found that SAP had ramped up very quickly. They also listened to us and brought the right players to the table.

My team has deep SAP experience, but some of us have memories of SAP from two decades ago when implementations took years instead of weeks or months. SAP has worked with us to stand up a prototype that was basically full-functioning, connecting the Leonardo platform to our field services system, our HANA database and the SAP Analytics Cloud. *They did it in three weeks!"*

This is where I wanted to ask the SAP team: "You did what?!"

"There were three things that were really helpful for us: Firstly, it was fairly easy for us to connect back to our SAP platform. Secondly, with us as a middle-market company, they brought value to the table by introducing us to the big hardware players. With regard to Edge devices, we did not have the market power to be able to talk to the big players. SAP got us to the table so we could select the right Edge devices.

Thirdly, they walked us through the different business use cases that we needed. In our business, we have some big players that we can get on a network. It makes sense where we have a large number of packaging systems and machines to have an Edge device on the customer's network and then send that information back. If it's a smaller mom-and-pop shop, it may not make sense to put a device there. In those cases, we used Edge services connected to the cloud. Finally, there's the use case where some of the really big players don't let us on their network and we don't have access to Wi-Fi either. There, we use cellular service and connect through the SAP IoT Connect 365 service.

As the competition grows, it's better for us as the customer because it is getting easier to get single function apps across different landscapes. We've been able to take single sign-on from our Microsoft stack and layer all these pieces together so that it's a good user experience. Then it is figuring out which of the apps from the Microsoft stack we can layer with SAP. On the SAP side, we have to make sure that it's compatible and creates a homogeneous environment. None of it is homogeneous yet, but it's a lot easier to figure out than it used to be."

Lufthansa

∧→

At Sapphire Now in 2017, I posed this question to a panel of Chief Digital Officers:

> "When you talk to CEOs, they look at digital transformation as smart products, smart services, business models, so its differentiation and revenue focused. Right? When you talk to technology vendors, in contrast, they're still trying to sell the same product to every customer. How do you reconcile the need for true differentiation that digital can bring you versus what IBM with Watson or SAP is trying to sell you, which they also sell to thousands of other customers?"

While everyone on the panel had good answers, I was particularly struck by the response from Dr. Torsten Wingenter, Head of Digital Innovations at Lufthansa, the airline:

> "Even in big companies, like Lufthansa and SAP, you have small nucleuses which try to do things differently. So, we worked with the SAP Innovation Center in Berlin to bring this FlyingLab together (as described below). These small groups have a different understanding than the rest of the company

about where we can try something disruptive. We have to acknowledge that the whole parent company is what it is, and has been successful for many years. But, at the same time, how can we help our companies? That is not an easy one. We can look at start-ups and say, 'Well, we have to be like them.' Now, as a company we have been around for decades. You have to find ways to turn the whole company around, and that is a challenge. And so, it helps us to exchange ideas with other innovative nucleuses in companies to see how they are changing things inside their [similarly large] company instead of saying, 'No, no, neglect the whole existing business.'"

The SAP Innovation Center, which Dr. Wingenter referred to, is led by Juergen Mueller, SAP's Chief Innovation Officer (not related to the Mueller at Pregis above or Mueller of *Constellation* in Ch. 2) and, at age 36, one of the youngest members of its executive board. Mueller, who learned the ropes at the Hasso Plattner Institute in Potsdam, has said, "I realize customers think of SAP as the ERP company. I want the world to also see what great, impactful innovations SAP has to offer — in addition to our ERP." He also said, "I consider it extremely important not to end up in an 'SAP bubble.' In my role, I need to be in constant touch with customers and partners — to understand what their needs are, what's going on in the market, and how we can start joint innovation projects. Meeting inspiring people that are bursting with ideas strengthens my own perception of trends in business and technology."[17]

What exactly is the Lufthansa FlyingLab concept? It is part of Lufthansa's plan to create conferences in the sky. On most days, LH 464 — a regularly scheduled 747-400 flight from Frankfurt, Germany, to Orlando, FL — carries plenty of tourists to enjoy Orlando's amusement parks. The in-flight entertainment tends to be kid-friendly. On May 15, 2017, this flight offered, in addition to the usual fare, the FlyingLab aimed at the business executives on board who were headed to Orlando for the SAP Sapphire Now event.

On that flight, thought leaders from SAP and elsewhere covered topics such as the future of work and technology. The speakers spoke in front of a camera on the jet, and passengers saw them and their slides on their mobile devices and could also pose questions. There was a specially optimized, on-board wireless network to ensure the quality of the video was consistent throughout the jumbo jet whether in the first row or last.

There had been three previous Lufthansa FlyingLabs. One flew to San Jose with a focus on virtual reality, another to Fashion Week in New York City and another to the South by Southwest (SXSW) event in Austin, TX. Each flight had a technology/innovation-savvy "audience."

Could conferences at 30,000 feet become a "product" for Lufthansa? Perhaps, but it got a chance to test it out with innovative passengers headed to Sapphire Now. The

---

[17] https://news.sap.com/2018/02/sap-cino-juergen-mueller-portrait/

Lufthansa team also got a chance to interact with a set of thinkers at SAP's Berlin unit. That was Dr. Wingenter's point: He got to interact with an innovative "nucleus" at another large company. SAP is, like Lufthansa, a company with lots of legacy baggage that is also in the middle of a transition.

Rainforest Connection

⌁➤

In a sector far removed from big-box stores, international airlines and the like, the next example is at a nonprofit which made me want to ask SAP "You did what?!" I met Topher White in Orlando in the summer of 2018. He was holding up a giant, black tarantula-like object. Upon closer examination, I saw it was a series of solar panels surrounding a smartphone. He explained that his nonprofit organization, Rainforest Connection (RFCx), makes devices, nicknamed "Guardians," that can hear the sounds of illegal logging up to half a mile away. The devices buy authorities like rangers of the Brazilian Tembé tribe valuable time to chase down such unauthorized logging.

White's group takes donated smartphones, surrounds them with seven solar panels (also recycled from industrial by-products), each of which has three photovoltaic strips. The panels power the phones even when hung on tall trees in the low sunlight of dense forests. The devices function as acoustic monitoring devices. They use a simple application that analyzes the live audio stream from the mobile device and isolates the sound of a chainsaw or gunshot from other noises.

An average of 100,000 acres of rainforest are destroyed each day, according to the United Nations. Since trees capture and store carbon (a key cause of global warming), logging not only removes natural carbon capture from the cycle, it actually increases the net carbon dioxide release.[18]

Working with SAP, RFCx took the technology further. Using predictive analytics on the SCP, they created a model that identified patterns among bird and animal noises. (They are also leveraging Google's TensorFlow ML algorithms.) Certain birds and primates that normally create loud and constant chatter in the rainforest often turn quiet if they hear human activity. That silence could predict a logging event. Rangers in the rainforest can now be notified in advance that someone may be starting a chainsaw and cutting down trees. Cell phone infrastructure keeps improving around the world, and many governments prioritize rural networks in their development plans.

Additionally, reports on illegal logging plus statistics on other events are available for local authorities and rangers in easy-to-use SAP dashboards.

Think about it — recycling discarded smartphones and other materials while protecting rainforests is certainly worth celebrating. It will further help tribes like the Tembé sell carbon credits to companies looking to offset their impact.

---

[18] https://www.snewsnet.com/news/topher-white-rainforest-connection-mountain-hardwear

Louisiana-Pacific

⋏⋏→

Lousiana-Pacific is in the building solutions business. They run an enormously complex supply chain with mills across North and South America. They tend to speak in terms of volume more so than pieces or units — as in shipping on tens of thousands of railcars and hundreds of thousands of trucks. Steve Fahey, Director of Logistics and Supply Chain Planning described to me their IBP implementation. What was particularly striking was the interaction he described with other SAP IBP customers.

"The IBP early adopter input has really come through SAP. I've been very fortunate to become involved with a focus group of about 30 companies. Through that group, we've been able to see, learn, discuss, and understand what each of our companies is doing. I have called specific participants to talk through various topics or decisions. That's proven invaluable to us and our implementation efforts. We were an early adopter of IBP based on how and when we implemented S&OP, Supply, IO and Demand in a combined solution. But, there are other companies that are far larger than us that have already crossed the bridge on some of the, "How do you scale?" questions and have already begun to implement some of the more advanced or newer capabilities such as demand sensing. It's very valuable to understand what they've done, how they approached it, and what kind of results they're realizing. The group includes varied manufacturers, CPGs, some high tech — a good mix of business scenarios. Within Europe, there are a lot of manufacturers that have done some pretty good things with IBP. Engaging with the IBP product owners has helped us learn from their experiences. Then it's very interesting in the sense that if you ask, "Who has really pushed the limits with IBP Demand?" you will come up with a set of companies to engage with, or as we began to evaluate procurement opportunities, I had references for those who had already integrated Ariba with IBP. There aren't as many that have done everything, obviously, but for each module, there tends to be two, three, or four companies that have gone pretty deep with it, especially if you find those companies who had joint development and requirements projects with SAP."

Listening to Fahey, I wanted to ask SAP a different question — why don't you do more of this? I thought about hundreds of other application communities that could bring together customers within a given industry, or across industries; within a given global region, or across regions. They need a "facilitator" like SAP which has the domain knowledge and reach across countries, industries and business processes. Why does SAP keep looking to its partners or keep making expensive acquisitions for these new applications?

Transitions Are Tricky

The customers showcased exhibit a remarkable diversity in industries and use cases. They represent a very different SAP than I have seen over the last 30 years. It is an SAP which is not just pitching out-of-the-box ERP or HANA.

Few vendors actually survive major architectural shifts. SAP was one of the few which actually capitalized on the move from mainframes to client/server versions — in its case R/2 to R/3 — and it was aided by a mass rush to become Y2K compliant. Can it survive a move to more contemporary cloud, open source and ML world? In the next section, we will see a changing cast of executives who are trying to make sure the answer to that question is a resounding "Yes."

CHAPTER 4

A Massive Pivot

∿→

On a clear day, you can see Lady Liberty from the SAP offices at 10 Hudson Yards in Manhattan. The 52-floor building is part of the largest, private real estate development in U.S. history. It is already reshaping New York's West Side. When completed, it will offer 18 million square feet of space.

Walk around the offices on the top floors of the building and you can see the city's many landmarks. In the distance, you see a steady stream of planes headed to the three local airports. Look down at the Hudson River and you will see a wide range of vessels on the water. On terra firma you see a new landmark, a funky honeycomb structure called Vessel that will soon allow SAP employees the opportunity to climb its 2,500 steps. Hudson Yards is designed to be for mixed use — some space residential, some recreational.

I always seem to meet Franck Cohen when I visit this office. Cohen has a long title, President SAP Digital Core & Industry

Solutions, but he is what Led Zeppelin had in mind when they sang about a "traveler in both time and space." I like to ask him where he has flown in from and where he is headed. Seemingly never jet-lagged, he will say he is headed to Shanghai or Tokyo, occasionally going to Paris where he lives, or to Tel Aviv where he studied. I don't think I have ever heard him mention Walldorf, Newtown Square, PA, or Palo Alto, CA — the three major SAP offices. These days Cohen spends plenty of time in the New York office, which has in little more than a year become a vibrant hub for SAP executives, customers and partners. It's just one small reminder that SAP has been through a lot of change since I wrote the first volume of *SAP Nation*.

Cohen tells about his conversations with customers. He has asked S/4 Cloud customers if they wanted to scale back from quarterly to semi-annual releases that are easier to ingest. To his surprise, their response was, "No, we want quarterly innovations — we'll even take them monthly!"

He spoke about lofty goals: "We expect to be the first ERP vendor to have zero downtime — and that means hot fixes, patches and upgrades can be done without any interruptions. We are aiming for 50% process automation in three years. That is 200 scenarios of hands-free ERP. Are our competitors talking about specific metrics? Everybody is talking about AI. We have clear objectives and metrics."

Indeed, Sven Denecken, Head of Product Management and Co-Innovation for S/4, describes SAP's vision of every process on a four-step journey. It evolves from digital to intelligent to automated to autonomous. Here is a depiction of how he sees the source-to-pay process evolving:

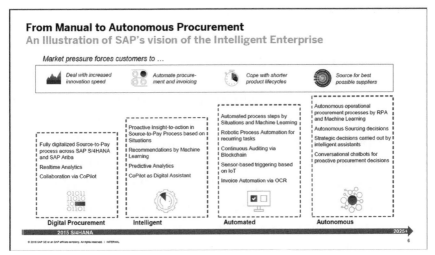

Figure 1   Image Credit: SAP

Cohen continued:

> "We are changing the partner economy. We are changing
> how they make money from SAP products. We have to
> realize that we're changing that radically, and we need
> to figure out with our partners how we can make money
> in this new [economy]. Today many are not convinced
> they can make money [in it]."

His customers empathize about the partners — but only so
much. They want SAP's direct attention to their needs.

He tells of a conversation with a large multinational who
noted that "to move to S/4, we calculate it will cost us US$120
million. Now how do I sell that to my board? How do we say,
'Guys we didn't finish the current SAP roll-out and now we need
to spend US$120 million to move to S/4.' I just cannot sell that."

Cohen's response:

"If you are only looking at the technology aspect, you won't find the justification. Now what if we can get rid of some of your customization? You pay US$45 million to manage a customization layer that you have developed over the years. What if we could cut that in half by moving the customized features to standard S/4 functionality? You mostly use SAP for back office and accounting type capability. What if we could move the custom manufacturing applications to standard SAP functionality?"

Denecken added that SAP has been investing in automating the migration. That includes remediation of previous customizations and obsolete code removal. He said they are reviewing 10,000 interfaces.

That argument works with some customers. Many point out that S/4 does not yet offer operational functionality for their industries. To which Cohen pushes back:

"Many customers have frozen their environment for years with so many modifications. I'm not even talking about moving to new S/4 functionalities. I'm talking about functionality they don't have today because their environments are stuck 15 years in the past. Just take a look at what you could have done with ECC6 in the last few years. I'm saying just take advantage of that with open eyes. They may already replace many of the customer modifications they have developed over the years."

Cohen's argument about retiring customizations makes a lot of sense, but bear in mind many of those modifications were written a decade ago or even further back. Will standard SAP software reflect 2009 practices or that of 2019? In the last decade, the shop floor has seen automation in the form of robotics, wearables, 3D printers, etc. As we will see later, global companies are moving plants across borders at startling rates and need agility they did not a decade ago. In fairness to SAP, Oracle and Infor have the same challenge. Also, many customers don't want to make big moves in ECC and then make a second transition to S/4. They would prefer a single move.

Cohen talked about a multinational customer who asked, "We love your public cloud but you have to offer us 189 countries localization out of the box." "I told him, 'I have only 64 today.'"

Customers don't want to regress from functionality in ECC and other current products. And they don't want multiple projects and change initiatives. As fast as he and SAP are moving, many of his customers want him to move faster.

Turnaround Artist

In his travels, Cohen follows a set of breadcrumbs Rob Enslin has been leaving for him around the globe. Enslin, President of Cloud Business Group, started his SAP career in South Africa. In an interview, he told me:

> "I tell people that the early days [in late '93, early '94] were interesting because I still had some R/2 customers and yet here was all this amazing amount of interest in R/3. I always remember thinking to myself, these UNIX systems are really going to run these business systems, and those mainframes are really going to struggle. People

don't believe it, but I can see this happening again now with the cloud model."[19]

He described two of his most challenging global assignments. One was when he was given a week to go run the office in Japan:

"I very clearly remember looking at [his boss, Léo Apotheker] and saying, 'I don't speak Japanese.' And he said to me, 'I know that.' And so — it was a Thursday night — I was like, 'Oh, shit. How do I tell my wife this?'

I ended up buying every book possible at Borders about Japan and living in Tokyo. Sunday night, my wife said to me, 'Okay, you've read every book possible. Are you going to say no?' I said, 'Um …' and she said, 'You're not going to say no.' She said, 'We're going to go, so just pick up the phone and tell him we're coming.'

We spent three years there. My daughter graduated from high school and my son had a blast there. We turned the Japanese business around in a massive way. I learned a lot about the culture, and together we changed it into a real growth business for SAP — it was very, very successful."

He then spoke about an even more challenging assignment:

"I came back to the U.S. running Latin America and building out a fast growth markets plan. And then,

[19] https://dealarchitect.typepad.com/deal_architect/2018/10/this-continues-a-series-of-interviews-with-tech-executives-who-have-seen-the-industry-evolve-over-a-minimum-of-two-decades-t.html

February 1st, 2009, I had the great fortune of becoming the president of North America. The previous president resigned, and it was just after the markets collapsed, so this was an interesting time to become the president of the number one market for SAP in the world.

We rebuilt our go-to-market strategy and we turned everything into selling to LOBs, building packages that were smaller, and changing the way we went to market. It took another six months before we saw the fruits of that strategy. But, once it turned, it turned strongly, and I don't think SAP has ever looked back after that financial market meltdown.

One of the things that really helped me was having had the breadth of growing up and working in Africa, understanding Europe, living in Japan, running Latin America, being the president and, obviously, living in North America. It really helped me understand how to grow SAP at a global scale for many years."

There are very few executives in the tech industry with that much global experience. Yet you could argue his turnaround efforts in Japan and the post-recession U.S. pale in comparison to his current role shepherding SAP's cloud properties like SuccessFactors and Ariba.

That's because SAP's cloud strategy and messaging has meandered for a long time. Sergio Segal, now an independent consultant, has watched SAP at competitors like Oracle and Infor. He can tell of mistake after mistake in SAP's cloud strategy:

"In April 2004, Bill McDermott said SAP had chosen not to get into on-demand CRM. He questioned whether hosted

CRM vendors would be able to retain their customers for long.[20] Then SAP organically developed seven SaaS products: CRM On Demand, 2006; Business ByDesign, 2007; BusinessObjects BI, 2010; StreamWork, 2010; Sales OnDemand, 2011; Travel OnDemand, 2012; and Financials OnDemand 2012. These seven products, along with two SaaS acquisitions — Frictionless Commerce (in 2006) and Clear Standards (in 2009) — showed total revenue of only US$50 million in 2013.

SAP acquired SuccessFactors in December 2011 for US$3.4 billion. McDermott explained, 'The big move was getting SuccessFactors because we needed the cloud DNA.'[21]

That was followed by more large cloud acquisitions, including Ariba for US$4.3 billion and Concur for US$8.3 billion. Wells Fargo confirmed in 2014 that 'SAP is paying the price for its inability to shift to the cloud. SAP is late to the cloud and missed the architectural shift.'"[22]

Segal can share more gory details on SAP's decade of slow cloud progress, but the reality is that in the last few years, Enslin has helped blunt the existential threat that pure play cloud vendors like Salesforce, Workday and NetSuite posed to SAP.

Phil Wainewright, of *diginomica,* who has watched the SaaS market for two decades, also used to be cynical of SAP's cloud

---

[20] https://www.informationweek.com/sap-maps-crm-push/d/d-id/1024780?print=yes
[21] https://www.informationweek.com/applications/saps-ugly-(bydesign)-baby-gets-prettier/d/d-id/1105551
[22] https://www.informationweek.com/software/enterprise-applications/saps-mcdermott-say-goodbye-to-too-complex/d/d-id/1269412

offerings. After SAP announced its C/4 offering, he wrote in June 2018:

> "This allows SAP to turn the tables on Salesforce, which for many years has talked up its ability to connect its customer-facing applications into SAP's less agile legacy systems of record. Now SAP CEO Bill McDermott portrays Salesforce as the "legacy CRM" system, unable to provide a rounded customer experience because it doesn't have those high-performance connections into the transactional systems that SAP now offers."[23]

The cloud turnaround story is still being written at SAP, but in many ways Enslin will likely look back and say his turnaround efforts in Japan and in the post-recession U.S. markets were actually easier.

One of the "Most Powerful Women in the World"

Fortune magazine included Jennifer Morgan on its list of 50 Most Powerful Women. It cited "Her sprawling territory brought in more than $14 billion in revenue in 2017 and accounted for some 70% of the company's cloud subscription and support revenue. The first-ever American woman to sit on SAP's executive board, Morgan is also known for investigating — and closing — SAP North America's gender pay gap."[24]

In her role as President, Americas and Asia Pacific Japan, Morgan's empire covers 43,000 employees and nearly 230,000 customers. Her career at SAP has been meteoric after she joined

---

[23] https://diginomica.com/2018/06/05/sap-turns-tables-on-salesforce-with-blueprint-for-end-to-end-connected-enterprise/

[24] http://fortune.com/most-powerful-women/jennifer-morgan-43/

the company in 2004. *Fortune* lauded her "speedy rise, at SAP, going from head of regulated businesses (till January 2013) to overseeing all of the Americas, Japan, and Asia Pacific in just five years."

She is another executive who has benefited from Enslin's work in Japan and Latin America. But she is blazing her own trails and has launched a weekly leadership podcast, entitled "A Call to Lead." At annual Sapphire events in Orlando, SAP has hosted panels on "the future of leadership in the twenty-first century. From former U.S. presidents, first ladies and secretaries of state to business titans from every industry and corner of the globe, the event has hosted prestigious leaders and has grown exponentially in the last few years."[25]

The podcast promises to reach a much wider audience featuring leading voices "from business, politics and culture — such as Arianna Huffington and Jill Biden — on what leadership means today. A unique opportunity to gain regular insights from female business leaders at Jen's level, the podcast will draw out stories, anecdotes, and lessons that will illuminate the changing face of leadership to help the next generation become better equipped for the future."

Don't Be Creepy

It became known as the "Don't be creepy" keynote. Alex Atzberger did not mean to upstage his CEO McDermott at Sapphire Now in 2018, but his accented "creepy" quote definitely perked up the audience. Atzberger, SAP's President of Customer Experience, was referring to how you collect and use customer data. The prominent security breaches at Equifax

---

[25] https://events.sap.com/us/call-to-lead/en/home

and other data custodians, the scrutiny focused on Facebook, Google and other social platforms, along with the need for GDPR compliance have brought a new focus on the protection of customer data. That gives SAP another reason to reopen the CRM conversation with customers and prospects.

Atzberger likes to use phrases like "Be Bold!" on stage. He is increasingly competing against Benioff, CEO of Salesforce, as SAP focuses, again, on the CRM/CX market. Benioff is a looming, booming presence in his presentations. But Atzberger is far more influenced by McDermott, for whom he has been Chief of Staff in the past, has run the Ariba unit and now is running the CX unit.

In person, Atzberger is subdued and thoughtful. Like many other SAP executives, he is a global citizen. He lives in New York with his Japanese wife. In an interview, he described his early days in Hong Kong:

> "What is so fascinating for me about this is that in many ways when I talk about global commerce, that's literally what I experienced as a kid sitting in smoky Chinese restaurants in Hong Kong, where my father was drinking rice wine with Chinese trading partners to sell machinery."[26]

As he told an analyst briefing, Atzberger is excited about the opportunity for C/4:

> "What I'm probably most proud of in 2018 is that I think SAP is now recognized as a credible player in the front

---

[26] https://www.forbes.com/sites/brucerogers/2015/11/11/alex-atzberger-leads-aribas-new-life-within-sap/#9974f845d08c

office again. I think that, through acquisitions, through the organic investments we have made in our solution set, the way we actually have now positioned the entire market opportunity of customer experience, and how C/4, our product suite, is addressing that opportunity, is resonating in the marketplace. I hope you see it in the number of inquiries you are getting from customers and prospects about SAP. I see it more and more that we are becoming a lot more competitive in the market. We are competing in a lot more opportunities than we ever did before."

Atzberger is fighting plenty of cynicism. Reaction from a couple of customers to the C/4 announcement: "five years too late" and "CEO McDermott arrived at SAP from Siebel 15 years ago ... what took him so long?" Several analysts reacted to my post, "Salesforce is Vulnerable" by adding "Yes, but not by SAP." One snarkily wondered if SAP's branding team had vetted the fact that C4 is a plastic explosive.

SAP is going after the CX market differently this time. It has lots of differentiated features, especially through its acquisitions of CallidusCloud, Coresystems, Gigya and hybris. The sales function is being redefined with Callidus's revenue recognition and sales commission functionality. Meanwhile, hybris Commerce, CPQ and NBA functionalities are much more relevant for newer outcome-based business models and a world where digital and physical are merging. The Coresystems acquisition offers customers an Uber-like platform to find available field service technicians in real time. So a customer like Siemens can use SAP functionality on a per-user basis for its own techs and pay for a marketplace for crowdsourced techs on an occurrence basis. Leonardo IoT capabilities allow for new service models as industrial assets get smarter and allow for more predictive versus scheduled maintenance. The Gigya acquisition, with its customer identity and access management capabilities, is more relevant for a world which is moving past email blasts and overused cookies. SAP CEO McDermott stood shoulder to shoulder with Shantanu Narayen, CEO of Adobe, and Satya Nadella, CEO of Microsoft, to announce their Open Data Initiative. It was also a vivid display of "coopetition": Adobe and Microsoft compete with SAP on many a CX opportunity.

In the analyst briefing, Atzberger commented on the top-of-mind issue for the audience: Will SAP be able to integrate all these acquisitions quicker than the others it has acquired in the previous five years? His reply:

"We published a C/4 roadmap around seven criteria that you see at the bottom of the slide (including harmonized user experience and platform services). This is particularly important because customers are asking what's the roadmap, what to expect, and most of the customers I'm speaking to expect integration from SAP for end-to-end processes. We have now, by industry, a co-innovation partner that we are working with to actually deliver more and more of this. But also, to look at the unified data model."

Will SAP get there this time? At least for now, C/4 gives SAP another talking point. You can never go wrong when you have something revenue-focused to discuss with customer executives.

Multitenancy at SAP

Another executive caught in SAP's cloud transition is Rainer Zinow, SVP Product Development of the Business One and ByD group. Business One is used by over 60,000 customers in 170 countries. ByD is used by over 5,000 customers.

Begeisterungsfähigkeit is one of those unpronounceable German words, which translates as "the ability to get enthusiastic." It is a trait most Germans will acknowledge they lack, especially compared to Americans who use way too many "Cool!" and "Super!" exclamations. Zinow does not fit that German mold. He is always smiling and enthusiastic, and he just keeps executing. ByD boasts a 30% increase in customers in the last year. He likes to say one of the best compliments he gets from customers is that their IT expense around ByD does not grow anywhere as fast as their revenues. He is also a shining example that SAP can actually deliver multitenancy and a public cloud offering.

But Zinow is clearly not loud enough. Both his products, sold by resellers, struggle for attention in SAP's dominant direct-sales culture. The products also focus on small to mid-sized customers and cannot compete with the attention SAP pays to blue-chip customers. Or the marketing emphasis SAP puts on S/4.

diginomica issued a nice summary of the twists and turns ByD has seen:

> "SAP Business ByDesign's tortured history within SAP is hopefully at an end. Launched with great fanfare in 2007, the product originally offered "mega-tenancy" — a kind of multi-tenancy where each customer's data was

physically separated on different server blades. The product was reworked to possess a more traditional multi-tenant architecture and to permit the solution to scale more effectively and cheaply.

The product's breadth and depth were expanded significantly over the years. It went from a solution that could support service firms and high growth start-ups to possessing a full manufacturing capability. But the product underwent other changes, too. The software was enhanced to make it viable in more countries. It also needed its underlying architecture to be upgraded to utilize the HANA in-memory database technology.

Each re-working of this product line made it stronger and better but it also put a cloud around it, too (no pun intended). SAP's internal support for this product line seemed to fluctuate over the years. These attitude changes were noticed by many analysts and, apparently, some partners, too."[27]

There are several analysts who think SAP should consider spinning off the Business One and ByD products. Their reasoning is that a more independent management team would put a lot more energy in marketing directly against Oracle (with NetSuite), Microsoft, Zoho and others, and likely would be much more creative with pricing.

Zinow just smiles at those suggestions. Customer compliments and 30% growth are pretty good rewards for his tireless efforts.

---

[27] https://diginomica.com/2017/01/17/finally-sap-business-bydesign-relevant/

The Wild, Wild UX Race

SAP has long been maligned for having an ugly user interface. When you listen to Maricel Cabahug, SAP's Chief Design Officer, you get a sense of the gut-wrenching changes that have been forced within SAP as expectations of user experiences gyrate wildly:

> "It's the new normal. There are new ways of interacting with systems, with intelligent systems now. What we're doing on the GUI side, although it's necessary, is actually solving the problems of the past."

Vijay Vijayasankar, a partner at IBM who has long worked on SAP projects, agrees:

> "Most customers are impossible to please these days around user experience. The general expectation is that whatever was the best UI that I last saw, generally becomes the minimal expectation for the next UI. It's a losing battle trying to keep up, and for a large company like SAP, at some point you have to draw a line."

Vijayasankar is only scratching the surface of the UX landscape. For example, when *Fast Company* named its "15 coolest interfaces of 2018,"[28] it included the Microsoft Canetroller, which allows someone without vision to tap their way through simulated 3-D environments, and a tiny sensor from researchers at Tufts University School of Engineering that sticks on your

---

[28] https://www.fastcompany.com/90278955/the-15-coolest-interfaces-of-the-year

tooth, tastes your food, and transmits its contents back via radio frequencies to your phone.

Vijayasankar said:

> "My general feeling is that it's an unnecessary battle to fight, because in the very short term a large majority of these transactions will be taken over by machines, in which case why bother with UI for those? It would be more prudent to figure out what is a small subset of transactions that will always be human driven and then just make them the best that they can be. Make it totally seamless, very rich, but don't aim for consistency across the whole suite."

As they continue to run on the UX treadmill, I hope they look back at an argument I made a decade back when I wrote, "The best UI is no UI":

> "… that messaging between machines, sensors, devices have for the last couple of decades outstripped human originated messaging traffic. Optimizing non-human interfaces is even more important than newer UIs.
>
> … that the "universal UI" is a holy grail. Traders, salesfolks, shop floor employees, the UPS delivery employees, are not homogeneous and will never use a single UI.
>
> … that amazon.com, eBay and Google have shown in the last few years that the best user interface is the one which does not require elaborate documentation — and does not generate tons of calls to some help desk.

... that we are already seeing a huge proliferation in mobile user interfaces. We are going to be swimming in way too many UIs in coming years.

... that the average CFO does not want a "prettier" user interface, but wants more productive accountants that can help compress the monthly closing cycle and help the company show in top quartile of best practice process benchmarks.

... that the average VP of Logistics is looking for tons of customer, shipment and other data — wants lots of reliable, bulk data, and in fact is suspicious of user touched data."[29]

Cabahug continued:

"Nowadays, it's the more natural way of interacting, like voice, chatting, typing, handwriting and so forth. We will take advantage of all of those. Of course, that doesn't mean that we don't do anything on the GUI. We will actually look end to end on how people work and do a combination of the graphical user interface with voice. It's no longer just replacing all of the screens."

The world of designing the user experience is mind-blowingly complex — mobile trends on iOS and Android; social/collaboration trends driven by Facebook Workplace, Slack and others; digital assistants like Alexa, Siri and SAP's own CoPilot.

---

[29] https://dealarchitect.typepad.com/deal_architect/2009/09/the-best-ui-is-no-ui.html

Listening to Cabahug, you see that expectations change dramatically as you move within an enterprise. Customer-facing marketers are far more UX-demanding than workers on the shop floor. As you move around the world, you have to reflect expectations of chat and emojis common in China:

> "Some of the customers say, 'No, I don't want CoPilot to be listening all the time. I want to actively say, "Okay, now I want to talk to you."' But, some customers, especially in the warehouse scenario, say 'No, I don't want to activate it all the time. I want it to just listen to me when I say this product, and this is the count, so it should just be with me as I go from one bin to the other.' It's just really different use cases and how we do this."

It is a bit ironic, then, as we will see later in the book, that even in the midst of all these exploding choices, many customers who are moving to S/4 are continuing with the old SAP GUI that has been maligned in the past. They are doing it to minimize the change impact on users.

The Changing World of Developers

The Register reported on a Microsoft event in 2000 which has since become a meme in enterprise technology:

> "A shiny-faced (Steve) Ballmer leapt around the stage clapping his hands and chanting the words "developers" to illustrate where Microsoft should be putting its attention. Ballmer was praised by some for his enthusiasm but the sight of him screaming at the audience with huge

sweat stains in his shirt spawned the "Monkey Boy" meme that still haunts him to this day."[30]

Thomas Grassl is a bit more subdued than Ballmer (who himself these days trains more of his passion on the LA Clippers, the NBA basketball team he owns). However, in his role as SAP VP, Global Head Developer & Community Relations, Grassl is just as passionate about developers. He calls developers "king-makers," invoking the title of Stephen O'Grady's book.[31]

"There's a big change in our industry — 20 years back, when companies bought software, developers were told, 'Please implement the software.' Now it has completely flipped. Developers are being asked, 'We're looking for a solution in this and this area. Can you guys come back with a recommendation?' Many of the evaluations are now being driven by developers.

Developers are getting ever more powerful. Two decades ago, the internet brought easier access to information. Then the open source movement brought access to software. Now the cloud is bringing easier access to compute capabilities. On top of this, now there is way more demand for developers than supply."

Throughout our research for this book, we heard customers like Paul Wright at Accuride, observers like Dennis Howlett at *diginomica* and talented developers like Hortovanyi discuss how

---

[30] https://www.theregister.co.uk/2013/08/24/top_10_steve_ballmer_quotes_from_microsoft_history/
[31] https://www.amazon.com/New-Kingmakers-Developers-Conquered-World-ebook/dp/B0097E4MEU

SAP and other enterprise vendors have a brand challenge when it comes to attracting young developer talent for themselves and for their customers.

Grassl agrees:

> "When I talk to my peers at developer relations in other companies, I get the same feedback. It's a very tough market to get and keep developers interested in your products."

He then countered with the following:

> "Let's start with who do we target. Does it make sense for us to go after a broad, less-professional developer? It doesn't help us to get a developer who knows HTML and can create a small app for a web page. We drive programs to show them the [enterprise] career path — but it also requires work on their side, to learn and build up the skills.
>
> At SAP, we accelerated our focus on developer relations about five years back. There are a lot more things available from SAP than in the past. Also, we use the term "developer" very broadly at SAP. It includes sys admins, technical people and business user-type developers.
>
> We have focused on three main activities:
>
> First, to drive *awareness* within different developer communities. There is the existing SAP community, those who are already touching some SAP software. We try to expose them to our new products. A good example is someone who worked on ABAP in an ECC setting. How do we get these folks interested to try out something else?

Or someone who has worked with Business Warehouse or Business Objects — what is interesting and what can I do with SAC? It's important to create awareness about the new technologies in these audiences. There is also the focus on "net-new" developers who have not touched SAP before, but that needs different tactics.

Second, is the *engage* phase. How do we move beyond awareness to have developers try out our software? We have opened up a lot of our software for free. In the past, you had to buy developer licenses. Now we give you unlimited access to software, including SCP. You can get a trial of the SAP analytics cloud. You get, for free, the SAP HANA express edition, which is a smaller scale SAP HANA with up to 32 gigabytes of RAM, and you also can even use this for productive use. Another big part in there is to give them the learning. This is where our tutorials[32] and openSAP[33] courses come in.

Then, finally, there is the focus on *adoption*. Developers want to know how they will be supported through the development lifecycle. I think SAP has had this focus going back to 2004 or 2005, with free public forums where people can exchange ideas. If someone has a question, they don't need to open a support ticket. They can pose the question in the forum and someone either from the community or from SAP is hopefully able to answer that. We have Developer Garages at our TechEd events around the world. Do you want to try out ABAP in SCP?

---

[32] in https://developers.sap.com/tutorial-navigator.html
[33] https://open.sap.com

Here are workstations and experts and tutorials to get started."

But aren't developer communities around Microsoft, Google and even Salesforce much more vibrant?

"We are doing a lot more in developer communities than people realize. Take open-source software. It's pulled in a lot, like in the start-up communities. Some of the more established, in-house custom projects are using open source. That's definitely an audience where you definitely want to play in certain areas. We have projects we're pushing out via open source. There is OpenUI5. There is Project Gardener, which goes into Kubernetes cluster management. It's used as part of SCP. You will see us more at events like OSCON. We are not there to find the next generation of ABAP developers. It's basically to get the brand of SAP out to the community, that SAP is very active in open source and to attract a new kind of developer.

Or take machine learning. What our products like Leonardo do is bubble this whole thing up that a regular developer can embrace machine learning functionality into the standard applications. We don't expect our developers to generate the next ML algorithm and work on TensorFlow in detail. There are not enough people — developers who understand this type of ML. For us, it's much more important that an application developer can use machine learning in a workflow scenario, like to do a prioritization or a self-approval based on ML. But, like I said, that's at a much higher abstraction layer.

We have other higher-level services on SCP. Compared to an ABAP developer in ECC who had to build it on their own, they can say, 'Okay, let's write a business extension in ABAP, but now I want to use a secure transmission of something to my business partner. I can use blockchain for that, and I use a service from SCP for it.' You need a simpler way of accessing the information or dealing with these newer technologies like ML, like blockchain, speech recognition, etc.

We don't talk much in terms of "low or no-code," but we see a lot of interest and we're reselling Mendix [a low-code development platform acquired by Siemens in October 2018]. Because the market for developers is so tight, all technology vendors need to make it much easier for someone who does not have a computer science degree to work with business applications. I think SAP was one of the first ones to actually implement that nicely. If you look at ABAP, it basically abstracts a lot away from developers. It was a 4GL language. It made all the screen painting and similar tasks very simple. Same today — if you go through the wizards in the Web IDE, some analysts might say, 'This is already like a low-code platform.' [SAP says it allows you to "develop applications rapidly using wizards, templates, samples, code and graphical editors, modelers, and more."[34]]

Then there is our Build service, which allows you to create user-friendly, interactive prototypes without writing any code. Let's say a business user — e.g., in

---

[34] https://developers.sap.com/topics/sap-webide.html

sales — has a new idea about improving a business process. We can sketch these ideas together and prototype it very quickly. You get feedback and iterate. Then when it's done you basically put it into the implementation. You have a very good spec and the whole lifecycle is much faster. We have seen with customers that you can have a brilliant coder or someone who implements something very quickly. But if it doesn't match well to the business need, it's a waste. That's where Build comes in."

Given the massive headache of customizations around ECC, should SAP be encouraging even more around its new products?

"We have learned the hard lesson in the past where we allowed our customers to do every crazy thing in ECC and upgraded them … it was a huge project. I think everybody out there has the same methodology. You keep the SaaS core clean to run your main apps, but then you need to build extensions around it to customize it and you push the extensions into PaaS.

Another thing with new technologies: If you go to customers in a specific industry, say in oil and gas, they are likely not sharing what they're doing with ML among other customers. It's their competitive edge, and I think that's where the developers are coming in, and that's where you also build these extensions."

What about trends around the world? Will China flood the world with new developers, especially around new technologies?

"For us, the three big markets are the U.S., India and Germany. These are very big and heavy developer markets. And broadly — Asia-Pacific is growing very fast.

Talking of younger developers: In Germany, we are very integrated with the student community. If you look at DSAG events, it's amazing how many partners show up. The ecosystem is very open and absorbs everything we roll out to developers. There's big adoption in India as well. Our biggest TechEd, by attendee count, is in Bangalore, India. It's bigger than the ones in Las Vegas and Barcelona. In the past, it used to be you outsourced legacy code to India. No longer true. We have seen it around HANA, around SCP; Indian adoption is as quick as the rest of the world. Whatever we roll out gets immediately looked at from these markets. We're tracking, for example, who is learning certain things. This is running on SCP, but an implementation team for me is working out of India and Russia. Developers want to be on top of things and learn the latest. They may work with ABAP in their day job, but they likely check out SCP on the side or in the evening.

We don't publish adoption numbers even though our numbers are very good. The last thing developers need is more buzzword marketing. The SAP Community has 2.8 million active users, on average. Our openSAP courses and tutorials are being used by millions of active users.

Instead of telling developers, 'Here's a great community and it's all great,' I'm telling them, 'If you want to learn X, Y, and Z, get started over there.'"

I have observed that the more things change at SAP, the more they remain the same in its customer base. This was especially striking as I spent a few hours at SAP TechEd in Las Vegas in October 2018. SAP had a series of bins with pins (to put on shirts or jackets) for developers to vote for their programming language of choice. I walked around the show floor with Brian Dennett, co-founder of Enable.Ai, who grew up in the SAP developer world at one of its biggest customers, Colgate-Palmolive.

Dennett proudly showed off his Python pin. I expected most of the attendees would similarly be showing off their ML chops or Java pins. I was blown away that the ABAP bin was empty. As ABAP migrates to SCP, the 35-year-old language continues to flourish.

I spent some time talking to Dennett about the changes he has observed in the SAP developer world over the last decade. He has presented at SAP Demo Jams and socialized with SAP Mentors (a cadre of well-regarded techies in the SAP community) and developers at several TechEd and Sapphire Now events. He had a very thoughtful perspective:

> "One thing to understand about SAP is there's always this weird tug-of-war where SAP is a technology company, and so they need to innovate. Yet, SAP is an enterprise partner, and so they need to placate their customer base which, in large part, still views IT as a cost center. That creates this weird pull and push that forces them to invest time and effort in technologies that seem stale. But, ultimately, that's their bread and butter, and so it's just like a box they have to check.

HANA was the underpinning and the way that S/4 cloud is going, they're basically jumping on the whole move to the cloud trend. Now the burden is shifting back to the customers to acknowledge what the new SAP world looks like, and I need to shuffle my IT resources more toward custom development, more toward modern development practices, more toward the API cloud-based application architectures.

I see initiatives around building new kernels into the HANA platform so that you can run JavaScript or Python or other languages, and so each one of those steps is an incremental step toward saying, 'Hey, SAP has a ton of data in it. SAP has a ton of business logic and business intelligence type components in it. You can take those choice parts and hook into them through a variety of modern techniques and now exploit the value that's in those and bring more value to customers more quickly.'

Over time, the numbers will just shift. Every SAP customer will over time organically end up with more non-ABAP developers as today's ABAP developers retire. Over time, it just becomes easier and easier to let ABAP go. I think that the tricky thing for SAP is, at what point do they start switching to other technologies to build out their own business logic because at some point they have to make that shift. That's just a hard decision to make.

I think it's going to be interesting to see how SAP navigates this fragmentation between ABAP, JavaScript and potentially Python or something like Python for the ML practitioner. Maybe SAP just doubles down on C++ or something more like that. But I do think that they need their Swiss Army knife language which, in many ways, may be JavaScript. Then they need their language for the machine learning practitioner that is going to drive a lot of value for IT organizations moving forward. I think that's just something that will organically solve itself one way or another as the customer base of SAP gets more savvy.

When it comes to ML, I think SAP has stepped out of the way and is allowing Google to make a lot of those calls. Google has this partnership, essentially, with the open source community around TensorFlow and there's the PyTorch community, which keeps TensorFlow honest in a lot of ways. SAP right now is still trying to run down the list of things that SAP can build ML models around and then package those into their solutions.

There's basically a hit team within SAP that's running around just getting as many ML wins as they can under their belt and their customer ecosystem is going to benefit from that practice. I don't know at what point that stops and SAP has to switch gears. I think they've acknowledged that they're going to have to at some point. I think, in the long run, ML, as it relates to business processes and to development, is going to have a much more significant impact than a lot of people are currently giving it credit for.

There's a guy from Tesla who coined the term Software 2.0.[35] His point is that if you think about writing a function as a developer, when you write a function, you basically define your inputs, you define your outputs, and then you write a bunch of code in between to get

---

[35] https://medium.com/@karpathy/software-2-0-a64152b37c35

that stuff working. Machine learning inherently does the same thing. You define inputs and you tell the model what is the correct answer on the output side. Then the model figures out all the stuff in between. And so, there is like a 1:1 corollary between what a developer does when they're writing a function and what a machine learning model can do. I think that there are comparable corollaries when you think about a business process expert or a functional person within a company when they're going through and filling out a GUI to configure a new SKU or a new vendor or whatever the case may be where they're given a screen. They put in a bunch of inputs and then some master data or a transaction gets generated on the other end.

Over time, I see a lot of enterprise solutions taking this ML-first approach where, if you put a model in front of everything, that model can learn what the right answer is most of the time. Now it becomes a game of how accurate are you at catching the exceptions and allowing the user to interject the nuance that the machine learning model may not understand — may never understand.

I think SAP has shown some signs of getting that. It's definitely a big part of the conversation that I have with SAP when I talk to them about ML. I'm very interested in seeing how that aspect of SAP evolves over time because I think that whichever vendor gets that first and rolls out those solutions aggressively first is going to have a huge head start on their incumbents.

I think, as ML has time to permeate different organizations, we're going to see a lot more machine learning practitioners. Those practitioners will speed up the rate of innovation that we see in the enterprise software space. I don't know if I have any strong bets on who is really going to win that race because, arguably, Salesforce has done some very important things there. IBM obviously has their whole Watson group. But I think, in a lot of ways, all the vendors right now are doing the same thing.

They're building ML products that are the end result of ML researchers pushing the envelope on state of the art. None of them have really switched gears to empower the machine learning practitioner and how to lay out all the moving parts in a way where it's super accessible to a more traditional developer to leverage those pieces. That is definitely something to watch out for, to see who is making machine learning most approachable to their ecosystem of developers."

A few weeks later at the TechEd in Barcelona, SAP announced (as was widely expected) ABAP in SCP. CTO Björn Goerke summarized: "There is no future for ABAP alone in SAP, but there's also no future without ABAP in SAP."

Matthias Steiner, Head of SCP Evangelism, explained the move to me:

"We are articulating that this is not your grandfather's ABAP. It still uses a lot of the common technologies that have been floating around within the SAP ecosystem for a while, like HANA core data services. Of course, we recommend using UI5 and Fiori, so it's just a stepping stone. It's just making it a little bit easier for our one million ABAP developers as they up-skill.

We still believe that for all those hesitant customers, the best way to get started with cloud is this whole topic of user experience, because the elephant in the room is data, security and information privacy. If you leave the data where it is and just use the cloud as the catalyst to expose this data to the outside world, make it accessible to the end users, and typically this is what we do with Fiori-type applications, then you can familiarize with the technologies. For these things, pick something which is not mission-critical, so you have a little bit of time and no pressure to familiarize with cloud."

While comforting to customers from a continuity perspective, the longevity of ABAP is a double-edged sword. How do you attract next-gen talent?

Howlett at *diginomica* told me:

"The question is, can they find the next generation of rock stars that can be part of that SAP Mentor program? The answer to that is unknown, because when you've got 90+% people worrying about running ABAP, where the hell are the Python guys? Where are the React guys? Where are the Angular guys? There are so many new platforms that these guys could be playing on that they don't even know about. It's like, well, guys ... wake up ... smell the coffee.

We've talked about 'bring your own language' for at least five or six years. How long before it actually gets there? They've got to look at Microsoft and see what Microsoft has done to even have a snowflake's chance in hell at being able to get that Mentor program back running properly. Why did Microsoft buy GitHub? Because the future is open source. Microsoft now owns open source for all practical purposes. It's open sourced a ton of its own technology.

SAP talks about itself being gung-ho on GitHub. Yet, if you look at the number of repositories that it's got out there, it's fractional."

Mueller of *Constellation* is more complimentary:

"I think SAP's making very good choices in SCP components. They're building on Cloud Foundry, which has largely won the enterprise. It's moving now to Kubernetes, which achieves lots of portability across the different vendors. In the previous generation, NetWeaver was an attempt to build things themselves. It was similar to what they did with R/3 presentation, display, execution services. This time, it is all built on open source.

They have learned from IBM, which in 2013 announced their PaaS platform Bluemix, which was completely in open source. It was clear that if IBM would not build that themselves and they're in the platform business, then pretty much nobody else could do differently. There's always a combination of open source and, if you compare NetWeaver to SCP, there are little things which SAP has done there which are proprietary similar to how they built NetWeaver.

SAP has open-sourced what they called Gardener, which is a way to manage the different Kubernetes applications like a gardener would across different flower beds. It's quite the reverse of what SAP knows and understands. We will have to see how successful they will be, but they're using it anyway and hoping the community will pick it up."

SAP has also open-sourced a project called Kyma which provides a lightweight framework to build custom extensions to the commerce portfolio in the C/4 suite.

Still, there is the talent issue. As Howlett said:

"The new generation doesn't know about SAP. They don't care about SAP. Why would they? They care about Google, and they care about Amazon. They care about Facebook. Even Salesforce.

I recall that when Salesforce created their Trailblazer community, they said, 'Oh, we're creating this wolf pack.' I said, 'SAP already owns it.' They said, 'Yeah, they might think they do.'"

Steiner spoke about the talent base in the SAP world:

"Will everybody move toward the cloud? Probably not. Some will say, 'I have done this for 30 or 40 years. I have 15 more years to go.' Hey, COBOL developers are still needed. They make a lot of money. So, they're good for the rest of their lives. But for everybody else that is younger, they need to realize there is continuous learning. It's not what you know. It's how fast you can ramp up this new knowledge.

The ABAP guys have the process know-how. They know how the back-end systems work. Now, we say, 'With ABAP in the cloud, we give you that nice stepping stone.

You can leverage a lot of the existing knowledge, and you have to just learn a little bit more about those components.'

In general, my biggest observation [from the Barcelona TechEd event] was that — and this is a little bit surprising for us — it seems that the European community is much more now getting into the details of SCP. They're much more interested in cloud than what we see happening in the U.S. Typically people think that the cloud in the U.S. is much more prominent than it is in Europe, but we're starting to see it the other way around."

Howlett agreed:

"I've met a number of 100-to-150-year-old German companies, the classic *Mittelstand*. They're saying, 'We recognize that there are challenges on the horizon for us. We're not in danger now and the sun is still shining. We're going to fix the roof while it's still shining.' And they are making significant investments. They're going both ways, right? They're going to SAP for some, but they're going elsewhere for others."

A Different Kind of "Open"

In over three decades of analyzing technology vendors, I have dealt with countless marketing executives. I don't recall a single time when such an executive has pre-briefed a couple of analysts on what his CEO was going to present at an upcoming conference. That is, until Nick Tzitzon, EVP, Marketing and Communications at SAP, gave us a preview of what CEO McDermott would be keynoting at the Sapphire Now conference in June 2018. Then he listened to our feedback.

We advised him to not go overboard talking about "corporate purpose and values." We told him, "You cannot go wrong with that, but don't dwell on it. Too many of your competitors are dwelling on it. Given that your audience is business executives, just be a little careful not to overplay that card." Tzitzon agreed: "Vendors come out and say 'We're changing the world,' and it pisses me off. You are doing exactly what a company and a business should do but what we can tell authentically is that we take pride in what our customers are doing. We have to make the customers the heroes and not SAP the hero of that story."

On another point, Tzitzon pushed back at our suggestions:

> "On the IA issue — I'm usually the guy in the company that wants to err on the side of candor and humility. But you don't see any other vendor going out in their annual show and saying, 'Let's just air all our dirty laundry and be honest about how shitty some of this stuff is.' I just don't want us to be meaninglessly shooting ourselves in the foot. Every time we go out and we say something about any freaking practice ... it's the only story people write about."

Then the week after, he did something else unique. I asked him to critique (on the record) how the event went. You can read the whole interview here,[36] but the one thing that really stood out was this comment:

> "Bill [McDermott] always says that SAP is at its best when SAP is at its hungriest. The company culture right now,

---

[36] https://dealarchitect.typepad.com/deal_architect/2018/06/sap-is-at-its-best-when-it-is-hungriesta-conversation-with-nick-tzitzon.html

and I think you felt it at Sapphire and in the lead-up, we are very motivated because we feel so strongly about the story we have to tell. We're very much in a "don't take anything for granted" phase. I love that scene from the movie *Any Given Sunday* with Al Pacino. The locker room scene where he says, 'You go the extra mile for that inch, to gain every inch. It's the difference between winning and losing.' We're in a mode now where SAP is going to go the extra mile for every inch. And there should not be any situation where you're asking us to help you cover SAP where we're not able to come through."

More signs of a very different SAP.

SAP's Own Digital Transformation

At 38 years of age, Christian Klein is one of the youngest executives on the SAP Executive Board. One reason he qualified for that honor is the digital transformation through which he has led SAP. When I met him, I told him I had written about Cognizant's (the outsourcing firm) own digital transformation and wanted to understand more of SAP's initiative. To me, vendors have more credibility talking about digital transformations when they have gone though the trauma themselves.

Klein is now using that experience to help market S/4 and SAP cloud properties to other global companies seeking similar transformations. He is on a quest to help them become what SAP calls "intelligent enterprises."

He described the transformation in an interview:

"We are tackling the whole value chain at SAP. We are looking end to end, looking at marketing, sales, finance, service and support, cloud operations and the cloud infrastructure. That's the first aspect of our transformation. Next, we are infusing machine learning, IoT, predictive analytics and these new technologies to bring the intelligence into play.

It's about adapting business processes to the new digital age. It's about fixing the data architecture. Last but not least, it's about change management, and taking the people with you. In the end, everything that we do in the cloud impacts our 90,000 employees and our 400,000 customers. Change management is a key aspect."

Benjamin Blau, on Klein's staff, shared with me details of multiple projects they have internally worked on, and the success metrics they can show across marketing, sales, finance and other business areas:

"If you look at what SAP has developed, our acquisitions, the new markets we enter, new geographies, new products, new services, there's a need to have flexibility in our processes. We did not want to have a centralized process definition for everything. We made some conscious decisions on which parts of the process in the value chain that we want the business units to define, so they can react flexibly to new market requirements.

First, it's about the customer experience. Customers want an omnichannel experience. They want an always-on experience. We are aiming for a seamless, harmonized, digital experience. Our statistics show that 57% of B2B purchase decisions are being made even before people talk to a human sales rep. This shows us that the complete digital experience on SAP.com, and all the different points of interacting with SAP, are getting more important. We need to re-innovate the whole demand and deal management process to make sure that it's a seamless digital experience that the customer expects. If you look at the post-sales phase, our statistics show that a customer is actually worth 10 times more than the initial purchase, which means we need to proactively cater for a good experience with a product. We need to make sure the customer is successful with the product. This needs to be the full focus in the lifecycle.

Second, there are employee expectations — and they expect a higher degree of automation. They expect to get away from repetitive tasks, spend more of their time and experience on more innovative, value-adding tasks, independent of the function they are in. They want built-in intelligence in the processes. They want to spend their manual, human effort on innovative stuff in cross-functional teams and not in siloed organizations.

Third, if you look at shared services, obviously there are high expectations about our cloud. We need to be profitable, to scale and also to free up cash. Those are the things that shareholders expect from us.

That triangle is the three-fold objective that we are after and that drove our transformation."

The transformation had a specific set of objectives such as "70% reduction in lead response time" and "2.5X increased automation of order processing." Blau shared with me the long list of project targets but did not want them published. He continued:

"To simplify incentive design and commission management programs, we implemented Callidus commissions. The intent here was to automate, to a great degree, the complete process — from calculation of commissions to the payout. It sounds trivial at a glance, but it's really complex if you go into the details. We also implemented Callidus CPQ to simplify selling. Callidus has the capability to show the account representative in real time, when they are shaping the deal, what it would mean for their commissions. I think that is a very strong capability if you want to drive appropriate behavior with the right incentives."

Step back and think of the complexity of the deals they are trying to digitize. As Blau said, "Deals tend to include multiple components from different parts of our portfolio: cloud, and on-premise software SKUs and consulting services. Should you set up cross-functional teams that approve it at one go, or should you set up multiple organizations and then route the different parts of the deals through different approvals? Besides, you have to layer on geographical differences."

Changing Partner Landscape

Diane Fanelli, SVP, has had a 25-year career so far at SAP. Her latest role is to recruit ISVs to develop apps using SCP. SAP showcases them in its App Center. She explained her drive: "The future is small, simple applications that snap into existing landscapes. You go shopping [for them] on your phone."

Examples include JDMS (Job Descriptions Made Simple) from HRIZONS, which extends SAP SuccessFactors with a fully integrated solution to manage job descriptions. Accenture has a testing app that anonymizes HCM data. Vertex has an indirect tax app which calculates sales and use tax for SAP's commerce cloud.

Fanelli says she has the opportunity to move partners from a historic focus on reselling and implementations towards a broader role in helping customers become Intelligent Enterprises. Partner performance will be measured on customer lifetime value and their success.

SAP has a long history of building similar apps ecosystems around Fiori apps, HANA apps, mobile apps, etc. This time around, the customer access is much more digital. SCP leverages a lot more open source, and the barriers to partner participation appear lower. At this point, it is a fledgling in terms of revenues for both the ISVs and for SAP (Fanelli says focus is adoption prior to monetization), but there is significant promise.

This time, she has new platforms to benchmark against. In the last decade, Apple has generated tens of billions of dollars in revenues for its partners and for itself from its iOS store. Amazon with its fulfillment engine has done the same. She can help SAP dream much bigger in this round.

Rethinking R&D

Goerke, CTO of SAP, describes the transformation in its development organization:

> "The way our customers expect solutions from SAP has been massively changing — whether it is cloud solutions or the current interest in open source. It's real-world awareness of solutions that you're seeing with IoT. There is customer sentiment from social networks or algorithmic improvements in machine learning and the impact

of automation on solutions. In the consumer tech space, it is ubiquitous and is also invading the enterprise space.

How we deliver support is now substantially different. In the old days, we were basically supporting IT departments to operate our solutions. In the SaaS world, you are supporting end users who have issues rather than dealing with IT departments as intermediaries.

We have also gone from a single-product company to a multiproduct company. In the old days, we used to focus on core ERP functionality; now we deliver a very broad portfolio. It's about an end-to-end process that customers want to consume.

You have to decide if we deliver software every two months or a service update every two weeks. The feedback from customers is also much more immediate.

In the old days, we had to maintain code lines of all the versions that were deployed. We had to down-port software. That forced you to think differently about security. These days, it's about having a single code line, pushing out changes immediately. It's a very different way to look at things. Then you start asking questions: What's the best way to market that solution? How do we get customers up to date on what's going on? How do you roll out that solution? How do you educate about it? At the end of day, how do you support it?"

On the people impact in the R&D function:

"How do we reward Scrum team behavior? I don't want to have individuals competing with each other and everybody trying to do their own thing. At the end of the year, how do you decide who did a great job and who didn't? If we want them to act as a team, we need team goals, so we need to evaluate people on team goals and not just individual goals.

What is the impact on compensation? What can we ask people to do? Is it a change in job description? How do you get people to volunteer to be developers or managers on duty over the weekend? There's related discussions with the workers' council, of course.

When they joined the company, it was about developing software. You would press a button and, at some point in time, someone else made sure that the customer got it and implemented it. Now we were asking them to move to a DevOps model. Development used to be 5×8. Cloud is 7×24.

Sometimes I think SAP's a dinosaur and we're pretty late to the game. We hear great stories about digital natives like Netflix and how they do things. But then, I look at how we're doing things internally at SAP, and I look at what's happening in our customers and I think we're way ahead of them.

I think it's a journey for us that will take at least 10 years. We started a while ago, but we're not through yet. It has to do with moving from on-premise to cloud, but also moving from an application company into an application and platform company, which includes how we engage with partners in the cloud."

The Eye of the Storm

I have what I call a SES (Short Email Service) relationship with many corporate executives. When I read or hear something that impresses me about them, I send them a short email. Given their busy lives, I don't always expect a response.

So I was sitting in the audience at a SAP event listening to CEO McDermott. As usual, he was positive and exuberant. His critics call him "glib" for being so positive. But I fired off one of my SES notes on the mobile phone, writing:

> "I was in audience this morning. So nice to see you so positive. I think unbelievably you are even more positive after your accident."

In 2015, McDermott fell down the stairs with a cup of water, and a shard of glass penetrated his left eye. He had 12 painful surgeries, which still could not save that eye. He was back at work more energetic than ever, saying, "I lost that particular battle, but I won a bigger one."

A few months earlier, I had seen him next to Jon Bon Jovi at another event. The hugely popular musician opened up about going through a very dark, personal phase. He was openly vulnerable. McDermott, in contrast, was positive as ever, quoting from Teddy Kennedy's "the Dream shall never die" speech. There was no mention of his own personal tragedy.

I am wondering "How does this man stay so positive?" when Bill responds to my email:

> "Thank you for your kind words, Vinnie. Gratitude is everything!"

It's not just this accident; the man has also navigated being a cross-border CEO. As he told the *Harvard Business Review*:

"I'm the first American to lead SAP in its 45-year history. I'm also the only American-born CEO leading a company on the DAX, Germany's stock exchange. I'm the only American on the European Round Table of Industrialists, a group of CEOs of Europe's largest companies. With a presence in nearly every country on earth, SAP has long been open to contributions by anyone, of no matter what nationality or background. Still, leading a company whose identity is rooted in a culture that's foreign presents unique challenges — which is why few CEOs do it."[37]

That interview was conducted before President Trump came to office. I imagine there are now additional challenges in being an American CEO of a European company. Of course, it helps that he has a team with global executives like Atzberger, Cohen, Enslin and Morgan.

I am only describing the tip of the spear — these executives are just a small handful of the 95,000 worldwide SAP employees. The pivot at SAP in the last five years has truly been massive. And the pivot will accelerate, as SAP announced in January 2019 a restructuring where it "will reassign some employees and offer early retirement to others, but still expects its overall head count to exceed 100,000 by the end of 2019."[38]

Let's next see if the customer base is keeping up.

---

[37] https://hbr.org/2016/11/saps-ceo-on-being-the-american-head-of-a-german-multinational
[38] https://www.reuters.com/article/us-sap-se-results/sap-plans-restructuring-after-signs-of-weakness-emerge-idUSKCN1PN0GD

SECTION III

The State of the Union

CHAPTER 5

Risk-Takers

∿→

One of the most interesting developments in the SAP customer base is the emergence of a breed of Risk-Takers who are using Leonardo tools, SCP and S/4 in the public cloud. While many of their projects are pilots and one-offs, these customers are showing up in industries and conducting business processes that are not traditional SAP strongholds. We profiled some of these customers in Ch. 3, and include more such customers in this segment.

However, they represent only the left edge of the customer bell curve (see illustration) which approximates the types of customer behavior we saw in researching this book.

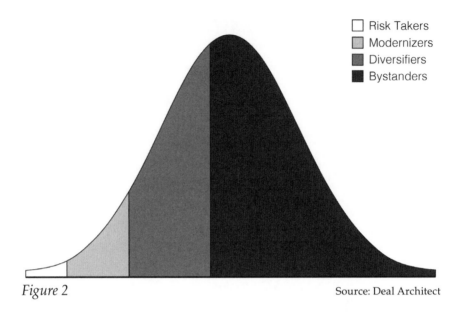

Risk Takers
Modernizers
Diversifiers
Bystanders

Figure 2   Source: Deal Architect

More widely represented on the curve are SAP customers that we call Modernizers. They are moving from legacy, on-premise technology to SAP cloud solutions like SuccessFactors and hybris. Many others are moving from ECC to S/4. But they are being cautious, deploying S/4 on-prem or in a private cloud, not in the public cloud. Many are sticking with SAP GUI and using traditional SIs like Deloitte, but in small doses. They are minimizing change, as they still have the muscle memory of painful, last-gen ERP projects. Seen another way, they may just be postponing the pain. And bypassing the gains — they may be missing out on efficiencies of multitenancy, and the benefits of ML and other innovations in the cloud. In Ch. 6, we will profile some of the Modernizers.

In the first volume of *SAP Nation*, we had described the early wave of Diversifiers. They were "ring-fencing" SAP with cloud solutions, trying out two-tier ERP models, TPM and private-cloud infrastructure. That group continues to expand and experiment. The big difference we noticed this time out is that in many cases they are returning to SAP products. Ch. 7 profiles several of these customers.

Bystanders are the biggest group of customers we observed during our research. They are waiting, and watching the other three groups. Some may call them "laggards", but I call this group "pragmatic." This customer behavior is not unique to SAP. Other on-premise heavy customer bases at Oracle, Infor and Microsoft are behaving similarly. Many SAP customers are based in Europe, and they often take a wait-and-see approach to new technologies. Motivating this group to try out SAP's newer technologies before they become enamored with competing alternatives will be a significant opportunity and challenge for SAP. We discuss this group in Ch. 8 to finish up this section.

Let's start off with the Risk-Takers.

Queensland OSR

⋀⋁→

They say everything is bigger in Australia. Queensland is an Australian state covering the continent's northeast, with a mainland coastline stretching over 4,000 miles! Its offshore Great Barrier Reef is the world's largest coral reef system, hosting thousands of marine species.

The Office of State Revenue (OSR), part of the state's Treasury department, administers a revenue base of approximately Australian $15 billion. OSR is tasked with delivering simple, efficient and equitable revenue management services for taxes, mining and petroleum royalties, fines and penalties. It also devises and delivers initiatives that support economic growth and job creation.

In recent years, OSR has faced key operational challenges, including the following:

- Data quality and accuracy to ensure the right amount of revenue is collected from the right person at the right time.
- Internal overhead costs due to time-consuming, manual processes.
- Increasing expectations of clients and other stakeholders for enhanced digital services.
- Cost of compliance for clients, which impacts their ability to grow their businesses and the Queensland economy.

These challenges led the Government to approve a significant transformation program at the OSR, and to allocate funding over five years (2017–2022) to support the effort. I interviewed Simon McKee, Deputy Commissioner, OSR, and Katherine Love, Program Director at OSR, about the program.

The OSR is running 46 digital initiatives or products. The SAP applications in the mix are currently run in a hybrid cloud model. The heart of the SAP transactional and data core is managed in an SAP-managed private HANA Enterprise Cloud in Queensland — soon to be moved to Canberra. OSR is also leveraging the C/4 suite of products that are more "pure" cloud based.

McKee is particularly excited about the ML projects.

One of the key business challenges that OSR faces is the late payment of taxation.

Land tax, in particular, has a high rate of tax payment default. This default comes at a considerable cost to the government, in terms of the opportunity cost associated with the delayed revenue and the cost in administering the debt recovery activities.

When OSR was looking to solve this challenge, they first needed to understand the factors that led some some taxpayers to pay on time, whilst others did not and gain better insights into the interventions that work versus those that are less effective.

In 2017, OSR ran an ML proof of concept with SAP teams from Queensland Innovation Centre and Palo Alto, CA. Despite what McKee described as limited internal sourced and not necessarily clean data, the machine predicted with 72% accuracy when land taxpayers would likely default on their payment obligations. McKee anticipates that with more internal and external sources and cleaner data they'll be able to get that number much higher, aspirationally closer to 100%.

The ML proof of concept highlighted to OSR two groups of taxpayers that do not meet their obligations. The first group has no intention of paying. Predictive technology can help with that group by sending out proactive notifications and campaigns to repeat offenders to encourage them to become compliant. The second group wants to pay, but is unable to do so for a variety of reasons. There is plenty of predictive work that can be done with this group, including reaching out to them with better payment terms or relief in case of natural disasters.

Love provided more details about the ML initiative:

> "SAP approached OSR. They knew that we had just commenced our transformation program. They knew some of the outcomes we were seeking. They offered us an opportunity to partner with them on a joint innovation project, leveraging some of the technologies around Leonardo.
>
> Over an eight-week innovation sprint, we developed a proof of concept on Leonardo ML, to see if we could gain the insights we needed. From an OSR perspective, we were so new to ML concepts that we leveraged heavily the SAP innovation team. We provided the data and our business knowledge,

and they provided the technical expertise. In eight weeks, they crunched 187 million records from 97,000 tax payers.

The product categorized all that data that we had — the 187 million records — into meaningful events in the taxpayer journey. Next, they matched the journey of each taxpayer with their event risk, over time, to be able to provide a prediction of what would happen next. The prediction was about the likelihood of default based on the taxpayer's unique set of circumstances. To measure the accuracy, the prediction was then validated against real data. That's how we derived the 72% accuracy metric.

We did look at some competing platforms. The advantage of SAP is that the solution could be run from our private cloud, so we didn't have to worry about any of the security issues associated with some of the competing ML offerings, where data would need to be sent to a public cloud and in some cases sent overseas. Given that we're dealing with taxpayers' data, that wasn't going to fly."

To clarify the point, McKee added:

"Because we have a stable SAP core, the integration aspects of the SAP Leonardo solution were attractive. With competing products, they would have been off the shelf. SAP built something which was fit for our purpose."

Love continued:

"Next, we deployed that solution into production. In less than six months, we have been able to stand up the production solution, and it's far more complex than what we deployed in pilot. We will have a solution that will provide real-time, live insights into our taxpayers. The business value of this is significant, allowing us to be more proactive in our responses and personalized in our treatment strategies, based on an individual taxpayer's circumstances.

We're looking at data as another key SAP project. As a tax office, we have access to vast amounts of data. So one of the first decisions that we made as part of our transformation program was to establish an enterprise data warehouse. When we looked at alternatives, the clearest option for us was to establish that on a very large HANA database. We are pushing the boundaries at the moment. We have a HANA Enterprise Information Management toolset. What we're trying to do is incredibly complex, given the data matching and the delta/change records flowing in real time from our transactional systems into the data warehouse, and the continuous matching/cleansing. When we started this project, I think we were one of only two organizations globally with that large a scale of EIM usage. Our team is regularly in contact with the product development team in Germany to resolve any issues as they occur.

We also have a series of initiatives around automation, and we're looking at partnering with SAP. One of that is around Intelligent Process Automation. So, rather than just doing Robotic Process Automation, we are exploring blending ML and RPA to get a better learned outcome. We receive a lot of manual forms. We are looking at the potential of using ML to interpret those manual, handwritten forms and then submit them into the system through RPA-style processes."

McKee described the most notable thing about working with SAP:

"I asked an SAP executive why, given we're a relatively small organization and we don't spend billions of dollars with them, the attraction of inviting us to partner with them in developing these bleeding-edge technologies? Their response was that they see us as quite a unique organization, relatively small and agile, that can rapidly pilot certain products. And, of course, if it works, they can commercialize it."

Bombardier

∿⟶

Delta Airlines is one of the launch customers for the Airbus A-220. Passengers will absolutely notice a very unusual feature on the new plane: There is more space onboard for carry-ons than those on similar-sized aircraft! The passengers, however, will likely not notice an even more consequential feature: The plane is actually developed by Bombardier, then marketed by Airbus.

Bombardier is a global aerospace and transportation company headquartered in Montreal, Canada. It started as a maker of snowmobiles, and is now a large manufacturer of trains, regional airliners and business jets. Bombardier Aerospace makes a variety of midrange planes such as the Challenger Regional Jet (its CRJ line of planes) and corporate jets such as the industry-defining Global Series. A joint venture with Airbus has led to the A-220, which seats 110 to 160 passengers and competes for the twin-engine, medium-range market against Boeing and Embraer products. With 40+ production and engineering sites in 27 countries, Bombardier Transportation is a global mobility solution provider with the rail industry's broadest portfolio. Worldwide, its installed base of rolling stock exceeds 100,000 rail cars and locomotives, and moves 500,000+ people per day.

When you listen to Global CIO E. Jeffrey Hutchinson talk about his company, you can almost hear the song *Tubthumping* in the background, which goes: "I get knocked down, but I get up again. You are never gonna keep me down."

As Hutchinson put it:

"When you look at the history of the company, we go through growth spurts and then, unfortunately, something hits us, be it war, economics or industry changes. And then, when that occurs, we have gotten knocked down, but we have this great tradition of climbing out and growing again. We have gone through this cycle many times in our 75-year history."

That pattern also explains the recent joint venture with Airbus, as he explained:

"[Bombardier] was almost bankrupt four years ago. It created a new transformation approach and is now going through and rebuilding its capabilities from an enterprise and corporate level. We make some of the coolest planes and trains in the world. This stuff is just incredible, and yet we did too much on spreadsheets!

We are in the business of what I call heavy industrial manufacturing. The largest part of our business is train manufacturing, which includes the engines and the passenger cars on the trains. At Frankfurt Airport, for example, it's our train that goes between two terminals. In New York City, most of the New York City subway trains are ours. Many of the high-speed bullet trains in France and Italy are ours. We make a large selection of trains, which is the largest part of our income, and we also make leading planes.

We have initiated an enterprise program that we call Polestar, focused on driving common business processes across the operational part of most of the corporation, enabled by leading technology. We're not the biggest player in our industry. As a matter of fact, we're probably small-to-mid-tier compared to Boeing or Airbus and some of the larger train manufacturers. Yet, we are large, and we're talking about a $16 billion business. Our challenge is to figure out how we're going to outperform our competition."

Hutchinson describes the company's approach to becoming an intelligent enterprise — but he makes a clear distinction between SAP's marketing and Bombardier's vision. He also explains why he doesn't use the term "digital transformation":

"We've got to be faster, more agile, and we've got to make better data-driven business decisions. We have to go from where we are today to becoming an intelligent enterprise. But it's not the definition that SAP will pitch for an intelligent enterprise, because we see SAP as an enabler to it, as a piece of it.

We have a business need to become more intelligent. In order to make that work, you've got to have good data. In order to have good data, you've got to have solid end-to-end processes. And, if you're smart, you'll have those processes leveraging leading technology. Most companies would call what we are doing a digital transformation program. We purposely don't use the words "digital transformation." We have a very narrow definition of the word "digital." To us, the term is way overused. We refer to digital as taking existing customer-facing processes and creating new products or services. Everything else is automation we should have done 10 years ago.

We don't even talk about SAP as part of the program. We talk about making better decisions. We talk about standardizing around leading processes, about being lean and more agile. We talk about leveraging a leading technology and the processes it brings with zero customization. And, by the way, it happens via S/4, but it's not about an ERP deployment. It's about driving the corporation to where it needs to get to.

For example, we just did a Polestar program status update. We purposefully had the Chief Operating Officer for that division give the presentation. I was on the call, but I purposefully stayed in the background. We're not making Polestar a software project. because it'll go back to the old ways that people want to do things. Unfortunately, our old ways included overly customizing our SAP environments over the years. This time, we are taking the approach we did at Maple Leaf Foods in Toronto [one of his previous employers]. In that one, it was like the old drug campaign, "Just say no." The CEO himself had to approve any customizations. This time the presidents of the business units and I need to jointly approve all customizations.

This is not a Canadian (headquarters) program. It is a global program that we are running out of Berlin, Germany. It's purposefully done that way so that we're sending a message to the rest of the corporation. This is truly a global effort and by working out of locations outside of headquarters, we're changing the mindset.

One of the things about S/4 is that because it's that new, the consultancies have limited expertise on the latest versions. Yes, we need to use consultancies, but there are two other core places I can get the latest knowledge. One is with ASUG and the other is working directly with SAP. We leverage ASUG to find out what other companies are doing, to find out who is actually where, and to get the networks and the contacts. SAP doesn't necessarily make that easy to do.

If I went to analyst firms, they will give me huge research studies. Or tell us, 'Go attend this conference.' Okay, but they don't easily help me navigate the world of finding out who else is doing something that I can go talk to, get my hands around. ASUG gives us access to such a network.

We leverage SAP to get into the development side of the house — what's included and what's not in the latest releases. We're going to spend the next quarter or so doing our high-level blueprinting with SAP, ASUG and one of our strategic SI consultancies involved so that we can make sure that we know not just what's available today in S/4, but what's also coming out shortly.

A little under two years ago, we outsourced application and infrastructure run and fix-it to IBM. Working with SAP and IBM, we transferred all our on-prem licensing to IBM. Because of the way it's set up with SAP through IBM, we have opened up our ability to move licensing around between on-prem and the cloud. This gives us the flexibility and support for what we have today and what we're going to need in the future.

We have a multitenant setting which is dedicated to Bombardier. I have five or six older instances of SAP today. I have 30+ other ERPs out there, and we're migrating to IBM's outsourcing support. They are also doing the application fix-it and support management.

In the first phase, we are focusing heavily on the operations side of the house. In the rolling stock side of our house, we don't sell a pre-built, pre-designed train. We sell a family or a model family with configurable modules, or only where necessary, customized components. When we are selling rolling stock it is unique to each customer. What I build for New York City is different from what I build for Toronto, which is different from what I build for the UK. It's very heavy from a product lifecycle management [PLM] point of view. We're also in the aftermarket business, which is also highly unique. For example, in the rolling stock side of the house, if you went to Frankfurt Airport, you will find the automated people mover is ours. We run it. We run the computer systems and manage the automation of it. We do maintenance on it. We do maintenance on the tracks. We do everything lock, stock and barrel. Many of these are 15-to-30-year type contracts. It almost becomes a job shop, with the one-off type approach for a lot of what we do.

On the other hand, on the aerospace side, especially if I look at business aircraft, we're kind of a final assembler. For those planes, the shell is standardized because that's what gets approved by the different country aviation authorities. The cockpit, the flight control systems are more standardized. In a business aircraft, it is the interior where the variation is immense. For example, if you're rich and famous, you may want a stationary bicycle in your private business jet because you want to exercise on the flight. Well, you can't just install one. You have to get governmental aviation authority approval. Anything that can move around on a plane — that's not locked in a cabinet — has to be approved. Then, you're getting into weight and balances. In that case, we have a highly customized approach to handle the variants. It's the PLM and CRM sides of the house that drives the process. Then, we release engineering and manufacturing BOMs to the floor through SAP."

Most early adopters of S/4 are focused on HQ functions. Yes, they need to standardize their financial requirements, but Bombardier is tackling operational areas first. And there, it is confident enough to implement S/4 out of the box, with limited bolt-on and/or customization. In addition, given the large size of the company, the global dimensions of the program and the innovative licensing and deployment model, Bombardier is in the Risk-Taker segment of our bell curve of SAP customers.

GEBHARDT

〜➤

Stephan Riemensperger, Head of Business IT, described his company, GEBHARDT Fördertechnik GmbH, where he has worked since 2007:

"We build conveyor systems and also write software for them. We are not tied to any particular industry. If a company wants to move a pallet or a box from point A to B within a facility, we can build the conveyor. We can also do the planning for the customer if desired, not just deliver the hardware and software. Our sales order starts with one line item and ends up with 2,500 component line items. The high complexity of each individual device is mapped with variant configuration functionality.

In 2007, we were approximately 170 employees; now we are at nearly 600. So, you can see, we have been growing rapidly. I am part of the business IT team, which is responsible for all the enterprise solutions in our company, including SAP ECC, C4C, JAM, Analytics Cloud, SuccessFactors Learning, an inbound marketing system and a live chat system — and we are responsible for the end step in product configuration for our sales and design department."

Riemensperger continued:

"Our goal is to have a very close partnership with our customers. It is a competitive market, and we want to be a strong partner to our customers through the lifecycle of our conveyor systems. So that led us to requests for IoT scenarios such as condition monitoring, predictive maintenance and also a portal to share equipment and service information with customers.

We looked at the market and compared SAP Leonardo to Siemens MindSphere, Microsoft Azure and some open-source solutions. We have had a very good partnership with SAP for a very long time. We have successfully implemented a number of other SAP solutions. The Leonardo IoT solution and roadmap SAP showed us was powerful and fit into our plans. Finally, the SAP headquarters in Walldorf is very close to ours in Sinsheim — only 20 kilometers away. So, for all these reasons, we decided to go with Leonardo IoT.

We developed a proof of concept in March 2018 with SAP and demoed it at LogiMAT, the International Trade Fair for Intralogistics Solutions and Process Management in Stuttgart. We branded it Galileo IOT and this YouTube video[39] shows all

---

[39] https://www.youtube.com/watch?v=1G8FebTEBoM&t=107s

our current IoT scenarios. We showed condition monitoring in an application that we built ourselves and continue to improve. The foundation was the IoT services and the application enablement was on the SCP.

We also developed our own sensor that tracks various metrics. We analyze the data from the sensor as time-series data points. Let's take temperature, in one minute you have — depending on transmission rate — 60 data points, and the sensor can summarize all 60 sensor data points onto one data point. That way, you do not have much traffic between the physical world and the cloud. In the IoT world, it is common to collect information on a million data points, and 990,000 are "noise" and only 10,000 are important. You just want to have the 10,000 data points in the cloud because data storage is money for a company.

We had to build that filtering capability and map it to our products. SAP just gives us the infrastructure. I think that is the next thing SAP will have to develop because that's a challenge for every IoT customer, especially for smaller companies. A very big company has specialists, a big IT department, who can do it. But for us, IoT or web development is not our main business. Our main business is to build conveyor systems.

Here was our experience with the different Galileo modules. We offer them to customers on a modular basis. Customers book them as part of their rental agreement with GEBHARDT:

Condition Monitoring

It wasn't easy to build a web application for condition monitoring. The approach to develop a web application is completely different to an ABAP development on the ECC solution.

Predictive Maintenance

We created various predictive maintenance scenarios. This required different algorithms and thresholds in the time-series data. If that exceeded a maximum or minimum value, it created a service ticket in our CRM system. It's a trigger. We can do other tasks with triggers, but in our scenario, we created a service ticket. That starts a process where a service technician goes to the customer site and helps them with the problem.

Augmented Reality Glasses

We created an augmented reality scenario using HoloLens [Microsoft's mixed reality glasses]. You wear the glasses, go to our equipment and scan the barcode with the glasses. You can see different controls for attributes like vibration and speed. We also transfer the data from the time series database to the HoloLens glasses — so that becomes the single source of truth.

Customer Portal

We use the SAP AIN as a customer portal. Our aim is that every customer who buys a conveyor system from GEBHARDT will have access to AIN where they will find manuals, data sheets, maintenance manuals and short animations for changing different components. We have a nice solution from SAP called 3D Visual Enterprise where we use the CAD model. We can show animations on how to change special parts in this CAD model.

Our second step will be to create "digital twins." In our business, it's not uncommon that we deliver the conveyor system but the customer has their own maintenance department. So, if the customer changes a spare part, it should be reflected in the bill of materials in AIN and so we then know that the customer has changed it. We would also like to offer the capability to easily order spare parts from AIN. We will have a shopping cart in AIN.

Our experience with SAP around IoT and AIN was very good. It was a similar situation with Cloud for Customer where we were early adopters in 2014. Very helpful, very friendly, a good and strong project team from the SAP side. For ECC, C4C, and so on (as that has matured), we use third-party partners. But the Leonardo portfolio is very young and so it's very hard to find partners who can help you.

We have not made the move to S/4, and I'm not sure when we will migrate. We don't have a licensing issue since we did a swap — we can also use our licenses for SAP ECC for S/4. The tougher issue to choose is whether to go with a brownfield or greenfield implementation. [In Ch. 6 we will see that every SAP customer is grappling with that choice.] We will deploy it on-prem or in HEC, not in the public cloud, but we are not sure yet. The move to S/4 is turning out to be a tough decision. It may be a 2020 project. Or perhaps even 2021."

It's not that GEBHARDT does not have public cloud experience. Riemensperger elaborated:

"Our ECC system is on-prem, but other SAP solutions are in the cloud — and the integration experience has been pretty good. We use the SAP cloud integration, SCI or the SAP Cloud Connector. Sometimes we find naming between products is not consistent. For example, in ECC you have one name for an object, and in the CRM you have another name for a similar object. But in the big picture it works fine."

Separate from the Leonardo IoT project, Riemensperger provided further input on their HoloLens experience. They also use it in sales situations. They show prospects a simulated plant and the conveyor system they are proposing. He would like the glasses to become smaller and more comfortable to wear. The next milestone could be glasses similar to those from Realwear with its noise cancellation features. Field technicians could control their glasses with their voice even in noisy settings, leaving their hands free to work on the machine.

For early adoption of C4C, Leonardo, AIN and other SAP products, for experimentation with HoloLens and other augmented reality glasses, and for pioneering IoT scenarios and new business models, GEBHARDT qualifies as a risk-taker.

Endeavour Energy

∿➤

Paul Coetser is a plainspoken Aussie who tells it like it is. His LinkedIn profile says: "Let me help you get what you asked for. Plain and Simple. I provide you with Design and Delivery Assurance. All my clients are reference-able. Pragmatic solutions to challenges are my bread and butter."

Over the course of writing this book, I had numerous conversations with Coetser. Many were about SAP project failures, but he raved about one client in particular, Endeavour Energy in Sydney. And with good reason — they are undergoing a massive transformation. Coetser said, "This is the biggest wall-to-wall transformation that I'm aware of in this region over the past 18 years from a functionality point of view. It includes almost every one of SAP's major product sets." He is playing the role of Chief Architect, and a broader role as adviser to the CIO and project driver.

> "We're a regulated distributor. We take the energy from transmission lines, put it all over the suburbs, with major commercial businesses and big industry all the way down to the meter at your house. We have about 2.4 million people in households and we're the fastest-growing Australian utility in our sector because of the growth market around Sydney, which we call the Western Corridor.

In turn, we also have a number of fundamental issues. We were government owned up until the middle of 2017 when a Macquarie-led consortium acquired a 50.4% stake. That effectively made us switch to being a privately owned entity.

Now, you can imagine pivoting from a government mindset to a privately owned mindset was a major change in itself. Macquarie also mandated other changes: 'The business will optimize and become more efficient. And, by the way, we also had a look at the business and many of your core systems are unsustainable. You'll have to undergo a transformation.'

The CIO, Andrew Bettenay, came onboard, and he is absolutely one of the most pragmatic CIOs I've ever worked for. He mandated the changes, wrote the services RFP, went to market, scored and selected a SI. We put all the commercials, constructs and frameworks in place over December 2017. We marshalled in all the troops and we kicked off the project in February 2018. We've gone through the standard project prep, blueprint, design phases. We're now in the *Realize* phase. Our first release is due in February 2019. Release Two, which has the lion's share of the capabilities and new system functionality, is October 2019. Release Three is due April 2020.

Our scope includes S/4, Ariba, Concur, SuccessFactors LMS, OpenText, Enable Now, BW and EAM. In terms of the customer-facing area, we have IS-Utility and the Hybris functionality. We're also using ClickSoftware, a SAP partner, for the field force and work scheduling. We decided not to go with certain aspects of SAP suite, like Fieldglass. We have deprecated some of the Ariba capabilities because we could not see the value proposition to the business.

We are using SCP. We've got SAP PO, the process orchestration engine. S/4 will be in a private cloud on Azure. We will own the solution and the extension framework.

Where we don't use SAP is in what is known in the industry as OMS (outage management systems) or DMS (distribution management systems). Those are in the control room where engineers and controllers physically shunt and control power between the power lines and the feeders. It's a highly specialized system and we are replacing our old systems with new ones from Schneider Electric.

We effectively have four GIS systems that we've inherited over 20+ years. We're going to a single GIS system, Esri, and new functionality from SAP called GEF which complements it.

This entire SAP footprint is only one of the pillars that we're busy with. In total, we have about 150 projects. For example, we have the Lights Up pillar which covers the Windows XP, 7, and 8 to 10 migration, standardizing the desktops, remediation of the network, rebuild and redesign of infrastructure. We are reengineering the data centers and the communications network. There's an ADMS (grid modernization) pillar. Under another pillar, we have security improvements — hardening the encryption and implementing defensive technologies.

I asked him how it has been to work with SAP.

"SAP terminology has been confusing. In our project, we call it ERP, IS-U, and EAM. It's the same system, but we have three streams and three project managers, and that's what the business thinks it is. IS-U is actually part of S/4. It's a common misconception. IS-U is not a stand-alone or a sidecar design. I ask SAP reps, 'Why do you do that? You confuse customers. You won't confuse me because I know better, but if I'm a net new customer, that looks like different systems to me.' It's the same code line. It's in the core.

From a user experience and a process execution point of view, the solution is complex and incomplete because you start a process chain — you may start in Fiori and then have to go to a different GUI, so it's a very disjointed, complex and expensive solution to own. The security model on GUI is different from Fiori, so when you're defining roles you have to apply two composite security frameworks so a user has a seamless experience. That's been a challenge.

Their licensing conditions can be — how shall I say this — esoteric. So when we licensed Concur, we told them, 'You know our business. Can you just bring us back some use cases?' We got this whole four-page response back quoting the license metrics. We said, 'No. Just give it to us in English, mate. If Paul goes to the U.S. on a trip, and Paul wants to submit the claim, how will that work and how would you then bill us for that?' But we got every answer except the straight answer, and that caused us quite a bit of distress. But SAP stood tall and fixed that, too.

We also reengineered the services agreement with SAP, which caused us a massive … disagreement. They told us, 'We've never had a customer try and make us change it. These are our terms and conditions, and we don't change it.' But kudos: SAP was willing to listen and change — and they did.

We mandated all processes and all artifacts to go into Solution Manager so that we can manage our entire business from one repository. To that end, we tasked SAP to provide us with documentation for Concur, Ariba and SuccessFactors, so we will be the first client in the world to actually have all that in Solution Manager. I pushed SAP really, really hard. But again, SAP came up roses.

Integration across all their properties is a work-in-progress. If you'd asked me about Ariba two years ago, I would have told you to put twice as much money into your integration bucket as the entire cost of Ariba. SAP has invested quite a bit in that respect. There are a number of things, though, that are problematic. You can't integrate those, all the SaaS products, into SAP IDM and SSO because the connectors are not created, so there are problems with that integration. We had to do some manual wizardry in the background to make all that play nice, and that is quite an expensive outcome.

The GRC stuff, from an integration point of view, is proving to be a bit of a challenge. You can see SAP hasn't invested in PO, so we use 7.5 single stack Java and nothing much has changed. A few bug fixes here and there, but the product is showing its age.

SAP talks up a good show on C/4. But when you try and integrate it, it's a messy affair. My perception is they're investing in flashy, front-facing stuff that gets them the most media time rather than knuckling down to get customers going. I did a quick exercise where I plugged all the applications into a capability matrix. Some of the areas have a 65% overlap … which goes where for what?

SAP is behind the eight ball on where the utility market is going. We're going to 288 reads a day per meter, and their systems just can't handle it. The sales guys will happily tell you IS-U is a solution. You buy these couple of things here, plug this in there, and it'll all work. But when we did the design I had to go, 'Geez, this isn't going to work, mate, not in a month of Sundays.' We had to come up with a custom solution. From the integration perspective I have to say it's a little disappointing. Overall, though, SAP is changing so I have huge respect for that."

Given the complexity of the transformation, Endeavour Energy was recognized as the Best Enterprise & IT Architecture in the Utility Industry at the New York ICMG Conference in November 2018. Bettenay and Coetser were also recognized with awards in other categories. Bettenay commented, "[There's] still a lot of work to go to successfully deliver but a great way to end the year and a ringing endorsement on the strategy and architecture that we have put in place."

I don't have an award for Bettenay and Coetser, but I can certainly recognize them as Risk-Takers for working with so many pieces in the SAP portfolio and hammering them together to make them work.

Restaurant Chain

⌁➤

Tara Gambill, Sr. Director of Enterprise Systems at a restaurant chain, described her journey to S/4 and SuccessFactors in the cloud:

"We had some of the challenges that came with rapid growth in a start-up mentality. I call them 'true crimes of passion.' You get to a point where, if the company wants to continue to scale, how do you provide some foundations and frameworks to enable that growth?

One of the first systems that we had already maxed out was our accounting system. It was a cloud restaurant-specific, SME-focused system, but more on the small side of scale and support, and we had pushed its limits.

We needed a system that was going to be fast to implement. Naturally, with our scale of data, we needed to be able to rely on speed of data processing, and we needed to be able to teach people quickly.

We are a SaaS-only shop. It was important that we find a tool that would sit in that space, that would provide that scalability, the right total cost of ownership and the ability to fit in our cloud architecture.

We had a number of people that were quickly solving a handful of problems. That leaves a wake of things that need to be standardized and automated. We also needed to raise the visibility and transparency of compliance, knowing that we wanted to effectively manage our controls.

But the system had to be something that was simple and easy to train on, whether it was our users or whether it was the technology team.

We had more of a bake-off than a full RFP. Some of us had worked with SAP before — we had some background with the ECC products. A few of us also had some background with Oracle and NetSuite. So it really became a compare-and-contrast activity between those three in particular. It was narrowed down to SAP and NetSuite."

They were such an early S/4 cloud adopter that the company had to figure out how to implement and then take advantage of the new S/4 system as fast as possible, all the while living "on the tip of the spear."

"I'm acutely aware that being on the public cloud, we are a minority in the S/4 world. I think we were one of the first in North America to go live with the enterprise management version. I know there were a couple of professional services firms that might have beaten us.

I did have a direct dial to a number of SAP folks because we were on this tip of the spear here. I don't think we fully realized how nascent the cloud product was when we signed the papers. I have lived it. Where it is today versus where we were when we went live a year ago, it's a night and day difference. It has been quite a ride, and it will continue to be so. I am excited to partner with SAP when I see their commitment to moving it forward.

The capabilities that we focused on were core accounting — GL, AP, and AR. We are starting to use the procure-to-pay capabilities. We also plan to use the project capability to manage the budget to actuals.

Also, the UI was not quite ready. That also has changed, but at the time, we had to make some decisions. Just given how busy our stores are and the demands of our general managers, that is a trade-off. We want the great data on the back end, but we can't give general managers a user experience that makes everything else suffer.

We want a P&L on every single store, and that tracks back to a plant. Each one of our stores is considered a 'plant' in S/4. You know if you're one of the bigger commerce or manufacturing companies, you're not spinning up two plants a week. They don't have our scale of opening stores. So it's not surprising that we were at the design table with SAP to rethink the organizational structure in S/4.

We found a great provider to help us with the implementation, and they were one of the few SIs that had any experience in the public cloud. Even the biggest SIs who have been doing ECC forever will have a learning curve with the public cloud.

Our SuccessFactors implementation was a little more challenged. As they have acquired these different modules, there's still a lack of that back-end integration. It's siloed. Even their API strategies are not consistent, so that brings another layer of challenge. The S/4 roadmaps are much more specific.

I was fortunate enough to be in Walldorf [SAP HQ in Germany] for a Cloud Day event and was able to participate in one of the SAP developer sessions and share my customer story. This is what I heard: Customers want more. We all want more. But make sure nothing breaks. Make sure it's perfect — especially in the multitenant space. I fully understand that, unlike in a private cloud or on-premise, you can't just get in there and rodeo these fixes and stop the bleeding. It's a different process.

It's a conversation that we had in Walldorf about the balance between quality and volume [of new features]. And, I remember they asked me, 'What's your take on that?' It was a *Star Wars*-themed event, and I'm a big *Star Wars* fan, so I kind of cheekily answered: 'It's like a balance of the Force.'"

She did have some advice for SAP:

"I don't see really big companies, for at least the foreseeable future, being able to unhook the tentacles out of a 10- or 15-year ECC implementation and plug it into preconfigured best practices. So, if you ask me, and you want to go big like Bill McDermott wants to go, it's going to be more customers like us. That is where the multitenant market is going to grow."

In being an early adopter for the S/4 cloud version, and for using a product she needs to adapt to the unique needs of the restaurant industry, Gambill definitely qualifies as a Risk-Taker.

Munich Re

∿➤

Munich Re is one of the world's largest reinsurers. At SAP's TechEd event in Barcelona in 2017, Andreas Siebert, head of the company's Geospatial Solutions division, described some of its challenges:

> "We are running a team of approximately 50 people focusing on natural perils worldwide. We are looking at earthquakes, storms, floods and wildfires. When looking at wildfires, we have seen an increase in claims during the last decade in North America. We have socioeconomic factors, with more settlements in risk-prone areas. We see some environmental factors like climate change, making the years dryer or hotter, and increasing fire activities.
>
> To model wildfires, we need land use information, altitude, soil moisture, weather climate — and much of this data cannot be delivered by earth observation."

So, they leverage data from Copernicus, the European Union's Earth Observation Programme. Petabytes of information from the European Space Agency are blended with Munich Re's own data. In a demo during the session, they showed a HANA system with data on 240,000 wildfires in the United States.

"We're now going to drill down into the Fort McMurray fire, which happened over two months last year [i.e., 2016]. These are some of the original photographs from the European Space Agency, and they have 12 layers that analyze different wavelengths of light. This one is focusing on vegetation, so this is the view here in April. If I scroll over, this is the view here in June. You can see the difference. The vegetation has grown. Munich Re wrote a REST-based API call to compare the foliage in those two photographs. They could then calculate with very great accuracy the footprint of the fire. Here you can see the footprint of the fire. Now, we already have a very accurate picture when a forest fire happens, immediately, what our risk and exposure is. We can take this data and take it one step further. We use these maps to predict where we think forest fires are going to happen. We have overlaid the actual Munich Re customers inside this area. If there are any fraudulent claims outside the red boundary, we will know about it. What we can then do is also instantly calculate the risk of exposure. Over here, you can see approximately how much money is at risk here, and you can see the different categories of businesses that are actually affected.

We take our learning from the United States, and we can apply that to the rest of the world. If we move to Spain, a neural network recalculates all of the points. What you see here is that every 16 square kilometers lots of different data points are calculated. We can pick any point here, and we can see why we think this is a danger area for a forest fire."

As Siebert summarized, it is allowing them to "improve claims management, portfolio management, the accumulation control, which is really key to our business and, last but not least, we can improve risk prevention and even mitigation activities."

It's not just Munich Re which is benefiting. Many other companies can use the API delivered through the Earth Observation Analysis service. Their use cases may include where to place new power lines, where to build a new store or when to harvest particular crops.

Another use case involving satellite data comes from the Waterwatch Cooperative.

Waterwatch Cooperative

∿➤

Waterwatch Cooperative aims to improve farming yields with more efficient use of resources such as water, fertilizers and pesticides. They focus on smaller farms, promising them a higher and more secure income and to help to make the farming value chain more sustainable. Using a variety of data sources from satellites and from farmers, they are developing a global vegetation database.

In collaboration with SAP, Waterwatch developed the Crop Disease Alert app, on SCP. The app records a crop's growing conditions and monitors it for signs of change in the growing environment like rain, humidity or change in temperature that might cause a specific disease to occur. The app then conducts a risk analysis for disease occurrence with each possible infection and rates them by risk level ranging from green (no risk) to red (high risk). The data is provided for a very affordable US$1 per farmer per year. It alerts farmers, the users of the application, about the condition of their crops so that they can apply appropriate treatments in time. They report 25–40% reduction in incidents of crop disease and more efficient use of resources.

More applications are being planned. Current projects include a crop selector for farmers in Burundi that advises them as to which crops to grow, based on soil quality, weather conditions, available seeds and market information. Another app offers coffee farmers in Vietnam a digital calendar of seasonal tasks.[40]

---

[40] https://www.forbes.com/sites/sap/2018/05/18/crop-disease-waging-modern-warfare-against-an-ancient-foe/#3e2dd3407a5f

Sports World

∿➤

Over the last decade, sports teams around the world have become early adopters of leading edge technologies like VR goggles and 5G networks and have been accepting bitcoin as currency.

Go to the annual MIT Sloan Sports Analytics Conference and you see how every sport has being reshaped with data. It's *Moneyball* on steroids. The best-selling 2003 Michael Lewis book has fired up the imagination of analysts in every sport.

There's ticketing analytics and dynamic pricing in the world of secondary ticket markets. There's injury data so athletes can bounce back quicker and better after major surgeries. There's "fanalytics" to measure sentiment before, during and after a game. There's scouting data on players for use both during drafting and trading athletes. There's in-game analytics which includes missile-tracking tech that can home in on a pitcher's curveball or the best position for a basketball rebound.

SAP has been working with a number of sports teams to help analyze this growing mountain of data.

San Francisco 49ers

Yosh Eisbart, CEO of the SI NIMBL, told me about their project for the Executive Huddle for the San Francisco 49ers, the U.S. NFL team. "It's located in one of their executive suites. It's a real-time data mashup of geospatial,

Ticketmaster, point of sale at their concession stands, parking information and other data. They act on the data during the games, deploying resources differently to try to bring up their average ticket spend or attendee spend."

The software behind the digital boardroom in the Huddle is based on SAP Leonardo and SAC. It ingests inputs from parking, ticketing, restrooms and other locations in the stadium. This synthesized data is then used to relay real-time instructions to 3,500 employees during each game. The 49ers previously relied on surveys to gauge the customer experience, but the data was too old to enable mid-game corrections.

Moon Javaid, Vice President of Strategy and Analytics for the San Francisco 49ers, told *ZDNet*,[41] "The at-home experience (with the TV broadcast) is so great that we wanted the in-game experience to be the best."

Of course, all this activity in sports analytics is spawning a number of start-ups and SAP is working with several, like RemIQz.

RemIQz

I had a chance to catch up with the Founder and Managing Director of RemIQz, Robert Slijk, and Huub Waterval, CEO of Nextview, an SAP Partner.

"RemIQz is a sports technology company which focuses on football [soccer] analytics & intelligence. We help clubs, players and other parties in the football industry to make objective decisions and enhance performances based on predictive data. Every day, we get to answer many interesting football questions!

In its most simple form, we created 'Moneyball' for football, based on SCP. If you buy or sell players, you need to take into account what they add to the team, and the ROI for investing in them. This has to be measured in terms of revenue from broadcasting, stadium attendance and winning trophies. We help calculate how a team will perform with or without a certain player, and then calculate his ROI.

The product became commercially available in August 2017. We have signed a number of professional football clubs across Europe, scouting agents and TV stations that are using our predictive analytics on a regular basis."

Industrie 4.0

∧∧→

Five years ago, in the first volume of SAP Nation, I wrote:

"I first heard about Industrie 4.0 from Dr. Henning Kagermann, former CEO of SAP, and now President of acatech, the German Academy of Science and Engineering. The first three industrial revolutions came about as a result of mechanization, electricity and IT. Now, the introduction of the Internet of Things into the manufacturing environment is ushering in a fourth industrial revolution. I conducted many interviews with executives at German companies like Daimler and Deutsche Bahn AG for the book *The Digital Enterprise* by Karl-Heinz Streibich, CEO of Software AG. I repeatedly heard about Industrie 4.0. They were describing how nextgen agile robots, urban factories, augmented reality training, 3-D printing, predictive maintenance and sensor technologies are reshaping manufacturing and logistics."

Those scenarios are showing up in a growing base of SAP customers.

Hoerbiger
Hoerbiger, headquartered in Zug, Switzerland, has been in business since 1895. It manufactures compressors, industrial

engines and turbines, automobile transmissions and multifaceted mechanical engineering applications. With 7,000+ employees in over 50 countries, it has revenues in excess of €1 billion.

A SAP customer for over two decades, Hoerbiger has been implementing S/4 to migrate from ECC. It has about 400 wellhead compression units in Argentina and Mexico. As gas fields mature and their reservoir pressure and production decline, compressors are designed to reduce wellhead pressure and allow for larger gas flow rates. These units tend to be in remote areas, and inspections require long trips and manual notations. If an inspection shows maintenance is needed, it entails a second trip.

These units are now being digitally connected to communicate with SCP. There, an algorithm splits the feed into two streams. One stream goes to the SAP C4C solution and the other to the SAP ERP system. If a machine goes down, a ticket is automatically created in the C4C system so the operator can evaluate whether it's necessary to travel to the unit. Timesheets feed hours into the ERP system to automatically generate invoices. Importantly, customers and not just Hoerbiger employees can now monitor the compressors remotely.

Kaeser Kompressoren

Kaeser Kompressoren, headquartered in Coburg, Germany, is similarly a century-old business. Its equipment also deals with compression. In their case, it is compressed air used in mines, refineries and other industrial settings. They have been moving to a new business model — compressed-air-as-a-service. As a result, servicing the machines is now a cost element for Kaeser, and so it works harder than ever to minimize service calls — and with the help of sensor data, it can predict needed repairs.

Like Hoerbiger, Kaeser had also moved to S/4. Additionally they have implemented SAP's Data Hub ties to stream IoT data for predictive maintenance and service. This allows Kaeser to identify and replace faulty parts during regularly scheduled maintenance — helping avoid unexpected, costly outages on customers' production lines.

Wearables and Mobile Apps

∿➤

Roche

Diabetes is a global epidemic, with over 400 million people suffering from the disease and projections of many more to be so diagnosed in the future. Roche, the giant Swiss pharma and medical devices company, offers a product called Accu-Chek View to help prevent and manage Type 2 diabetes, which is often caused by unhealthy lifestyles.

Accu-Chek View bundles a blood glucose monitor, a wearable fitness tracker and an app developed by SAP. Using a lancing device, users put a drop of blood on the test strip in the monitor, view results on the mobile app and transmit the information to their doctor. The data is securely stored and processed via SCP. The tracker collects other vital stats so the doctor can also monitor the patient from other health perspectives.

Satellites, sensors and wearables — products not tradition-ally associated with SAP. The customers above are definitely Risk-Takers for partnering with SAP for these emerging catego-ries of applications. However, most of their projects are pilots. McKinsey, analyzing IoT projects, said, "Many enterprises have launched pilot projects to develop IoT-enabled products and services or use the IoT to achieve operational improvements. Of these, less than 30& have taken their IoT programs beyond the pilot phase, according to our research."[42] You can substitute PaaS, ML or blockchain for IoT and get similar results across customers. That will also be SAP's challenge with these Risk-takers — how to take their pilots beyond their proof of concept projects.

Let's next look at what we call Modernizers. Like the Risk-Takers, they are trying out newer SAP products — but they are being much more cautious, like implementing S/4 in private cloud and minimizing process or UX change.

---

[42] https://www.mckinsey.com/business-functions/digital-mckinsey/our-insights/what-separates-leaders-from-laggards-in-the-internet-of-things.?cid=other-eml-alt-mip-mck&hlkid=6e4d05a8320e4413b4a3065bfc3a9b84&hctky=2428411 &hdpid=55f995b7-10a7-4fe0-9618-999f03e7315c

CHAPTER 6

Modernizers

∿➤

Migrations from ECC to S/4 are reviving the old Miller Lite "Tastes great! Less filling!" debate. Michael Broberg of Bluefin Solutions describes what he calls a "stark choice."[43]

"When they eventually implement SAP S/4, do they treat their prior investment as a sunk cost and re-implement their business model on S/4 (greenfield), or do they largely ignore the market-leading business capabilities S/4 offers and do a technical conversion of their present ECC system (brownfield) — and then he asks, "or is there a (third) alternative?"

SNP Schneider-Neureither & Partner SE calls their third alternative "bluefield."[44] What color is your migration from ECC to S/4? It doesn't matter — you qualify as a Modernizer by this book's grouping of SAP customers. Other modernizers

---

[43] https://www.bluefinsolutions.com/insights/michael-broberg/february-2018/sap-s-4hana-greenfield-and-brownfield-implementati
[44] http://www.snpgroup.com/en/bluefield-for-s/4hana

are moving from legacy, on-prem to SAP cloud solutions like SuccessFactors and hybris.

In the migrations to S/4, most customers are being cautious — deploying S/4 on-prem or in private cloud, sticking with the SAP GUI, using traditional SIs like Deloitte and mostly implementing accounting and inventory functionality. They are minimizing change and risk. The color coding, however, repeatedly comes up, as we will see throughout this chapter. Let's start with one of the earliest SAP customers to adopt S/4.

Johnsonville Sausage

∿➔

Johnsonville started as a small family-run butcher shop in 1945, and is now a global leader in the production of bratwurst and dozens of other sausage products. The privately held, family-owned company employs more than 1,800 members (employees). Johnsonville products are served in more than 40 countries and in more than 130 professional, college and semi-pro sports stadiums throughout the U.S.

Ron Gilson, VP and CIO, said:

"Johnsonville has been an SAP customer since 2003. We started with HCM Payroll and Benefits. We then followed it up with the APO products — Demand Planning, Supply Network Planning and a Vendor-Managed Inventory deployment that we integrated with a legacy ERP. We started our ECC implementation in 2006 and went live in 2008 with all the core functions of ECC — order to cash, procure to pay and plan to produce. We implemented a number of other products from 2008 to 2017, such as Business Objects and BW on HANA, Plant Maintenance, BPC, Global Trade, Global Batch Traceability, PLM, etc. We also use a number of the cloud products including Concur, SuccessFactors and Cloud for Customer (C4C).

In 2016, we started taking a look at our overall SAP roadmap. We had a significant list of new capabilities that we were looking to roll out: capabilities like extended warehouse management, yard management and transportation functionality. We stepped back and asked, 'How do we want to go about adopting that functionality over the next three or four years?' We can either build that on top of the existing ECC framework or move to the newest release of S/4. For us, it just didn't make sense to put it on top of ECC and then migrate a few years later to S/4. So, for us, a technical upgrade to S/4 was the most logical path. We did not attempt to calculate a financial justification or ROI for making the investment in S/4.

For context, ever since going live in 2008 on ECC, we would do a technical upgrade on an annual basis. For us, this was normally an enhancement pack upgrade that took six-to-eight weeks to execute. We have no modifications to the system. And we have a relatively low amount of custom code. We are, primarily, an SAP shop with almost 90% of enterprise application functionality delivered via SAP technology. There is limited third party or other best-of-breed solutions. So, since 2008, our upgrade cycles have been relatively minor and low effort.

The upgrade to S/4 was a significantly larger initiative than the annual enhancement pack upgrade, and that was primarily driven by the changes to the S/4 code-line. First, you had items that were deprecated, which is also known as the infamous SAP simplification list: the 300-page document that lists all of the code that's been deprecated to eliminate redundant solutions with the introduction of S/4.

For instance, in ECC Johnsonville relied heavily on Rebate agreements which was redundant with the newer feature known as Condition Contracts. SAP elected to deprecate Rebate agreements, forcing customers to move to Condition Contracts. Similarly, they had a product called Easy DMS, which was a graphical front end for SAP's DMS. Easy DMS was deprecated and replaced with a newer product called Mobile Docs. These are not one-to-one functionally equivalent products. Implementing Easy DMS or Condition Contracts requires significant process change, configuration changes and some retraining of end users. So, that is an effort we would not usually have to address in a typical ECC upgrade.

Additionally, third-party-certified applications required significant work. When we started our S/4 project in early 2017, SAP required that third-party applications be certified for every release level of S/4. Vendors had to recertify on release 1511, then 1610, then 1709 — which requires an investment in time and resources for those vendors. They were also forcing the third-party vendors to wait for GA [general availability] of the S/4 release before they could start the certification process. That created a seven- to eight-month delay in getting many products certified. As you're going through a migration project, you can't continue the process if it encounters a noncertified product in the stack. Ultimately, some vendors simply elected not to certify for S/4, requiring Johnsonville to source alternate solutions. We worked with SAP and the vendors over the first six or seven months of the project to evaluate the certification process and encourage a more customer-centric approach to certification.

Most of Johnsonville's configuration and development work for the migration centered around the required migration to the Business Partner entity. In the legacy ECC world, we had Customers and Vendors. In S/4 SAP requires the use of a Master Data entity called the Business Partner for both customers and vendors. At the end of the day, we kicked off the project in February and went live in October.

There are SAP-provided pre-checks that identify custom objects that could potentially have an issue. For us, approximately 2,200 custom objects were identified as potentially having issues. When we dug into those, only about 200 of them actually had to be touched. The rest were just warning messages based on change in item number length which really wasn't an issue for us. The actual remediation for those 200 objects was relatively simple and did not require a lot of sophisticated skills. Most of it required modifying SQL statements. There was work to do and it was time-consuming, but it wasn't difficult work, and we handled most of that internally.

There were some sizing issues. The actual migration required more CPU and memory on the ECC servers than we had anticipated or estimated. So we had to add some hardware to improve performance of the DMO (Database Migration) in order to meet our scheduled downtime window. The sizing of the HANA environment was accurate — we had no issues during conversion or post go live with HANA sizing or performance."

Next, Gilson described the difference in the way Johnsonville thought about its move to S/4 — as an upgrade — versus the way SAP talks about the transition. He also mentioned his decision on whether to embrace SAP Fiori or stick with SAP GUI.

"Overall, I think SAP has done a good job. The move to HANA simplified the database, but they left compatibility views in place. So, even though they eliminated tables, they left a logical view of the data that looked just like the old physical table so it helped mitigate the code remediation.

SAP doesn't want to position the move to S/4 as an upgrade. They really focus on making folks aware that this is a different code-line, it's a different SKU and it's a different product. So it's a migration to a different product. However, we treated it like an upgrade; our environment was suitable for that approach. We were current on ECC, we were on Enhancement Pack 7, and we had consistently done upgrades. We had minimal custom code concerns, a single global instance, and we were already Unicode compliant. Additionally, we were relatively small, with a database under a terabyte in size.

We also elected not to implement Fiori, the new business processes or best practices that are baked into S/4. Today, we are running S/4 with the SAP GUI and the business processes we had configured in ECC. We have about 12 transactions based on Fiori that were required because there wasn't a corresponding SAP GUI transaction available in S/4, but that is it. Everything else is running SAP GUI on top of S/4. We made that decision because we were treating it as a technical upgrade. One of our project goals was to have our end-user experience exactly the same as the ECC experience when we went live on S/4 (no retraining or change management requirements).

This is a database migration, so we had to find a suitable downtime window. We negotiated a 72-hour downtime window with the organization. We basically shut the business down for three days. In order to hit that downtime window, additional hardware requirements were required to get through the migration tasks within that timeframe. It wasn't huge. I'm not saying we had to spend millions of dollars on additional hardware. It was primarily a matter of tuning the memory to CPU ratios to dramatically reduce the conversion time.

I guess that's the key point here: It was an upgrade to facilitate future roadmap items. And our go-forward strategy is to evaluate the best practices and Fiori, as we implement new capability in a specific area. Our next big task is a significant procure-to-pay project. We'll take a look and bring in best practices in that business process. So, kind of a gradual move into Fiori versus the Big Bang major change-management project.

We implemented BW on HANA over five years ago. From a skills perspective, it gave us the ability to scale up our internal Basis and infrastructure teams on HANA in a less mission-critical environment. We had three or four years of experience with HANA on the BW side before we began implementing HANA for S/4. We didn't have to hire any new specific skillsets and we took our existing BASIS resources and skilled them up. We're still running with the same two BASIS resources we had prior to the migration. In the environment we came from, we were running SAP on SQL Server with data compressed on a Dell EMC Flash Memory storage array. We were essentially running SQL Server in memory. From a performance perspective we have experienced mixed results — minor improvements in some areas and minor degradation in others. Overall, there was not a significant impact either way. We just don't have a big enough database to realize the performance improvements promised by HANA.

We licensed and run HANA as a runtime database, we're not doing any major HANA-specific development. There may be other technical skillsets required if you're actually leveraging HANA for custom or net-new development.

While I wouldn't say our go-live was 100% issue free, we had zero major issues. The technology works — HANA and the S/4 code line have proven stable. I think there's a lot of concern that S/4 is still new and there's going to be immaturity or bugs in the code. We've had a rock-solid experience with the S/4 code line and HANA as the database.

I do think that there's value in collapsing some of the various SAP landscapes. I also think there is big value in bringing EWM [Enterprise Warehouse Management] and PPDS [Production Planning and Detailed Scheduling] back into the core.

I don't think SAP's public cloud offering today is an option for most manufacturers, and I think they're really targeting that at service- and consulting-type organizations or very small organizations with limited requirements — not at manufacturing or CPG organizations of any significant size or complexity.

We will step back and try to do a TCO of a cloud deployment. We'll work with the Microsofts and the Virtustreams of the world and see if we can't understand the TCO of migrating. In the initial analysis we did three years ago, we found it was way more expensive to be running in a cloud outside our four walls. My perspective is, if I already have a modern data center and I've done a decent job of keeping our infrastructure current, it's hard to justify. I've got a small staff, and I'm not going to get rid of a bunch of people if I move my workload out. So I just don't know where the cost savings would come from. But we will go through the exercise.

Most of the organizations on S/4 we talked to executed a greenfield project. I don't think we talked to anyone that did an actual ECC to S/4 migration. Given the lack of true migrations at the time we elected to use SAP as our primary partner. We utilized components of their Value Assurance team as well as SAP Consulting. We did look at other providers, but we were one of the first, if not the first customer, here in North America to go through an actual migration to S/4 1610.

From the reference calls I do with my peers, a lot of folks are surprised that you can run SAP GUI on top of S/4. Many look at S/4, and they see Fiori and get spooked. But it seems to me even within the SAP sales organization it's like an 'Aha!' moment, that 'Hey, you know what: this doesn't have to be a Big Bang massive change management project. We can run SAP GUI and get folks into S/4 over time.'

Folks do have to be aware that there are licensing implications, not just for the HANA database but as SAP has deprecated functionality, some of the replacements require new licensing. Even some of the existing ECC-based SKUs have different SKUs in the S/4 code-line, so that requires a licensing conversion. If you're looking at an S/4 project, you should get started early on understanding the licensing impact and negotiation.

A lot of the code remediation can be done in ECC prior to starting an S/4 project. You don't have to wait to have the S/4 code-line there to get that done. So you can be working on that over the next 12 to 18 months as you're prepping for an S/4 move. Things like business-partner conversion, which caused a lot of work in our project, can be done in ECC. Business-partner resides in ECC today. You can convert and have that done before you start S/4. There's a lot of that type of prep work and remediation that can be done and pulled forward before launching an S/4 project.

So has S/4 moved the ball forward? I don't have a great perspective on that right now, because we really did not dig deep into the new business processes or business best practices, or Fiori.

Cintas

∿→

Cincinnati-based Cintas, with 35,000 employees, is one of the largest corporate apparel providers in North America. While it is a long-time SAP customer, running SAP systems like AFS and APO, Cintas is not moving to S/4 because it will not support the apparel and footwear market right away. But they are doing other things to modernize like deploying Fiori and mobile apps.

A group of analysts met with Matt Hough, Senior Director, Enterprise Applications, at Cintas and Eisbart (previously introduced) of NIMBL, Cintas' SI partner. I then had a follow-up conversation with Eisbart where he told me about other NIMBL work, including that for the San Francisco 49ers (described in Ch. 5) and how he sees S/4 as a way to modernize the services world.

Hough began by describing the company's push to modernize, which included Fiori-based dashboards and the mobile enablement of 7,000+ field service workers:

> "The service reps see the customer every week. They drop off, replenish and sell. The mobile functionality allows them to immediately address any issues. They can also order in real time through the mobile device. It increases Cintas's speed of execution to revenue, and improves customer satisfaction. They are our competitive differentiator."

As of now, Hough said, even if they wanted to move to S/4, the industry functionality they need isn't there yet. They are working with SAP to understand roadmaps and forward options on ECC, and on S/4, for AFS and APO. Hough said they are working with Adidas to advocate their retail roadmap needs and concerns to SAP.

He then described how NIMBL has evolved with Cintas:

"They used to focus on core ECC and CRM. But those systems are a lot more stabilized. So the focus is more about leveraging new technologies — whether it's filling out Fiori or working with our data warehouse and the analytics systems we're building."

Eisbart told me about NIMBL's role:

"NIMBL is leveraged as a support mechanism to help with the ebbs and flows of work that internally Cintas doesn't tackle. We act as a 30% overflow mechanism, which is flexible in how we support them. Sometimes it may be via projects or via break/fix or via enhancements. Cintas has given us the opportunity to evolve our own expertise and learn side-by-side with their team. I think that may be unique since most AMS models and customers look at their AMS provider as a commodity."

New England Biolabs

⌁⟶

Next, let's look at New England Biolabs (NEB), which has taken a different journey than Johnsonville to S/4. Sharon Kaiser, its CIO, has had a long career with SAP products. Her SAP experience ranges across industries like oil and gas at CITGO, apparel and footwear at Timberland, and medical devices at Abiomed. She described the company's business model and technology path:

> "New England Biolabs is a life sciences company. We make enzymes that are used in research for molecular biology applications. In short, our products cut, copy and glue DNA. We have expanded into other areas too, and provide solutions supporting genome editing, synthetic biology and next-generation sequencing.
>
> What we make are products that are used in research. Our primary customers are from research organizations, pharmaceutical companies and in research labs at academic institutions.
>
> We have around 500 employees, and all of our manufacturing and production is here in the U.S., in the Ipswich, Massachusetts, area. NEB currently has seven subsidiaries: three in Asia, three in Europe and one in Canada. We ship product out of the U.S. to the subsidiary offices, where they warehouse and ship product to their customers.

NEB is known for our product quality, technical support and quick delivery, which is primarily overnight."

Kaiser described the internal challenges that she and her colleagues had to overcome in order to overhaul long-standing manual processes by research and production scientists who were used to doing their jobs in a particular way:

"Our challenge at NEB is that we operate more like a research institute than as a biotech company. We have brilliant scientists — over 100 of them. The company is under 45 years old and has an average tenure of over 17 years. Scientists come here for life because it's such a great company to work for, and we do amazing research. They are interested in working on the science, not on SAP. For many years, their recipes and how they created their products were either kept in their head or in their lab notebooks on a shelf. There was no system that documented the bills of materials or the routings on how to make these products.

In 2014, the company went through the first phase of implementing ECC6 for finance, SD and MM at the finished goods level.

Over the last couple of years, I've been working with our executive director of production to determine how we can digitize this product knowledge. We had to get the information out of the heads of the scientists, out of their paper note-books and into the system. This would allow us to provide full batch traceability for our products, a better understanding of what it takes to make our product and the costs involved. We needed inventory management across our components and raw materials, and not just for our finished products. Once all the data is accurately in the system, our MRP runs would be usable.

We've been working on digitizing the product information for the last two years, and it's all about the master data. In the meantime, the IT team focused on preparing our SAP environment to migrate to S/4. We first brought our system up to Enhancement Pack 7, then we upgraded to Suite on HANA. Both were fairly smooth upgrades since we did not introduce any new functionality. In fall 2017, we upgraded fully to S/4 v1610.

I joined NEB right after the go-live of the first phase of the SAP deployment, understanding that we needed to bring our production and manufacturing onto SAP. This was a decision point for us. It did not make sense to bring all the production to ECC6 knowing that at some point in the future we'd have to upgrade to S/4. We decided to bite the bullet and migrate all of our business functions to S/4 so that our production and manufacturing areas would only have one big transition. In talking with the executive director of production, he said, 'If the product can do what we need, I'd rather go once and not multiple times.' To confirm the robustness of the solution, we conducted a proof of concept with version 1610 to make sure that S/4 could perform every major NEB production business process.

We did consider the S/4 cloud version, but it wasn't robust enough for us. It didn't have all the features and functions that we needed at the time, so we decided to stay with our hosted environment and moved to S/4 for our phase one functionality. In May 2018, we brought in all of our manufacturing and production processes live to S/4. We wanted our production customers to have a better user experience than having to learn how to use the typical SAP GUI transactions. So we started using the Fiori apps. Each production person has maybe two or three Fiori apps that they work with on a daily basis. Every once in a while, we find features that don't work as they should. Sometimes these are problems our implementation partner can fix, and sometimes we have to go to SAP support.

We have a partner that provides hosting, Basis and security support. Functional support is provided in house with a small internal team and supplemented with external partners."

Kaiser offered practical insight on the decision to make the move to S/4 that many other long-time SAP customers are facing today. She also detailed how NEB is preparing for its future across the globe with SAP:

"I've talked to my colleagues here in the Boston area, and it's very hard to develop a cost justification and ROI. Moving to S/4 will enable you to take advantage of new features and functions that SAP has invested into the product. But, to say, 'Tomorrow we upgrade to S/4/HANA, and then I'll have all these new benefits on day one' … it's not going to be there.

Each company will have different considerations in making their upgrade decision, and the level of difficulty and complexity will also be different. Companies with a lot of customization, user exits or that are on older versions will have to do more detailed planning and analysis on what an upgrade would take. In NEB's particular case, going from ECC6 to Suite on HANA to S/4 was not technically hard. We conducted a series of technical upgrades with no major changes to business processes. There were changes in S/4 that we had to accommodate in our processes and user exits, especially around the new business-partner functionality. It requires analysis, planning and lots of testing.

A major part of our project was regression testing. We have not had any business disruptions caused by S/4 — business continues on as it should. I think one of the things that really helped us a lot, because we were one of the early adopters of S/4, was that we qualified for SAP's customer care program. Every week, we had a conference call with our SAP customer-care manager to review and discuss any issues that we might have with our implementation. Because of this program, NEB had direct involvement with the SAP developers who worked with us to keep the project on track. Since we were implementing one of the earlier versions of S/4, version 1610, some of our issues were with the new technology and SAP generally responded very quickly.

A different use case took us to SAP Hybris, now part of the C/4 product line. We were looking for a PIM [Product Information Management] solution because we have hundreds of products each with very specific, scientific metadata that requires strict management. If you go to the NEB.com website, it is chock-full of charts, diagrams, scientific information, protocols, tools and videos. The NEB website is a reference library for scientists on how to find and use our products. All of the information about that product has to be stored somewhere. We needed a PIM. As we started looking, one of the solutions that popped up was the Hybris Product Content Management solution.

We also have this pretty innovative freezer program, called NEBNow. Many of our customers are in big research labs and want immediate availability to NEB products. With the NEBNow freezer program, NEB products are close by and immediately available. The scientists log into the freezer app, review what's in the inventory and select the product. The app unlocks the door, and the scientists take the product out and scan it. This information is then fed back up as a replenishment order into S/4. It is an example of the Internet of Things. The freezers have sensors that warn us if the temperature gets overheated, or when the door is left open. It's not only the product information, inventory and sales — it's also letting us know the health of the unit itself.

A key initiative for NEB is to continue our journey to globalize our system portfolio. All of our other seven subsidiaries have developed their own system solutions over the past 30 years. They have their own ERP systems, their own warehousing systems and their own websites. Here in the U.S., we have invested in a strong infrastructure and integrated application portfolio. We have SAP as our core back-end transaction system, Salesforce as our CRM solution and our website for content management and e-commerce. We have completed our CRM globalization and are now embarking on extending our SAP and web solutions. NEB is opening a new subsidiary office in Australia where we will deploy our full application suite. After Australia's deployment is complete, we will offer the package to our other subsidiary offices so that they can take advantage of the applications and integrations that the U.S. office has already invested in. In our efforts, we have ensured that we always designed 'global' so that we could deliver 'local.'"

NETZSCH

∿→

As the need to coordinate the view on its global customer base has continued to grow, NETZSCH's Business Unit Pumps & Systems also felt the need to improve transparency across its products.

Bernhard Diemer, SAP Senior Inhouse Consultant, provided details of the company's work with SAP's Digital Business Services organization to deploy the AIN. He described how the cloud-based network is designed to share with operators access to up-to-date maintenance strategies and manuals from manufacturers. In turn, manufacturers also automatically receive asset usage and failure data from assets in the field.

"Our company NETZSCH Pumps & Systems leads a global sales organization serving a variety of industries and target groups. We are a leading manufacturer of industrial pumps, which are, deriving from a platform strategy, mostly custom built for customers. I'm part of the SAP ERP team and have been involved in the roll-out of the SAP AIN project over two years.

In our business, we sell directly to some of our end customers but for the most part we don't have much contact with customers because we sell through distributors and our subsidiary network.

So we know our sales partners, but we don't have as much visibility to the final destination of our pumps. What we want to gain is a better knowledge of how the pumps are used in the field and to gather data to make our products better. So far, we only have information on about 800 pumps in the system, but we sell at least 50,000 units a year.

In phase one of our AIN project, we have been able to provide operating and maintenance manuals to our customers and service partners. In the past, those often 'got lost' on the way to installation. We are also planning to get remote support to our service partners. Today when customers call they often don't know, in detail, which pump they are referring to — they can only refer to the number plate on the pump. Our field service has to gather relevant information for the pumps at the customer. It would be easier for the service tech to get direct access to all the information before they show up simply by entering the serial number from the specific pump into the system.

We can also start to provide visibility to the whole service process over the network. We have scenarios where the customer upgrades his asset, but not all involved parties know about the upgrade. AIN will help us to get a single point of truth. In the next phase, we will be collecting IoT data from installed pumps. Our ECC system continues to be the book of record for the assets.

The AIN system has had some quality issues. SAP did a really, really good job and made a lot of features available in a very short time. However, it would have been better to slow things down a little bit and take a little bit more care in quality and documentation issues."

Terumo BCT

∿→

Unlike other customers in this chapter, Terumo BCT modernized only its HCM processes. Christine Reynolds is a Senior Manager in the HCM area at Terumo BCT in Colorado. She was joined by John Brooks, who is a Senior Manager for IT Applications, as they described their SuccessFactors journey:

> "We are a medical device manufacturer, and we are a leader in blood component technology, therapeutic apheresis and cellular therapy technologies. We are part of a global company based in Japan. Our global headquarters is in Lakewood, Colorado, and regional headquarters in Argentina, Belgium and China. We manufacture medical devices, and we follow FDA regulations. Outside the U.S., there are other authorities that regulate us.
>
> We have quite a large global footprint and have six manufacturing sites in six countries. We have about 7,000 employees worldwide, with about 2,500 based in Colorado. Roughly two-thirds of our employee population is in manufacturing. They are hourly workers, with little to no computer access at work and so they are not the target users of the tool. We track their records and ask them to interact with it in the U.S. probably more so than anywhere else.

We had hired an implementation partner two years ago to do an analysis of our HR technology capabilities. They measured us on a variety of technology enablers. Their ranking put us lower than where we want to be. We also knew that it was time for us to upgrade. We hadn't upgraded our U.S. HRIS software in about 10 years. It was outdated. We're outsourcing our payroll function in the U.S. Outside the U.S., we manage them regionally, also with other outsource providers.

We used a maturity model to create a business case for our executive team. When it came time to look at other solutions, we did a gap analysis based on our requirements. SuccessFactors came out at the top of the list. We had 365 requirements and, when compared to SuccessFactors, there were only 30 gaps, so it was a 91% fit.

We were already using components of SuccessFactors, including the LMS on-premise, the Performance & Goals module and the Compensation module. In addition, outside of the U.S., we were using EC as the HRIS. We were pretty well committed to SuccessFactors at the time that we did this analysis. We had also implemented SAP's ECC ERP, a couple of years prior.

We had gone with Plateau LMS back in 2006 because it was the most suited to a regulated industry like ours. SuccessFactors acquired Plateau shortly after we went with them. Even when we were evaluating other human capital management systems, we knew we would keep the LMS because as a regulated customer, we are very invested in it, and it has worked very well for us."

Reynolds then talked about some of the issues from the global rollout:

"We have had challenges with global deployment. There are several data fields that are not being used consistently around the world, and we're now making a list of any field that has missing data for a large population plus any field that may not be used consistently, which then creates confusion. In terms of helping us hire and recruit for that talent, we haven't been able to use the tool as thoroughly because we went live only with English, and therefore we can only recruit in English. For most of our offices, if you don't speak English, you're not using the system.

Also, if you're going to apply for one of our jobs, you must have an email address. I know, in India, this was a big challenge. We wanted to assume that everybody has a mobile device, that everybody has internet access. In India, they said that is not the case with many of the candidates. We have a lot of issues with the phonetics and spellings in the India site. Names and titles aren't accurate. And so, we are currently undergoing a project to clean up that data. It is much more complex because this is a company that our parent company owned and then transferred into our organization. Their processes and systems were very different than ours. India is not yet using global job codes that the rest of our organizations are using. It's an internal process issue, and it is a matter of us then cleaning up the data. It is not a SuccessFactors issue.

But, it's something to consider ahead of time if a global organization is going to implement a system like SuccessFactors. Our implementation partner alerted us to the issues around March. We had about six or seven months to go before we had to go live. We said we'll worry about it later. We had plenty to worry about then, and so later is now. This is the project we are exploring for 2019. That will clean up all our data and also help us decide what happens with the processes at the Indian plant."

Reynolds shared other learning from the project:

"Our post go-live was pretty intense. As we were implementing, we had a team of five analysts managing the work around the LMS migration and the implementation of the other modules, as well as migrating our U.S. HRMS into EC. It was really demanding. Then, shortly after we went live, we had turnover. Two of those five people left the organization. The loss of knowledge and lessons learned set us back as well.

During implementation, we shortened our training process. Our budget didn't allow for us to use our implementation partner for training. And so, we made the case that we would rely on our testing to be the training. They made the best of it, but we had mistakes and had some data integrity issues.

After we went live, I would say the biggest pain point was not having good knowledge transfer. Post go-live, we only kept our implementation partner for one month. We also had our turnover, so it was intense. I would say now, two years later, we've got it more under control. We've found it difficult to find people with SuccessFactors experience in the Colorado job market where unemployment is low, and we've had some challenges getting experienced system analysts and system administrators.

I would fall into the category of people saying quarterly SuccessFactors releases are too frequent. We have a core number of settings that we test before it hits production, and that's about all that we can handle. We haven't had too many things break. But, it's a constant worry. And we're regulated so, fortunately, the LMS upgrade cycle is annual. But even so, it means we spend about half the year preparing and testing for that annual upgrade, and that's just for the universal features. We were used to updating the on-premise LMS every three or four years, so this annual routine is significant.

We are active in the SuccessFactors community, and so we try to stay abreast of the chatter throughout the community. Like I said, we have a core set of functions that we test on our own, and if we see something that's a little off, we turn to SuccessFactors. We have two people at SuccessFactors that we meet with regularly. They'll point out, 'Hey, this release is coming and it affects these types of clients, and I think you should look for it,' and that gives us a heads up that we should take a look at that while it's still in the preview environment and before it hits our production environment.

Another major learning — we did not do an instance refresh after we went live. We waited about a year. That entire time, we did not have a sandbox or test environment that matched production at all. They were so far apart that you couldn't even use them for accurate testing. We had to do most of our testing in production because our sites weren't matching.

Now, we have done a lot of research, spent a lot of time in the community and chatted with other customers to get a cadence for when we do those refreshes. I would say it was a huge eye-opener, the whole management of the separate instances. Again, it's not a SuccessFactors thing. I think it's any cloud-based system. When we started, we didn't really have an appreciation for how important it is and how much work it is.

Our IT strategy as a whole is to go cloud first. We have Salesforce. Our quality application, which will be going live next year, is Windchill by PTC and it is also in the cloud. We have a couple of others as well.

At the time we went live, SuccessFactors might have been either our first or second implementation of cloud-based software. I remember having many conversations with IT about how to support this system. It was kind of a unique business model. It was a great conversation, but with the perspective that we hadn't had in the past.

We realized early on that we were going to have to maintain a relationship with a partner because there are just some things that we flat out can't do without one. Therefore, we found one who could support us in an ongoing way, rather than just for our implementation. A big portion of our implementation partner's resources during our go-live was offshore, so we had considered extending it but cost was a big consideration. When our Indian operation gets built up and their infrastructure is improved, we think we might hire there to give us that 24-hour clock. But, it wouldn't be an outsourcing relationship. They would be internal resources.

Finally, we had some challenges with integrations. [Dell] Boomi is our current enterprise IPaaS tool. Back then, Boomi came packaged with SuccessFactors. And so, we were forced to learn it as the IPaaS tool. There was a period of teaching and learning that we had to go through to do these integrations. It made that work a little more complicated than it needed to be.

Overall, we consider our implementation a success because we have the full suite of modules. While it was challenging, we are satisfied with the decisions we made."

Carpenter Technology

⌁→

Carpenter Technology, headquartered in Philadelphia, is implementing S/4 — albeit cautiously, given the company's lack of significant experience with any prior ERP system. CIO James Johnson provided an account of Carpenter:

> "Carpenter Technology is a 130-year-old, $2 billion public manufacturer of specialty alloys. We are a recognized leader in high-performance specialty alloy-based materials and process solutions for critical applications in the aerospace, defense, transportation, energy, industrial, medical and consumer electronics markets. Carpenter has evolved to become a pioneer in premium specialty alloys — including titanium, nickel and cobalt, as well as alloys specifically engineered for additive manufacturing [AM] processes and soft magnetics applications. We recently expanded our AM capabilities to provide a complete "powder-to-part" solution to accelerate materials innovation, offer rapid prototyping, and streamline parts production."

Johnson has spent a lifetime in the process industry, with Honeywell and spin-offs from Dow Chemical, mostly working with SAP's ERP:

> "Five years ago, I had the opportunity to come here to Carpenter, for a CEO who was the business unit

lead when I was at Honeywell. Part of my job is to help this company develop and execute its enterprise systems strategy. Today, the company runs a number of disparate systems including SAP. Over the years, we've looked at ERP solutions and didn't really ever take that plunge. We acquired a business about six years ago called Latrobe Steel that was running SAP. They were on ECC6. So, that was Carpenter's first business that was running on a proper ERP.

About four years ago, we started the journey to Suite on HANA for a very small segment of our business, just to dip our toes into the waters. Now we're in the midst of our multiyear implementation to place the entire company on S/4.

Compared to ECC, S/4 with its better UI and less complex back end, has been beneficial. Obviously, there's a learning curve that everyone has to go up, but overall, it's been positive. We are pushing the S/4 boundaries in some areas and are working with a SAP partner to implement functionality specific to our industry.

An additional complexity is that we're keeping a portion of our legacy system that handles the shop floor and manufacturing functionality. We could replicate the functionality in SAP, but it is a risk we are not willing to take right away.

We are also running Workday. The business case for this system was completed as I was joining the company, and I had also used and implemented Workday at my last company. We've been able to use it pretty effectively. Over time, I'm sure there may be more integration that we would want to take advantage of, but for now it does what we need.

S/4 is in a private cloud deployment. A partner hosts my environment and provides my Basis support. I have my own functional team that does the configuration. When SAP tries to package this and sell this concept of one-stop shop [in the public cloud], I don't see what it does for me. Workday works for me, because it's a multitenant solution, and we're doing mostly standard activities — HRIS and payroll. How do you take that into a complex manufacturing environment? Now, I may be completely off base, but I wonder how they're going to get there."

Johnson is not the only executive we interviewed who has the same worry about manufacturing and other operational functionality in the S/4 cloud version. In contrast, as we will see in Ch. 7, Plex is supporting a number of complex auto industry manufacturers in their cloud.

Johnson continued:

"We partnered with a global SI on the implementation and on the AMS portion post go-live. The SI has been here two-and-a-half years now, and over time they have built up more dexterity with S/4. In general, I would say there is a learning curve that these SIs are going through to bring their consultants up to speed and to be able to unleash the value that is espoused for S/4.

In my past, I've also implemented and run Salesforce at Honeywell and other companies. Here, in the last year, we have deployed SAP's Cloud for Customer, C4C — but only the salesforce automation functionality. I have to think hard about how much I would extend it based on the user experience. The integration piece should continue to improve to my back end. With Salesforce, that integration was not out of the box.

On the C4C side, I could see doing more. Carpenter's value is that we are a solutions provider. It's nice to be able to understand customer issues and route them back to our quality, technical or R&D groups. How could I leverage technology to be able to get to that solution faster, get it to our R&D people quicker and allow them to turn it around?

Bottom line: C4C has to become more stable. Every few weeks I'll get an alert that it was down for some reason, which I never ever had with Salesforce. They have to get that improved to be a player in this space because that's like air. Those are things that I should never have to worry about."

Johnson said his expectation going into his S/4 implementation was that many of the challenges he would face would have already been detected and fixed by SAP or its SI partners. But that wasn't always the case:

"To me, there is this gap between what SAP espouses, what end customers might do, and how we tie all that back to ultimately some bottom-line impact. That to me doesn't always resonate in their messaging. We're kind of late to the game as a company with implementing SAP. My assumption would be that some of the things that we're dealing with would have already been solved, and they could have quickly referred us to those companies. But they were unable to.

The relationship I want with SAP is a more symbiotic one where you explain to me what your wares are and what you bring to the table. In turn, I explain to you a business problem, knowing that I already have implemented your solution, and I've already spent a lot of money on your solution. I want you to help solve my business problems. I do not want our conversation to center on how I can now spend more money with you to fix a problem that I thought should be able to be solved by leveraging the system that I have already implemented.

I wish SAP would leverage ASUG to have a conversation around, 'We're thinking about doing X. How would X fall on you?' Get that voice of the customer from the person or groups that are actually using their technology. They do that for much larger customers. I do not know if that cross section is broad enough in terms of truly understanding the needs of a US$2 billion company versus a US$20 billion company or a US$200 billion company. I think there's opportunity there. To me, that's where ASUG can play a role because we have that cross section."

Old World Industries

∿→

Over the course of 45 years, Old World Industries (OWI) has transformed from a small chemical trading company into a billion-dollar global powerhouse for the automotive, chemical and agricultural industries. Old World moved to S/4 from a highly customized and aging AS/400 system.

Sameer Afsar is the Managing Partner at 4th Wave Solutions, which helps clients with CX projects. I met Afsar in the summer of 2018 when he was employed by Old World Industries, and he recounted their ERP modernization journey. He started by describing how two entrepreneurs started the company during the petrochemical crisis in the 1970s:

"They were opportunistic, formed a lot of great relationships, hustled and bustled and tried many different things. They purchased the PEAK brand franchise, and PEAK antifreeze has been their main product. Since then, they have added brands like BlueDEF diesel exhaust fluid and EiKO Lamps. Now that the North American market had been saturated from an antifreeze perspective, what's next? They brought in a consulting company to develop a roadmap for the future.

We had been on the AS/400 for the past 20 years, with a highly customized system. Companies enjoyed working with Old World because of its nimbleness, and exemplary service. Customers got exactly what they needed when they needed it.

However, that nimbleness required processes and internal systems to be highly customized, with continuous change to meet customer demand. So if the CEO wanted a report on various KPIs, there was no true ERP system and no single source of truth. To scale to that next level, to change the way we did business, to standardize business processes while still meeting customers' demands, we decided to look at an ERP solution.

The evaluation narrowed down to Oracle and SAP. This was back in 2015. SAP had a core roadmap for a future. They had just come out with S/4, and at least a few companies were using S/4 Simple Finance. Oracle didn't have a clear roadmap on what that future looked like, especially with their JD Edwards product. That worried the executive team.

We approached this project as a business transformation opportunity. So yes, we were implementing SAP and we were decommissioning a 20-year-old customized ERP system, but the CEO approached this project as if we're transforming our business, and we were not just doing a technology implementation. And that set the mindset for the rest of the organization — by saying this is the catalyst for that business transformation.

We sent an RFP out for the implementation and got 30 responses from the major players, like TCS, Accenture, Deloitte and several boutique shops. It was early 2016 and S/4 was still fairly new. This was a greenfield implementation, so everyone wanted those credentials. So as a mid-market company at US$1 billion in revenues we were surprised by the attention we were getting from the bidders. We narrowed the initial 30 down to eight vendors, went through in-person presentations, and short-listed to three finalists. These firms brought their A-teams, which was pleasantly surprising. We eventually decided on Deloitte. SAP was also very invested in making the Old World implementation a success story as well.

We started the S/4 journey in July of 2016 and blueprinted for four months. Executive leadership wanted to use SAP out of the box, but the people in the trenches would push back. We showed those folks a new way of doing business the SAP way. I have known of ECC implementations where they have hundreds, even thousands, of WRICEF [Workflows, Reports, Interfaces, Conversions, Enhancements and Forms] objects. We have only about 50, and most are interfaces to other applications. To the maximum extent possible, we stuck with the standard S/4 implementation.

OWI uses a wide range of modes of transportation — parcel, LTL, full truck loads, rail, barge — so we did have to look at best-of-breed transportation management systems. We looked at MercuryGate, Manhattan and Oracle. Ultimately, we went with SAP Transportation Management [TM] functionality because of the breadth of functionality it covered along with the prospect of converting to the embedded version in S/4 in the future.

In 2016, when we did the analysis from a cost and SLA perspective, we didn't find the cloud service mature enough, so we went with the on-premise version. We were one of the first customers to implement S/4 logistics, and we wanted to make sure we had complete control over the functionality and in environments to be able to update quickly.

We went live in September 2017 and there were plenty of challenges from a business process perspective. Again, Old World had been in siloed business units for 20+ years and was introducing a system which is completely integrated end to end. There was a dip in productivity for a little longer than expected because people were working together in ways we hadn't before, adjusting to a new business process and a new technology.

Deloitte helped with offshore application management. During the implementation, we had limited their onshore component to make it economical for a smaller company like ours. And being one of the first S/4 HANA implementations, we negotiated good pricing, which they likely wouldn't offer others.

Fiori was one of the major reasons to go with S/4. We were fairly disappointed in what Fiori 1.0 had to offer; Fiori 2.0 made it a little bit better. SAP would do well to make it a lot more standard out of the box."

Graham Construction

∿→

Founded in 1926, Graham Construction got its start building railway stations for Canadian Pacific. Today, they are a leading employee-owned, fully-integrated construction solutions company with revenues in excess of C$2.5 billion. They have more than 1,500 employees working in 17 major professional, technical and administrative categories at 14 offices across Canada and the U.S.

Graham Construction was an early S/4 implementation in Western Canada. Unlike many other S/4 customers we have discussed in this segment, they mostly did the project with internal resources. Susan Park, Manager of Business Applications, and David Grenard, Solutions Architect, described their company and its SAP journey:

> "Graham is in vertical buildings, industrial and infrastructure construction markets. I think we do everything but residential. Two years ago, we moved to Business Suite on HANA. At that point, we implemented our on-premise infrastructure. And so when we migrated to S/4, we stayed on-premise, which actually made the migration really very simple."

Modules implemented included: Finance, Sales & Distribution, Material Management, Plant Maintenance and, critical to their sector, Project Systems. They also run SuccessFactors, Concur and Ariba, and have Fiori Launchpad on cloud for business partners.

"I believe ours was the first brownfield implementation of S/4 in Western Canada. We achieved it within seven months using a very small, highly skilled technical team of 16 people. Our implementation approach was to minimize impact to our business users by focusing on a purely technical upgrade. This made change management very easy as business impacts were limited to small groups of business users. It's funny, because when we went live, we were asked by several users from the business if we had launched yet as it was so quiet.

In parallel with the migration we also completed a 'return to core' activity, during which we were able to clean up earlier custom developments where they were no longer providing value or alternative standard functionality could be provided.

Our biggest struggle was the S/4 data model changes. We rely very heavily on controlling for reporting. The move from all the controlling tables to the Universal Journal caused us issues. SAP provides compatibility views for custom code but they are not a complete solution. The compatibility views perform poorly, and so in many cases we had to swap those out for the core table. We extensively use HANA Views for our BI solutions. The compatibility views did not help there either as they are not available for BI reporting. Virtually all of our management reporting had to be redone.

We also had to reengineer several of our pricing processes because data model changes to core sales tables removed fields used in our pricing access sequences.

We have custom applications that handle project estimating for construction. We've partnered with InEight, leveraging their core Hard Dollar Estimating and Project Suite software. The SAP solution for construction engineering leaves a bit to be desired. InEight provides us an integrated project management suite that is specifically tailored for our methodology.

When it comes to our SAP cloud solutions, we have been faced with some challenges, particularly around communication outages and downtime.

Throughout our S/4 implementation, SAP has been very responsive and collaborative when it came to issue management and resolution. SAP has issued 23 brand new notes specifically for our implementation [help documentation of known system issues]. One of the best outcomes of this collaboration was around resource-related billing, a key area of our business. Working with SAP, we were able to optimize core code to decrease by up to 15 times the runtime."

Naturipe Farms

⚡︎➤

Naturipe Farms, working in a perishable-product sector, moved to S/4 to improve its responsiveness.

Carol McMillan, Director of IT, described the company:

> "We have been growing produce since 1917. Our main revenue sources are berries, avocados and value-added products. Naturipe is owned by four different companies: Munger Farms is family-owned; MBG Marketing is a cooperative of growers with over 300 members; Naturipe Berry Growers is a cooperative of growers based in California; and Hortifrut, in South America, is a blend — it is family run, and also sources product from other growers.
>
> Naturipe represents all four companies and acts as the sales and marketing branch for them. We oversee inventory management, especially for the product that arrives from South and Central America, and handle all of the sales, marketing, accounting, grower liquidation and finance. Millions of pounds of product go through Naturipe Farms a year, and the vast majority is in berries. Naturipe has only about 140 employees.
>
> We implemented ECC about 10 years ago. We've been using it with an Oracle back end. With perishable products, we need to be able to make decisions

much quicker. The BI tool that we use, Dimensional Insights, is only refreshed once or twice a day, and that often isn't enough for our needs. Along this journey to S/4, shortly after we had our development environment set up, one of my developers called me up. He said, 'This is incredible. We had this query that was taking more than 30 minutes to run, and it just ran in 30 seconds.' That is one of my favorite stories from our journey to S/4.

We decided to do a migration, not a greenfield implementation, because it would mean less impact to the users. Within Naturipe, we have a number of employees who remember the pain of implementing SAP 10 years ago, so we wanted to try to make this as seamless for them as possible. Honestly, it's been less work on our end. Yes, there's more testing involved, but as far as the master data migration, it's overall been less work.

The vision that I've been sharing with the business users is that we are moving to a platform that allows further growth. SAP is our system of record, and I want to bring in the capabilities that they have with predictive analytics, which are now being more integrated into business applications. I'd like to take advantage of some of the financial tools that are available through Simple Finance.

We are going to continue using SAP GUI. It really is a comfort factor, and I think any time you're making a change like this, you need to give users something that they're still familiar with. Throughout 2019 and 2020, we're going to work on a Launchpad, mobile applications, and improved reporting. Those are some of the promises that we are making to our users.

We did consider a cloud deployment, but we already have a data center, and for us it became a financial decision. It was actually more economical to purchase our own hardware. We may consider the cloud in another three to five years once our equipment has depreciated.

Velocity helped with the implementation, but it was only a modest effort. We work for the growers, so we try to keep costs at a minimum. We told them, 'We want you to do 100% of the technical migration, and then we would handle all of our custom code changes.' They continue to help us with Basis support.

The SAP migration tools were very helpful. The migration team on the technical side used them more than we did internally. But internally, we used the Code Checker and the Simplification Items Report, which SAP provides, and that has been very helpful with identifying items that need to be fixed.

SAP has replaced obsolete tables with compatible views. I think some of it was mentioned in the Simplification Items, but it's not until you really get into the migration that you find what is most relevant for your company. We were also affected by some of the deprecation. One of the biggest impacts on us was credit management. We were using Simple credit management. That functionality is no longer available in S/4, so we have to migrate it to FSCM [Financial Supply Chain Management] and there's a significant learning curve there. The material item number has gone from 18 characters to 40, so you have to make sure that you've defined it correctly.

We are heavy users of Order Processing, Materials Management and Accounting functionalities. Those are our main modules. We do use some Quality Management for our value-added products, for some of our frozen products. We use it to keep track of quality data.

Our industry is becoming more demanding. We want to be better at forecasting, and at demand planning, and we should be better prepared to take on some of those projects now that we've gone through the S/4 migration.

Grocery chains are customers for our products — we are exploring Leonardo blockchain with SAP. We participated in a proof-of-concept project with SAP that ran last year and we have joined the consortium for blockchain that they put together for CPG and agribusiness sectors."

McMillan presents on her S/4 project at a number of SAP user events, and I asked her to summarize the tips and traps:

> "Perform your steps ahead of time, test your readiness and correct your code. Plan for issues. Test and test again. And identify any obsolete code that you have. Don't try to just migrate everything, because we found that a number of programs that we had were not being used. Finally, over-communicate."

Global customers?

We have seen a nice sampling of ECC customers migrate to S/4, but are SAP's very large, global customers ready for S/4? Eisbart, CEO of the SI NIMBL sees a two-tier opportunity with much larger companies:

> "The S/4 cloud product, which is one that NIMBL specializes in, is to create a multitenant solution for companies under US$1 billion in revenue to be able to "rapidly" implement ERP. We're finding, from our own experience, that if it's a business fit, which is sometimes a big "if," projects could be done in truly a matter of weeks. We mean 14 weeks as opposed to 14 months or 14 years.
>
> Large enterprises will look to implement it in a two-tier model. And so, an ExxonMobil will not go multitenant in the S/4 cloud without industry

functionality for oil and gas. However, ExxonMobil would implement it in their Angola or Uzbekistan facility when that site is primarily a finance implementation. They don't need to roll the behemoth SAP on-prem for a unit of 50 people. Instead, they could implement on S/4 cloud rapidly and then integrate.

The S/4 cloud customers are opening up other Application Management Services (AMS) opportunities for us. They want someone to help them with the quarterly releases. And so, we're in discussions right now with a global company on an Italian S/4 cloud instance, They're looking to roll out 22 more countries in the next four years. That's a volume play for us as opposed to S/4 on-prem or ECC, which could be 2,000 hours a month. Now we're talking about 1,000 hours a quarter. It's significantly different.

It provides tremendous opportunity because there still are a ton of customers out there that are on ECC, and they may be migrating to S/4. However, they don't want to build out a production support internal mechanism of ten people at a burden cost of $160,000 a person. Instead, they can leverage us, and we're able to provide fractional resources. For us, it's exciting for a couple of reasons. One, it's a volume play. Two, it candidly provides us an opportunity to train up project resources via our AMS offering, so it's a career path for our consultants."

In Summary

A growing number of SAP customers are modernizing with S/4 and SAP's cloud properties. With S/4, it's encouraging to see customers are not being too ambitious. They are implementing core functionality, sticking with older GUI, deploying on-premise and using their service partners cautiously. On the flip side, many customers are postponing implementations in operational areas where the payback will likely be higher. They are missing out on benefits of multitenancy and SAP's innovations, which are increasingly in the cloud. In some ways, they are postponing the pain but also the related gain.

Most of these early S/4 adopters report similar issues — redaction of previous functionality, confusion caused by introduction of compatible views and with hardware sizing, and much less functionality on public cloud releases compared to the on-premise versions.

Next are the Diversifier customers. In the first volume of *SAP Nation*, we had described the early wave of Diversifiers. They were "ring-fencing" SAP with cloud solutions, trying out two-tier models, TPM and private-cloud infrastructure. This group continues to expand and experiment. The big difference we noticed this time around was in some cases they are diversifying back to SAP products.

CHAPTER 7

Diversifiers

〰→

Every year, *Consumer Reports* magazine catalogs new car models. During a recent listing, they showed 450 new cars, SUVs and trucks.[45] In a way, that's not surprising, given that every auto manufacturer wants a piece of the large U.S. market which has been averaging 17 million annual units for the last several years. In enterprise tech, there is a similar growing amount of choice. Vembu of Zoho has watched the growth: "Cloud app development has become objectively easier. I mean we've been in the software business for 32 years, so I know. There are a lot of infrastructure pieces that have been figured out more and more and more. And it is becoming easier and easier and easier. I saw a figure for 30,000+ VC-funded cloud start-ups in the world now ... it's even harder to pin down

---

[45] https://www.consumerreports.org/buying-a-car/new-car-buying-guide/

because it's global and there are integrators everywhere."[46] Switching enterprise systems is not as easy as switching cars, but with so much choice it is no surprise that customers are starting to diversify their technology portfolios.

---

[46] https://dealarchitect.typepad.com/deal_architect/2019/01/zoho-day-the-long-shadow-of-amazon.html

The Churn

∿→

Unilever

Unilever is one of the world's largest consumer product companies, with 2.5 billion consumers across 200 countries who use its products on a daily basis. They include more than 400 brands, like Lipton tea, Ben & Jerry's ice cream, Dove soap and VO5 shampoo. Unilever is also one of SAP's flagship customers, one of its top 25 around the globe and a frequent co-innovation partner. At Sapphire Now in 2014, Unilever's then-CIO, Willem Eelman, shared a stage with SAP's Cohen (who was featured in Ch. 4). Unilever's emphasis on sustainability as a critical company KPI came through in that conversation.

Fast forward to 2018. At Dreamforce, Salesforce's annual conference, current Unilever Global CIO Jane Moran played a prominent role in a keynote demo that highlighted Salesforce's Heroku, Commerce, Einstein and MuleSoft products. She was joined on stage by Peter ter Kulve, Unilever's Chief Digital and Growth Officer. The demo focused on an app to increase consumer engagement. It allows customers to make their own flavors of ice cream while teaching them about sustainability practices around the ingredients. Four years later, the company was still committed to sustainability — but had it changed course on SAP?

In the hypercompetitive software vendor world, Unilever could be construed as giving up on SAP. Actually, like many CIOs, Moran is merely diversifying her portfolio.

Moran told *CIO UK*, "Working with SAP, they helped us put together the internal business case to move forward with S4/HANA. We've found that having HANA on our databases has increased performance five to 10 times when we have HANA sidecars."[47] In that article, she also talked about her other strategic partners: Microsoft, AWS and increasingly Google. Unilever also has a Foundry that, since its launch in 2014, has facilitated 100 pilots between start-ups and Unilever brands — stimulating and facilitating experimentation across the global footprint. It's all part of diversifying the portfolio, and SAP continues as a key component.

---

[47] https://www.cio.co.uk/cio-interviews/unilever-cio-jane-moran-developing-agile-platform-for-innovation-3675637/

Under Armour

Under Armour has grown like a rocket over the last two decades, even in an athletic products world dominated by companies like Nike, Adidas and Reebok. Founder and CEO Kevin Plank has called SAP his "big, bad technology partner." In a 2016 TV campaign, he said, "What SAP has really done to change our business is the ability for us to dream ...."

A year later, Patrik Frisk, the company's President and Chief Operating Officer, was telling Wall Street that "the struggles with the July 1 launch of its integrated ERP business solution 'negatively impacted' third-quarter results by causing disruptions in Under Armour's supply chain."[48] On LinkedIn, Under Armour had a job posting which highlighted its decision to invest in the Salesforce Commerce Cloud, as several of the job requirements indicate:

- "You are well versed in Salesforce Commerce Cloud (Demandware) and will be a driving force behind launching new sites, growing existing ones, and architecting a global delivery model.

- You are to be the Salesforce Commerce Cloud subject matter expert.

---

[48] http://ww2.cfo.com/applications/2017/11/armour-discloses-hiccups-sap-implementation/

- You are a principal implementer of new features on Under Armour's Global Ecommerce sites."[49]

Like Unilever, Under Armour remains committed to SAP and Plank told Jim Cramer on the *Mad Money* show, "We upgraded our systems; we implemented SAP, so we're never going to have to do that again. We have the scale of a great company that can give us that pliability as a business to be able to grow forever."[50] SAP CEO McDermott continues to sit on the Under Armour Board of Directors.

[49] https://www.linkedin.com/jobs/view/salesforce-commerce-cloud-sfcc-architect-global-ecommerce-at-under-armour-764821979/
[50] https://www.cnbc.com/2018/02/28/under-armour-ceo-on-2018-outlook-leadership-changes-and-improvement.html

Pregis, again

In Ch. 3, we introduced Mueller of Pregis who described their move from Microsoft to SAP around their IoT initiative. He also told me about another move in the CX area:

"We moved sales functionality from Salesforce to Hybris. We used the technology as an opportunity to get everything into a system that all people across the sales team could use. It was really about moving accounts, contacts, activities, leads and opportunities into the sales cloud so that we could get to a 360 view of the customer. A year later, we moved field service onto the service cloud. Now we'll be looking at extending that platform to our distribution partners and moving forward with the partner portal. We are opening that up to partners, not just Pregis employees.

So we are using more of what is becoming C/4. The question that we'll come to eventually is data orchestration. In the immediate future, we're not ready to move there because we don't yet have a big data problem, but we know that's the next thing that we need to figure out. How do we get four verticals of systems as opposed to just one vertical of machine types and our packaging machine types connected so that we can start working through all of that information? We'll have to figure out where the data lives and how that works."

CLP Power

⌇⟶

Blumberg at CLP Power, introduced in Ch. 2, had provided a glimpse of his diversification efforts in the first volume of *SAP Nation*. He provided an update for this volume, and as his industry rapidly evolves you can see the acceleration in his diversification:

"We haven't had a major ERP change, and we continue to use our existing SAP ECC footprint. It's just as well that it's reliable … but we haven't really seen or observed SAP very much for our recent software requirements. We're planning to look at a more holistic ERP platform strategy in 2019-2020. This is where we really want to take a step back and look at our company strategy, industry disruption, process improvements and automation. This will be driven from our business requirements rather than solely from SAP product changes.

We already have a diverse portfolio. For asset management in generation plans and transmission and distribution assets, we run IBM Maximo in China and Australia and SAP in Hong Kong and India. For customer care and billing, we run Oracle in Australia and SAP in Hong Kong. As part of our ERP strategic review, we can leverage our learning from across the CLP Group to assess what is the best way forward.

On the other hand, when it comes to cross-industry processes such as HR, procurement and finance, I think there's even more choice nowadays and most of that is cloud-ready. We've been reviewing in some detail the pros and cons of a single integrated approach versus a best-of-breed approach. Today, the world looks a lot different than in the early 2000s.

The more interesting project which is our focus now, is to look at global disruption, industry changes and technological innovation. When you look at the Apple iTunes store, the Google Play store, Amazon, Alibaba, etc. you see how the platform business model has disrupted many industries. We've been looking at what a platform business model could look like for our sector — so what is the "energy internet"? What is the Amazon equivalent for a utility company? We are working on that now and how we can bring ecosystem players together to provide added value for our customers. How can we establish that on a modern public cloud PaaS platform so that any third-party ecosystem player or start-up companies can join our platform and work with us? That way, we don't limit ourselves when it comes to innovation. That's a much more exciting discussion and we're working primarily with proven public cloud companies, particularly Amazon Web Services. It will be interesting to see how the global public cloud providers play out in the Asia-Pacific region over the next two to three years.

If you look at our sector, you see similarities with the telecom and mobile industry. So, it has evolved from where you used to pay for minutes of voice and then you had a package for unlimited voice, and then certain data, and now you have unlimited packages. Similarly, you could plan for a flat fee from your utility company ... small, medium, large and extra-large, and everything included, so as a customer you can budget much better. Look at the potential there is in combining the smart home around energy, security, content, internet access and so on. The idea really is to leverage your customer relationships and the brand that we have, to move into some of these new markets. There's also a lot of opportunity in terms of energy efficiency and energy management services, especially with commercial accounts and large industrial accounts."

Sanofi

∿→

Paris-based Sacré (who we met in Ch. 3), VP, HR Services, described his life sciences company, Sanofi, and his role as they implement global Workday-based HCM processes:

"We are one of the largest pharma companies in the world, along with Johnson & Johnson, Pfizer, Roche and Novartis. We are very strong in the countries with large emerging markets, and that includes China. We are a company of 110,000 employees and have revenues of about €35 billion.

We started an initiative in 2011 to create a global platform for core 'hire to retire' processes. We now have a global Workday footprint. We have deployed everything that we set out to deliver in our initial investment proposal. The last segment went live recently and that will be used for the first time at the compensation year-end cycle. We're live with performance and talent management. We are live with recruiting. We do have absence management, leave of absence, vacations and approval by managers. Next year, we will introduce Workday's Prism analytics.

I lead a team of about 25 people, which essentially does four things — and they're all related to Workday. Some configure and own the processes within Workday. Others provide tier-three support, which requires deep Workday expertise in terms of support and change. They help manage evolutions that Workday proposes. I have a number of project managers who help us manage the big changes and the new functionality that we want to introduce, and I have a change management team."

He explained his rationale for going with Workday:

"We wanted cloud computing solutions which allowed us to make changes via configuration, but not customizations. Organizationally, it is better to bring my team closer to the business, where users get the agility to align their business processes to business requirements as opposed to being further away in IT. That is one of the main reasons why I'm in HR, not IT.

We started to look at software options in 2012. Due to acquisitions, we had several systems on SAP or PeopleSoft, and the landscape was very fragmented. We had a couple of large systems, but nothing that was truly global. We wanted global processes for talent, performance, recruiting and core HR, particularly for internal mobility.

We were at the start of a four or five year project, and we did a program review when SAP acquired SuccessFactors in late 2011. SAP told us, 'By 2020, we expect everybody to have moved to the cloud,' which in their mind, of course, meant

SuccessFactors. 'We will not be innovating much in the (on-prem) SAP HR from this point.' To be honest, it's not like we felt that they were innovating anyway in SAP HR. We felt, to a large extent, that SAP's HR product was more of a by-product that they had developed mostly to please their large customers. We never got the impression HR was a core and strategic project to SAP. By the way, we continue to be a very large SAP customer in finance and supply chain areas.

We concluded that if we stayed with SAP we would be at the start of this four or five year program to create our global footprint for HR processes, and then we would have to follow up quickly with another program that converts all of that to the cloud. Shouldn't we do this in one single step and start a deployment in the cloud straight away?

That's where we started to challenge ourselves. In 2012, Workday was at a pretty early stage in Europe for a company of our size. Should we take a risk on them? There were a few customers that were based in the U.K. but in continental Europe, there was literally nobody. Workday had only just launched their office in France.

We concluded that doing the two-step with SAP was a bigger risk than going with Workday, which was relatively new to globalization. We wanted to get to the cloud right away. We were fortunate enough to be in the healthcare industry where quite a number of large U.S.-based companies had already implemented Workday. Bristol-Myers Squibb was one of them. Abbott had also selected Workday. Another was Johnson & Johnson, even though they took quite a lot of time to deploy. In the UK, GlaxoSmithKline had also implemented Workday. So Workday was not completely alien to our industry.

At the core, SuccessFactors was weaker than Workday. It had a good learning module with the acquisition of Plateau. They had a good compensation module. They also had a good talent module, but they were quite weak at the core. Back then, Employee Central did not really exist. I appreciate that since then, SAP has massively invested in creating that, but from the beginning our belief was, as Workday says in their advertising — start with a blank sheet of paper and create it from the inside out, from the core to the other functionalities. For us, that was quite a powerful starting point.

We also liked that in response to our question, 'If we insist you tweak the system for our benefit, what would you say?' Workday told us an absolute 'No,' which is the answer we wanted to hear. Their response was, 'It's an absolute *no* because all our customers share the same system. We encourage you to influence the design, lobby us and interact with other customers in our community. If you guys convince Workday that it is missing functionality and that is absolutely critical to a number of you, we are happy to look at the request, make it go up our priority list and eventually deliver it to you. This is how we work. It's a joint co-creation process, but *no* to the idea of customizing or tweaking the system just for you.'

On the other hand, SuccessFactors said, 'Well, you know, we might find a way. If it's really that critical to you, we will probably find something.' That's not the answer we wanted to hear. We wanted to hear an absolute 'No.' Same thing with Oracle, which said, 'We'll bring 50 people to develop it with you.' That is not what we wanted.

Payroll is done locally. The footprint of Workday is everything that we call a global process. There were a few countries which needed to replace their time-tracking system in the context of the deployment of Workday. We told them we would look at Workday and, if it suits you, we will help you deploy, but it's only in five countries. Outside of that, we limited the footprint to our global process and for us payroll is local.

We haven't had a global approach to contingent workers. This is another thing that we are starting now. We are working with other parts of Sanofi to have a fully integrated on-boarding process that is not only about employees, but also about contractors.

We have a very large SAP consolidation of about 13 financial systems. For us, when I say finance, I mean finance and supply chain because they are so intertwined. There is no way we can do finance alone. Nobody at Sanofi has bothered to look at

Workday finance modules because they don't have the supply chain capabilities yet.

Generally, we are very happy as customers and users of Workday. They reward collaboration. The day that you desperately need them to make a difference for you, I am confident they will."

Motus Integrated Technologies

∿➤

Garn Evans, CIO of Motus Integrated Technologies, described his company and the move from SAP (and QAD) to Plex:

> "Atlas Holdings LLC, which is our private equity company, formed Motus from four plants that were owned by Johnson Controls on June 1, 2014. They are located in Holland, Michigan; Ramos Arizpe, Mexico; Creutzwald, France; and Uberherrn, Germany. Two are visor plants (which have been divested as of this point) and the other two make overhead systems.
>
> Johnson Controls ran these four plants, along with many others, on platforms such as QAD MFG Pro, which is a manufacturing and operations platform and on SAP Financials. So, Johnson Controls was using two very large platforms. As Atlas and Motus personnel went through the selection process (I arrived after the selection), they were looking for something more nimble, and selected Plex to be that platform.
>
> I think right off the bat, it was recognized that Plex capabilities from a manufacturing cloud provider — as well as inventory management, built-in AP, AR and customer-supplier integration platforms — offered us more in-the-box capabilities. Motus took the approach of trying to do away with processes that were along the lines of, 'Hey, we've

always done it this way, so that's how we're going to do it.' We tried to break that model as much as possible, by saying, 'Is that a business differentiator? Do we need to keep doing it the same way? The process that's embedded into operations or finance, does it really give us a better margin on our services and on our products, or can we take what Plex offered out of the box and save both money and implementation time in terms of getting it out to our plants as fast as possible?'

There was, however, a motivator behind all that, which is called a TSA [Transitional Services Agreement] with Johnson Controls. This required Motus to be off Johnson Controls' systems within a year from the close of the divestiture. It was a huge motivator to our executive team because the penalties for remaining on the Johnson Controls systems were extensive and expensive.

Plex offered both the software and professional services. We didn't meet that timeframe of 12 months, but we did do it within 16 months. From a Plex perspective, I think they oversold their product, at least what they had in 2015. We held them accountable to developing some of the things that they promised as part of the package and out of the box before we were able to implement, and they delivered on those things.

The positives were Plex embeds the manufacturing, operating business model, inventory management, serialization of inventory, ability to track raw materials all the way to finished goods, and the ability to have an integrated system from both a manufacturing and a financial perspective. As we refined our process here at Motus, we're still seeing benefits of the integration between their financial and manufacturing functionality. Some of the things that they're still a little bit weak in is their European customer and supplier integration. From an EDI perspective, they seem to really struggle on the European EDI maps.

My internal IT team has just three people who support Plex. They support our Plex efforts globally. That meets all of our needs from a manufacturing and a financial perspective. We do reach out to some of the Plex partners from time to time for help.

SAP was previously used for financial reporting and forecasting, AP, AR and supplier integration. MFG Pro was the MRP and MES, highly customized for each and every individual plant. I interacted with the teams that supported both, and they were large and costly. I replaced that with a team of three people that support Plex for Motus.

I think there are some technologists, as well as maybe some other people, who believe that a cloud solution for the shop floor would mean too many outages. Quite honestly, we've not seen that from the Plex perspective. Now, keep in mind, that in every one of my locations I have both a primary and a secondary internet circuit. We've had times when the primary circuit provider will fail, and we've had to utilize the secondary circuit provider. Typically, that happens without incident. There is no maintenance or manual steps in our local service hubs or out on the plant floor where we have to make adjustments. Our infrastructure is built so that if the primary fails, the secondary comes up automatically.

We've hedged a little bit against that notion of, 'Hey, what happens when the internet is offline? Maybe Plex isn't offline, but local service … a line gets cut or what have you.' We've put in a little bit of a guarantee with backups to make sure that we can successfully do manufacturing operations in the cloud.

My global infrastructure team consists of two people and they manage all my security, and user and application provisioning. From a global perspective, I just have two people. I do have local support team members in each plant that support the operations on the plant floor. But, again, my total team here in western Michigan consists of three Plex ERP program managers and two global infrastructure people.

After the initial investment, we acquired a second company that had four more plants. We closed one down here in western Michigan. We converted the others to Plex in a similar manner as before. The project started in the April/May timeframe. We implemented the three Mexico-based plants on September 1, October 1 and November 1. The spread was 30 days apart for each plant, with a start-to-end of about six months.

Then we divested of our plants in July of 2018. The Mexico plant went live on a new Plex environment end of September 2018, and the France plant went in at the end of October 2018. So, our model is one of a couple months of initialization, preparation, education and then we roll out a plant every 30 days. The software is localized — Mexico is in Spanish, and France and Germany were both in French and German.

When compared to legacy systems that Motus could have continued with, Plex has turned out to be much more integrated and more nimble. It has provided great functionality that has allowed us to be successful with our acquisitions and divestitures. Finally, it has been a much less labor-intensive solution that has provided us with the great business system."

EBSCO

∿➤

This example illustrates diversification around the maintenance and support of SAP software.

EBSCO Industries, headquartered in Birmingham, AL, is 166 on *Forbes'* list of America's largest private companies. It is a diversified company with the primary business providing discovery services, databases, other information resources and services for libraries worldwide. Other industries include real estate, promotional products, manufacturing, distribution and insurance.

Bryan Bee, Vice President of Applications and Service Operations, joined the company in 2014, after nearly a decade consulting for SAP. He found that EBSCO had expressed some concerns with SAP's cost of ownership, especially around the cost of running the software:

"One of my first tasks was to look at cost optimization and where we could add value. We started with our hosting provider and we saved over 20% and received better services. The next line item was our SAP shelfware — what we owned but haven't implemented.

Through that process, we looked at a couple of different applications. We may own their licenses, but when we looked at the implementation cost, it generally would cost more to implement from a service perspective compared to a metered cloud solution for the same period of three or five years. Also, we found integration aspects could have both positive and negative consequences. Typically, the shelfware was not fit-for-purpose given our profile.

We went down that path a few times, and it's funny because, you know, I was with SAP when TomorrowNow started. Then I read your book, *SAP Nation*, and I went, 'Oh yeah! I forgot about this TPM option.'

So we looked at Rimini Street and at Spinnaker Support. I also talked to a few peers and brought the idea back to my leadership. It was the cost optimization perspective that grabbed my attention.

We had a healthy skepticism when we started the process. It took us a while to get our head wrapped around the service provided, the risks, and interoperability issues. As we went through that journey, we became comfortable and we concluded going with Rimini was an acceptable risk. Once we did our initial due diligence, we engaged both our business stakeholders and our developers. We did multiple reference calls and each time it was like, man, this is too good to be true.

Even though we have complexity and run SAP, we're not necessarily a huge SAP shop. For example, complexity exists via multiple countries, statutory reporting, consolidations and multiple currencies, but we are not utilizing SAP in areas like SD and SCM. This relieves a level of complexity that we would have to deal with otherwise.

Simultaneously, we were also talking to SAP about options for shelfware. All we really wanted was for SAP to provide a good faith offer — to show us they're our partner. It came down to small items we were not using, like Adobe Interactive Forms and the HP Quality Center. They wouldn't even give us a $20,000 credit. We reached a point where we said they're not able to work with us and we have limited opportunity to implement shelfware. We now have this other viable alternative, and it will save us money. From our peer conversations, we expected better service, especially since they support customizations, unlike SAP's maintenance option.

One of our biggest risks was that we were using BSI [a SAP partner] for payroll taxes. Payroll is certainly something you must get right. The conversion was done early and on budget.

Another risk was vendor viability, given the Oracle lawsuit against Rimini. We brought in our legal team. We did a lot of work on our contract to protect ourselves.

Would there be problems if we needed to go back to SAP in the future? Would there be back maintenance or interoperability issues? We decided they were acceptable risks. We're now in year four with Rimini. Our shared service stakeholders are happy while completing several upgrades and migrating AIX to Linux. We continue to enhance.

We had challenges with SAP maintenance but were able to find an alternative for that service while SAP remains a key partner. As we move ahead, we will continue to look for the best solutions for EBSCO. Some will come from SAP, some from other vendors. We are doing new business with SAP via Concur and moving our on-premise HCM to SuccessFactors for talent management. We have evaluated HANA, BW on HANA, and we've considered S/4. But each time, it hasn't made sense for us to make the investment.

Rimini has been a good partner. It's not like, 'Well, if it's not in the agreement, it needs a change order.' I can think of at least two different instances of specific help in our international offices where Rimini was able to help us out. In my opinion, we underutilize Rimini Street. When I presented at their sales kickoff event, I heard how other customers were using them. Our account rep has told us, 'You guys don't use us as much as other customers.' So, I came back to our team, 'Hey guys, I want to start using Rimini more.'

Rimini provided an opportunity to create cost efficiencies with stable support so we could invest in innovative areas — i.e., cloud products — while still partnering with SAP. What's next? We continue to assess our long-term ERP strategy and whether we will move to S/4 or evaluate other market options. We know we will eventually move to a new platform even if it is S/4, so let's save the money until we are ready so we can invest in what makes sense."

Bruce Power

∿➤

Jeff Holland is Senior Controller at Bruce Power in Canada, which he described as "an eight-unit nuclear facility on the shores of Lake Huron in Ontario, Canada."

"We have four nuclear reactors at the Bruce A Station. That's units one to four. Our Bruce B station has units five through eight. In total, we have eight units —

Our focus is to generate safe, reliable and cost-effective power for the Province of Ontario. We are quite proud of the fact that we generate 30% of the province's power and we do so at 30% below the average residential price.

Bruce Power is also a significant source of Cobalt-60, a radioisotope used for the sterilization of medical equipment around the world as well as a specialized form of cancer treatment called the Gamma Knife. We're proud of the fact that not only are we safe, reliable and cost-effective, we're also literally saving lives, globally, by providing these isotopes that are used in radiation and cancer care.

Our site in Ontario is over 50 years old. We completed our refurbishment of units 1&2 at Bruce A in 2012. We are going through a Major Component Replacement Program on our other six units over the next 10 years. We have partners investing billions of dollars in our units with the Unit 6 MCR starting January 1, 2020.

The finance team saw this coming, and the CFO said, 'We've got to get ready as we have a lot of folks trying to take our market share, whether it be wind, solar or the gas companies.' The CFO recognized that finance has to play a role in providing valuable insights and strategies to our leadership team in order to secure our long-term future.

We made the strategic decision to partner with human resources and IT. And so, we went live with Workday and created a partnership between finance and HR. We put both systems on the same trajectory, and both went live on the same day.

We have 4,000 full-time employees. With Workday, one of the big things we wanted to focus on was, What are our people doing? Not only how much are they costing and how much overtime are we spending, but what are they working on? What is the cost of our equipment, systems and units? How can we get more wrench time and more time on the tools? How can they improve?

Workday's 'Power of One' was a big selling point because we were frustrated with our legacy system. It was not easy to stay on the current platform. We had to bring in consultants every couple of years. They would have to essentially do an overhaul of our legacy system to get it back up to the most current version. We'd also customized quite a few functions in our legacy system and it was really hard to stay current.

The Power of One was a big draw. The fact that it was in the cloud and that every Friday night they would do a refresh, meant that every single customer would be on the same version. The twice-annual version updates would essentially happen overnight. We would always be current, and that was huge for us.

The other big thing with the Power of One was the community. It's the fact that Workday pretty much opens the book and says, 'We're so confident in our product and we're so willing to learn from our customers and work with them that we're going to just open the doors and have a portal where our customers can talk to each other and remove the middleman.' We don't even need Workday as the intermediary when we're speaking with other customers.

We have a Canada user group. Typically, we go down to Toronto once a year. We get together with other Workday users in eastern Canada and talk about lessons learned and best practice on the Workday platform.

We do everything in Workday from a finance perspective. We do our allocations in Workday. Our AP flows into Workday. All of our cost accounting is also done in the system. We also signed up for Workday planning, where they've recently changed their strategy. They've bought Adaptive Insights now and we are waiting on that. Then we made a massive overhaul to our expense reporting and that's in Workday. That was the first big win for the whole organization, as people were frustrated with the old system. It was mostly paper-based, and now we've completely automated it with Workday and it's pretty slick and easy.

We haven't adopted Workday Time. We have a heavily unionized environment here, and we've got collective agreements with complex shift schedules. And so, one of the things we've been working with Workday is to get their time system up to snuff to accommodate a very complex timesheet organization.

We signed on with one of the Workday partners, PowerPlan, for asset management. In 2015, Workday did not have the functionality and implemented PowerPlan, which integrates into Workday.

As one of the largest nuclear sites in the world, we can benchmark against ourselves. We can compare unit one against unit two, look at the systems in each unit, and say, 'The boiler system on unit one costs us $5 million in maintenance this year, whereas that on unit two cost us $7 million.' Then we can dig in and our analysts can go with the click of a button or two and say, 'Oh, well, look at this. We had a lot more corrective maintenance on unit two, and that's what drove up the cost. I wonder if we have a different predictive maintenance schedule on unit one that's preventing breakdowns.'

We're getting to the point now where finance is becoming a valued business partner with the line organization. Our analysts aren't spending 70% to 80% of their week trying to transform data into information. Workday now does the dirty work for us. Our folks are able to take that information and start to develop strategies and provide value-added insights to the executives they support. That is helping finance become a valued business partner.

One of the big things we do is work with our financial reporting team to develop meaningful dashboards for the internal client organization. With Workday, because it's such a nice, simple and slick interface, when we create a dashboard, say, for a plant manager or a maintenance manager, we work hand-in-hand with those guys. Then it feels like it's their own.

Such dashboards are our first line of defense. When they have a question, it's a lot more pointed. Instead of asking, 'Why was my overtime over by $50,000 this month?' they can navigate the system on their own and in a couple of clicks, they can answer that question. They're instead asking, 'Why am I spending so much time on corrective maintenance overtime?' What are we doing wrong from a predictive maintenance strategy? It's a big change. And so, the beauty is, because it's relatively intuitive and relatively easy to use, people are actually using it.

Our IT security and our regulators made it very clear. Yes, we've done our due diligence. Yes, we're comfortable with the cloud and with Workday's security. But because of the U.S. Patriot Act, we were not allowed to have our data hosted in the U.S. So, our data server is actually in Ireland. We're affiliated with Workday's international data hosting.

We looked at SAP, Oracle and Workday. Workday blew them out of the water on economics and then you add all the intangibles I mentioned. Other than getting comfortable with the cloud concept, which was new, it was a no-brainer for us."

PBF Energy

∿→

Another TPM customer is PBF Energy, one of the largest independent petroleum refiners and suppliers of unbranded transportation fuels, heating oil, petrochemical feedstocks, lubricants and other petroleum products in the U.S. PBF currently owns and operates five domestic oil refineries and related assets with a combined processing capacity, known as "throughput," of approximately 900,000 barrels per day.

Yael Urman, former CIO, said:

> "PBF is a relatively new company — it was founded in 2008. In retrospect, we could have gone with a SaaS solution, in the cloud. But we had a very stable SAP environment. When we first moved to Rimini Street, we had only one instance of SAP. We had been on various ECC versions and realized that SAP was not investing in ECC and had moved its focus to S/4. We didn't have any appetite to move to S/4. I know one company in our industry, very similar to PBF, that is in the middle of an upgrade to S/4 and they have already spent $300 million and they are not close to the finish line. How can you justify such an investment?
>
> We acquired a refinery from Exxon and as part of this acquisition we got a second instance of SAP, which joined our support agreement with Rimini Street. Then, a few months later we acquired another

refinery from Exxon. Rimini supports all these instances.

Since we moved to Rimini Street, we have bought an Ariba subscription. SAP was happy to sell us the Ariba subscription, no issue there. We have purchased other licenses but they were for the same products that we had already licensed. When we started to discuss purchasing new products they said that we could not do that. We discussed buying a HANA appliance, and they said 'No.' I suspect because HANA was on-premise and Ariba is a subscription.

We have a big offshore team and it was rare that they would open a ticket with SAP. It was too painful to deal with SAP. Still, this team was concerned about how we would manage without SAP. Once they got over their concerns, we encouraged them to open tickets with Rimini. I think we doubled or even tripled the number of tickets that we opened with Rimini Street compared to what we had opened with SAP.

The goal was definitely to save money around maintenance fees. In terms of our own L2 and L3 [level 2 and 3 support], however, the plan was not to save money but to free up people to do enhancements. So, with the same budget we now have more people doing enhancements instead of SAP support.

BPC was always a painful system. Half of our tickets are related to BPC. SAP struggles even today with BPC. We get much better service from Rimini

Street for this product. In niche areas, Rimini has struggled a bit. As with BusinessObjects, and especially Analysis for Office. The integration with Microsoft Office requires both SAP and Microsoft Office skills.

I have talked with many of my peers in the SAP world, and to be honest it's more emotional than logical. People have been with SAP for 30 years and many are afraid to break this relationship. But I think that in many, many cases it's emotional and not logical.

We are very happy with Rimini Street. We have a better relationship than what we had with SAP. PBF is a company that tries to maximize and optimize for the short term. And Rimini Street is a perfect fit for the PBF strategy."

Accuride

ᐧᐁᐧ→

Accuride Corporation is a diversified manufacturer and supplier of commercial vehicle components in North America. Based in Evansville, IN, the company designs, manufactures and markets commercial vehicle components. Unlike many other customers, Accuride diversified into SAP and not the other way around.

In many ways, Paul Wright is the prototypical CIO in the SAP world. He is comfortable anywhere in the world, and has had several operational roles in the manufacturing sector. However, unlike other customer executives in this chapter, he got introduced to SAP much later in his career.

> "In 2017, we acquired mefro wheels GmbH, headquartered in Solingen, Germany. It's now branded as Accuride Europe. It was a family business that grew through acquisition, and while still making wheels, they didn't just make truck wheels, as we did in North America. They made small trailer wheels, passenger car wheels, truck wheels and off-highway wheel products. It was a global organization, with a few plants in Germany and others in Argentina, China, France, Turkey and Russia. When we acquired mefro, we did not bring the Argentinean asset with us. The original family business, mefro Metallwarenfabrik, still remains with the founder of the company.

They had started implementing SAP for the same reason I think that anyone chooses to do ERP projects. They wanted to get all of their businesses into one common system of management. I think if I'm a German company then I'm probably going to start with a German product, and they started with SAP ECC 6.0, which is still the platform that they're on. They have implemented what I call core functionality of SAP across the different sites. They hadn't taken on Russia yet. That's something that we are going to do next year.

They use another third-party software that's integrated with SAP to handle the majority of their shop-floor interactions. Maintenance and quality are handled in outside systems. I'd say their back end is pretty functional, but I can't say I'm a huge fan of the approach of not doing everything inside one system.

We found we had bought a distressed asset. There had been a lack of investment in the factories, the people and the technology. The SAP system is one of the significant issues of the entire business right now. SAP works but the hardware that they were utilizing hadn't been changed at all since 2006. There also hadn't been a lot of data archiving.

And so, you've got 12 years' worth of data of an expanding factory and, all of a sudden, the hardware is grinding it to a halt. Sometimes you'd enter a sales order and, as you would expect, it's click-click-click and go. But, on other occasions, you'd be going click-click-click, and you'd wait 35 minutes, literally 35 minutes, to get a response from the system.

One of the first things we did was to invest in new hardware. We're seeing some transactions going 10 times more quickly in terms of processing. With the new hardware layer, more complex processes are now running 30 times faster!

Step two will be to put in the HANA layer. It's better technology to use as a foundation. I'm expecting, again, that the system will function better. We've got to go back and win the hearts and minds of the users who use the system instead of just downloading stuff and doing everything in Excel, which is where we are right today.

Then, when we're through that, it's the Russia implementation. Next, it will be time for us to look at S/4 and not just migrate what we have today, but take a hard look and ask, 'What should we be doing in SAP and what should we be doing somewhere else?'

You lose all of the efficiency that you were supposed to get from using ERP because you're waiting for the ERP to respond to you. There's an argument for cloud right there because you remove the hardware issue. The only thing that you need is a solid network connection. Again, even that is more of an Op-Ex expense where you can make choices without a huge capital investment."

Accuride has been running most of its operations in the Plex manufacturing cloud. It had decided to go with

Plex after a market evaluation and had looked at choices like Infor, Oracle and SAP. Rick Dauch, President and CEO of Accuride, had previous experience with Plex which also factored in the decision.

Wright continued:

> "In North America, we're moving a lot of our financial functionality to Workday. We're certainly doing all the analytics in Workday. We have our consolidated financials for both Europe and North America rolling up through Workday, and we'll be doing all of our plant performance analytics through Workday. With their Prism product, we'll be able to do even more analytics in Workday. Now, they can only go so far right now based on the amount of data that we're going to throw into Workday, and we are going to throw in a fair bit through the Journal Connector.
>
> What I've seen in ECC 6.0 is that the GUI is just terrible. So, you have people doing everything on the command line in SAP because that's better for them. Because of that, you've got people doing the same function multiple different ways and getting different results. The beauty of a system like Plex is that it is so intuitive. If you want to run a sales report, you hit Control-M, and you type in 'sales report.' In SAP, you've got to know the exact transaction you're looking for and, if you don't, navigate through to try and find it, which is a nightmare.
>
> Now, my guess is S/4 is better. But, right now, it's awful. With Workday, they've absolutely designed

it so it is easy to do all this stuff, and the analytics is drillable by nature. As long as you build it the right way, then you can do whatever you want with the data. And so, because of that, it's likely that I'm going to move more and more of the functions in SAP, and do them in Workday.

We also have to think of reducing the number of people we have inside our IT group because we're not an IT company; we're a manufacturing company. This has always been our mantra. With the acquisition, I've inherited a team of 34 people inside those plants working on IT on a revenue base of $450 million. In the U.S., I have a revenue base of $750 million, and I have 18 people. The math just isn't right for SAP right now.

Functionally, there's no doubt in my mind that with SAP, we'd be compliant anywhere we wanted to go in the world. In today's world, that's important. We had a choice when we were going to Russia. I had a choice. I could have said, 'Let's figure out how to do with this with Plex and Workday. Or, let's do this inside SAP.' I mean, at some point, unfortunately, the government regulations are going to drive what you can and cannot do as a business, and it was just too risky to do something else in Russia, even if we wanted to, so we stayed with SAP.

However, it's not an innovation driver. And, you know, I'm not your typical IT guy. I don't wake up and say, 'You know what? I am going to go and comply the heck out of this day.'

I'm exposing my German team now to a whole bunch of different technology, and the young, eager ones are lapping it up; they want to use it and they want to learn about it. If you're recruiting now, are you going to get the brightest and the best if you say we're an SAP ECC 6.0 shop? You're not. You're just going to get the dudes who know how to do stuff. And, there's nothing wrong with them. But, if you're looking to transform an organization digitally, that's not it.

Let's say we bought another company, and their footprint was U.S., Britain, some Europe and China. I tell you right now that my bias would be to find a way to implement Plex and Workday because I just like the complementary solutions they represent. I don't want to spend a gazillion dollars in new capital on servers. I've already got a team that gets more done, especially now with both Plex and Workday's emerging platform-as-a-service.

I just don't feel excited about what SAP is doing. One of the more powerful messages in the recent Workday event keynote was, if we find a bug, we fix it, and then it's fixed for everyone. How does SAP compete against that? How do you do that if you're not cloud, if you're not SaaS? It's just that innovation multiplier. SAP's advantage is it's the biggest [application] software company in the world, so they should have more engineers doing cool stuff for their customers, right? That's their value proposition, I think."

As I was finishing up work on this book, I got an update from Wright. "We have updated the server hardware, archived the data and moved to HANA since we last spoke. Not an inexpensive endeavor but the users certainly are feeling better about their experience than they were when we started."

More TPM

Like Rimini Street, Denver-based Spinnaker Support provides TPM to over 1,000 Oracle and SAP customers from their nine regional support centers. I caught up with Matt Stava, CEO, and Shawn Du Plessis, VP of their SAP unit:

> "SAP customers understand that SAP is aggressively pushing cloud adoption. Many, especially those with more complex environments and landscapes, feel like it could be another four to five years before SAP cloud reaches sufficient maturity. Those customers are going to wait until cloud is ready. While they wait, they want to save money, get more value for their maintenance spend and make a smart cloud adoption decision later.
>
> To counter, SAP is offering incentives to drive early adopters. Not every customer is interested, particularly those who have been through long, costly and disruptive SAP implementations in the past.
>
> It's not like customers have the choice to easily move their on-premise applications to the cloud. Many are choosing a hybrid approach, gradually migrating to cloud solutions. The question is, how do

you best support that hybrid environment, ensuring you choose the right business solutions and making sure those technologies are seamlessly integrated? Is SAP 'lock-in' best for the business or is it better to combine best-of-breed point solutions? These are very challenging questions to answer for SAP customers.

These and other circumstances regarding the on-premise to cloud journey are boosting TPM adoption. Many SAP customers are opting to take a 'maintenance vacation' in order to increase service quality, reduce maintenance fees and buy time to make informed cloud migration decisions. We are helping SAP customers fund cloud and providing them additional options, whether SAP, Workday or other best-of-breed solutions. TPM is enabling freedom of choice where SAP customers are not locked into premature or inferior versions of cloud. After a few years on TPM, customers can easily reengage with SAP to migrate to SAP cloud.

Organizations that make the switch to third-party support fall into three main categories:

- They are under some form of financial pressure and need to quickly reduce costs.
- They are moving to new on-premise platforms and see no need to pay exorbitant maintenance fees during the migration process.
- They are sustaining their on-premise software with plans to migrate to cloud.

In the early days of TPM, most customers were under very strict cost pressures. Nine years ago, the economies across the world were in trouble. But now, increasingly more enterprises are on the journey to cloud. Saving money is important, but they love the higher value they receive from TPM providers.

In the past, it seemed that SAP would engage customers they wanted to retain, typically the larger customers or the more recognizable brands. In the last two years, SAP has become aggressive to try and keep every customer, irrespective of their size. Of course, the larger customers still get more attention, but there has been a change in focus such that no customer should be lost.

Besides offering aggressive deals, SAP customers complain about intimidation tactics from the software vendor, including IA audits. Of course, this didn't go over very well with the customer base. Such actions actually benefited TPM providers.

There's no doubt that TPM alternatives have increased in popularity and adoption. Both SAP and Oracle are fighting harder than ever before to keep their massive support revenues — and the resultant 70–90% profit margins. Drivers like more personalized service for a fraction of the cost plus maintenance vacations resulting from ongoing cloud adoption will keep us very busy for the next 10 years or so."

To Sum Up

The diversification continues, but in many ways SAP is holding its own and even regaining some ground. As SAP's Tzitzon observed in Ch. 4, it is a game of inches. The war is being fought in the trenches, and SAP's competitors are much smaller, much less global and often siloed.

In some ways, far more worrisome for SAP are what we call Bystanders. They are waiting and watching the first three groups. This customer behavior is not unique to SAP. Other on-premise heavy customer bases at Oracle, Infor and Microsoft are behaving in a similar manner. The one big difference is many of SAP's customers are based in Europe, and they usually take a wait-and-see approach to many new technologies. Motivating this group to try out SAP's newer technologies before they get enamored with competing alternatives will be a significant challenge and also an opportunity for SAP.

CHAPTER 8

Bystanders

∿→

For years, Gartner and other analysts have been telling customers they have accumulated "technical debt" to vendors because they have not been upgrading to the latest releases of software. I personally don't like the term. Vendors should be enticing customers to upgrade to newer releases and products, not *guilting* them or behaving as if customers are indebted.

Besides, we do not talk as much about the "other" technical debt. We have forgotten what Ward Cunningham said in 1992, when he is credited with having coined the term:

> "Shipping first-time code is like going into debt. A little debt speeds development so long as it is paid back promptly with a rewrite. The danger occurs when the debt is not repaid."[51]

---

[51] Learning Agile: Understanding Scrum, XP, Lean, and Kanban By Andrew Stellman, Jennifer Greene, O'Reilly Media, November 2014

Vendors have been racking up this "other" technical debt by not keeping the software current with the times, even though customers keep paying them maintenance or annual subscriptions. You see it manifested in many ways:

- Vertical applications which continue to only be supported in on-premise mode when vendors have been pushing cloud and in-memory versions of horizontal applications for years.

- Significant customer customizations continue because the functionality delivered by vendors was inadequate. Vendors glibly claim their software reflects "best practices." Often it is practices from the 1990s.

- Large number of "ring-fence" tools and applications, because the core functionality delivered by the vendor was inadequate or has not kept up over the years.

- Wave after wave of UX struggling to keep up with what consumer tech has been delivering.

- Vendor investment in platforms and tools, when customers would prefer the money went into application functionality.

- Continued customer use of spreadsheets, often large ones, when analytical tools were supposed to have replaced them.

So, it is not surprising that only a small fraction of SAP's 400,000+ customers have migrated from ECC, Business One,

BusinessObjects and other products to its more modern S/4, SuccessFactors, ByD, HANA and SCP.

In fairness, Oracle, Infor, Microsoft, IFS, Unit4 and other vendors have the same issue with their legacy customer bases. You also have to ask why after 20 years Salesforce, NetSuite and other SaaS vendors have still not converted millions of customers from the on-premise world.

It is a vexing challenge. You could cynically argue legacy vendors are happy to collect maintenance checks from those customers who stay in on-premise mode. So, Oracle's Applications Unlimited[52] for its PeopleSoft, Oracle E-Business Suite, JD Edwards EnterpriseOne and Siebel products claims its "commitment to continuous innovation while also providing a commitment to offer Oracle Premier Support through at least 2030." In the SAP customer base, the years 2025 and 2030 have near-mythical significance as deadlines when major on-premise products are scheduled to be de-supported.

Wall Street, on the other hand, wants to see more cloud revenues, so vendors are eager to see these customers migrate. I turned to several industry observers to get their take on why these customers are migrating so slowly to modern cloud and in-memory solutions.

Mueller of *Constellation,* with experience in development at both SAP and Oracle, said we "live in the era of business process uncertainty:"

> "If you look at past migrations, customers made these moves when two things were present: when the cost

---

[52] http://www.oracle.com/us/products/applications/applications-unlimited-1970561.pdf

of ownership of the new solution is significantly lower, and when it is functionally good enough. SAP won in the client-server world thinking that they would offer two options, the mainframe R/2 for large companies, and R/3 for smaller ones. R/3 was Hasso's foresight, banking on client-server architecture and betting that mainframes would not be attractive to SMEs. In the German *Mittelstand*, there are a significant number of SMEs.

The thinking in the early '90s was that large companies would use the mainframe R/2 version, and smaller companies the client/server R/3 version. However, because of the TCO advantage and good enough functionality, large companies realized they could run a number of subsidiaries on client-server architecture at significantly lower costs than they could run them on the mainframe.

SAP stumbled on what is called a two-tier model. IBM and JD Edwards had done well selling AS/400 solutions to subsidiaries in the 1980s. Something similar is happening today again in SAP world, to some extent, with its ByDesign product.

Soon, these large customers were grabbing SAP by the throat and asking, 'Hey, when will R/3 be broad enough like R/2 and replace everything, not just at the subsidiaries?' SAP went on what I call the 'death march.' SAP was reprogramming during long nights, and weekends, porting the R/2 capability over to R/3. That is why SAP is the number one ERP vendor now — because they brought the mainframe 'functional equivalency' to the client/server world.

Of course, the irony is that SAP missed a few markets because they were so busy expanding R/3. So, in the SCM space, i2 and Manugistics clearly got away from them. CRM had Siebel, Clarify and others. Procurement had Ariba and Commerce One. SAP paid the price for not having the functional equivalency in those areas.

Now they're in a similar situation. I think SAP pulled a fast one, saying, 'Oh, don't worry. We copied all the code. S/4 is not a new system. S/4 is just a new implementation where we simplify things and get rid of old things.' To some extent, it was a technical argument as you got rid of these nonrelevant tables. The simplification ran the system better, and you got better business intelligence because there was no need for a data warehouse.

However, for SAP, just copying the code wasn't that easy. Technically, you had to examine the code and truly simplify it to make it work. Besides, the public cloud is not offering the dramatic TCO advantages that R/3 did relative to R/2.

Importantly, I don't see the functional equivalency. When SAP was started, Hasso has said, he went to ICI, the launch customer, and met a person in the finance department. 'He showed me how he worked, and I rebuilt that in software. It took us a few months, and then we had that.'

Today, you cannot go to a finance department and ask, 'How do you use machine learning? What do you do with data science? How do you use the cloud? What are your FP&A best practices?' These practices are still being distilled. We're in the era of experimentation. That is terrible for any SaaS vendor, because they want to build standardized software for hundreds and thousands of customers. That's how the traditional model worked.

Few business users really know, and the ones who have figured it out, and where it's working really well, don't particularly want to tell you. It's not a mature-state best practice, in which tons of people have left my company and built it up the same way. There are different ways of doing it.

That's already a gap on the horizontal capabilities. We haven't even reached anything on the vertical side with S/4 and they may never get there. You need to have the capability to build software again. Which is why every vendor is offering platform capability.

One of the big gaping holes at SAP is Big Data strategy. Dr. Plattner's fixation on in-memory computing is good, but he cannot hold all of the world's relevant data for business automation in enterprise memory. Memory prices haven't fallen fast enough. You need the spinning of disks and the benefits that tools like Hadoop give us. Users can store all the relevant electronic information without knowing, at point of entry, how they want to access and analyze it.

That's important to have because then it also feeds your deep learning with machines continuously learning on all this data, which you have to do on the cloud because the computer is cheaper."

Cindy Jutras, President of Mint Jutras, told me:

"I do an annual Enterprise Solutions study. One question I've been asking for 12 or 13 years in my annual surveys is, 'If you were going to evaluate a solution today, which deployment options would you consider?' When I started back in the 2006, 2007 timeframe, less than 10% would even consider SaaS. Today, that's the single most popular choice. But that does not mean they actually then go out and implement a SaaS solution.

Anecdotally, the biggest thing that stops them is the perception that they need all their previous customizations. I would argue they probably don't, partly because new solutions today do more than they did back when they implemented. Plus, they have more ability to configure without invasive custom code changes. Partly, it's because they just didn't need those customizations. They did it because that's the way they always did it, and they weren't willing to bite the bullet and do something even better or different.

I was at a Unit4 conference last year, and I was in a session meant to collect information from customers to help them move to cloud. It was almost like a focus group with product management. The big resistance to moving to cloud is customization, because for so many years Unit4 had the BLINC message — an acronym for "Businesses Living IN Change." With their SDKs, they actually encouraged code changes, but code changes that would move with upgrades. Now, in a multitenant SaaS solution, even those kinds of code changes are discouraged. But those customers are all sitting on those kinds of code changes, which is making them very resistant to moving into the cloud. I have asked Steve Miranda at Oracle a similar question. Basically, what he said was,

'I strongly encourage customers not to inventory their customizations and to move forward.'

But I really think it is inertia. People have bad tastes in their mouths from having gone through the blood, sweat and tears of an ERP implementation years ago. I don't think it needs to be like that today, but that's the perception.

I honestly believe they think of it like brain surgery: You don't do it unless the patient is dying. My recommendation is they're better off thinking of it as a joint replacement: You replace a hip or knee when it either becomes too painful or when it prevents you from doing what you want or need to do. I try to get people to look at it from that perspective.

The bottom line is, even if they're upgrading to a solution from their incumbent vendor, the same kind of solution, I always encourage them to look at a reimplementation as opposed to just a migration or an upgrade. If they don't, they're dragging a lot of old baggage with them. For many years, and with good reason, people avoided 'rip and replace' at all costs. They would go through all of this pain, aggravation and cost just to get back to the way things already were. This was in the context of rationalization at large companies, getting to common standards, and things like that.

Today's solutions are better and provide you with much more interoperability, connectivity, flexibility and agility. Now, you can go miles further with an innovative vendor who offers a modern technology-enabled solution. It is worth it, but it's still a struggle to get people to buy into that and make that move."

The "leave your customization" message works fine for HCM or CRM functionality where the cloud offers many choices. Many vertical and country-specific processes have few options in today's cloud application market. What should customers do about customizations in those processes?

I asked Scavo, introduced in Ch. 2, why customer bases are moving so slowly. Scavo, who is also President of consulting firm Strativa, replied:

"For many years, we've been helping companies select new enterprise software, whether it be ERP, supply chain, CRM or human capital management. I would say that, particularly with ERP systems, companies try to avoid making a wholesale change if they don't have to. Certainly, there are many things that are more attractive about cloud ERP compared to on-premise ERP or even hosted ERP. But that's not enough to drive a company to say, 'You know what? The advantages of the cloud are just so great. Let's go ahead and either upgrade our current system and convert to a cloud version or select a new system that's entirely a true cloud ERP, and let's go with that.' That's not enough of a reason.

As we all know, ERP implementations are painful. They can be quite disruptive. They divert resources from other things that organizations want to do, and of course everybody has limited resources, whether they be people or budget. Companies will always have something more immediately important or desirable to do than just making a change for no other reason except that the ERP system will now be cloud-based instead of on-premise.

When you get it all done, it's still basically an architectural change. You may get some additional functionality or ease-of-use and the other things that go with it. I can't think of any company that's just made a change to cloud from on-premise or hosted ERP to cloud ERP, just because they wanted to get to the cloud. It's always driven by some other event or driver.

Vendors like Infor and Oracle have tried to move legacy customers to the cloud with initiatives called UpgradeX and SOAR, respectively. The reason you don't have very many SOAR and Upgrade X customers to talk to is because there are not that many of them. Existing customers do not make that cloud conversion routinely.

Suppose you are an Infor customer on an old version of ERP LX (formerly known as BPCS). If you're looking to get off that system, the door is wide open to anything at that point. You don't necessarily need to stay with Infor. Infor makes it very attractive to stay with them from an economic standpoint. However, if you're going to consider migrating from that system to one of Infor's CloudSuite products, you're also going to look at Oracle, SAP, Microsoft, Plex and other cloud solutions. The incumbent vendor is not going to win 100% of those customers. They're probably not even going to win half of those.

With SCM, HCM and CRM, most of the leading solutions today are in the cloud. Nobody wants on-premise anymore. They all want cloud solutions. But not with core ERP. The attitude is if it ain't broke, don't change. If there's any excuse that business executives can find, they will take it. Even when these systems are really broke, they're still trying to find a way to put off the decision.

We see this all the time in our ERP selection services. Often, we go through the whole proposal phase and then the prospect says, 'You know what? We don't have the bandwidth for this right now. We're going to push this off another year. We know we need to do this, but not now.'

Some of these companies are running on operating systems that aren't even supported anymore, so they're running patched versions. They're not getting vendor support, and they are running in emulation mode. A "last legs" kind of thing — and still, they will try not to make a conversion.

What are the kinds of events that finally force a company to go to a new ERP? There are several:

- We did an acquisition and we're now on two ERP systems and this is just not tenable for the long term. We've got to standardize on one.

- We expanded our business into Asia and this ERP system is not double-byte or doesn't support localizations.

- We went into a new line of business that has subscription billing. The [current] system doesn't do this.

Those are the kind of events that force companies to make the move, and then they're much more open to cloud ERP."

The German-speaking SAP user group, DSAG, runs periodic surveys of its members, and summarized the findings:

"Like every year, members were asked about migrating Business Suite to S/4. The figures show that companies have extensive plans in this respect. Five percent aim to migrate this year, and 39 percent plan to in the next three years (+6 percentage points). A further 30 percent want to do it after this period (+10 percentage points). 'All but one-quarter of companies have made the decision to migrate,' says Marco Lenck, highlighting the results. 'Despite this, the number of those having actually completed such projects remains stagnant at 3 percent.' This could be due to the fact that businesses are currently starting projects that take longer or that they are doing Brownfield implementations where the complete conversion of one system to another is complex. It is also possible that they underestimated the amount of work involved."[53]

Mueller of *Constellation* talked about the European IT psyche and that may explain why SAP's European customer base is migrating slowly:

"Well, there is a slow reaction to innovation, which often saves Europe from all the changes common in U.S. IT and technology management. Sometimes, you sit some things out and it's good for you because it fizzles and you

---

[53] https://www.dsag.de/pressemitteilungen/more-information-required-digitalization

didn't spend money, time and effort on it. On running ERP in the cloud, Europe is definitely behind because there's this resistance to innovations and change.

Four years ago, I was at an Amazon summit in Berlin, talking to German CIOs. The interesting thing I heard was, 'We'll never put our customer data in the cloud. We won't put our employee data in the cloud.' But they were there at the Amazon summit to look at IoT. That's the interesting thing. All the big manufacturing base in Europe, and particularly as a manufacturer in Germany, I need to have my IoT strategy. When I have my IoT strategy, I run into this thing, which the cloud takes away, where I don't have to size how many machines I have, right? I don't need to go to a board and say I need five million or 10 million for more infrastructure.

The funny thing was that all these CIOs in the same conversation over the same coffee cup were saying, 'Never going to move my customer and employee data on this.' For IoT, they had to do it because of the technical necessity.

It was the flipside for the ERP stuff, where you could still size and justify the machine. It's the modus operandi. You have the data center. Utilize it. You have your people who know ABAP well, who know the platform well and who are doing your customizations well.

To be fair to many of the European CIOs, the vendors also have not done a good job bringing data centers across the ocean.

Germany is the largest European economy. Where else should your data center be? There have been so many ones opened in the UK, which makes sense for banking and financial services vendors, but Paris and Frankfurt are much bigger than London. That's not even an argument.

There is xenophobia at many of the U.S.-based vendors. You see this pattern. They go to Canada because it's across the border, and then it's the Commonwealth. How many people go to Australia and New Zealand with crazy distances, costs and time differences, which are not justified by the size of the economy, but simply because people speak English?"

Good point, and possibly SAP may be able to lead its European customer base since its U.S. competitors have not tried to.

Bystanders are clearly not rushing to SAP's new solutions and, like Wright of Accuride (profiled in the previous chapter), they worry that staying with older products hurts their IT employment brand. However, they hear mixed messages. They are told to decommission older customizations even as they see SAP encouraging a new generation of customizations with SCP. Ironically, they had a hard time getting SAP to support customizations to ECC while paying full maintenance rates, so many moved to TPM vendors who support them *and* at lower rates. SAP's automation tools clearly help moves to S/4, but they are told don't use those tools — do greenfield projects. The Risk-Takers in Ch. 5 are trying out many of SAP's newer technologies, but mostly can show early pilots and POCs. Many of the Modernizers in Ch. 6 are being cautious in their moves and continue with on-premise deployments and with SAP GUI. You go to Sapphire and see the massive SI booths, and the muscle memory kicks in of the large, painful last generation projects. Can you blame the Bystanders for taking their time?

It's a bit like visiting Cuba. Sure, GM and Ford take pride in the Buick Roadmasters and Ford Edsels that are still running seven decades later, but they would also like to see their current models running there. And they know that when the island eventually opens up, the competition will likely include Japanese, German and Korean models.

That is the challenge for SAP. And in fairness, it's also a challenge for its competitors with their own Bystanders.

A Plethora of Strategies

In the first volume of *SAP Nation*, we had described several strategies that customers were trying out to optimize their SAP investments. They included HP which was ring-fencing SAP with cloud solutions from other vendors, Embraer moving to TPM, AstraZeneca changing its talent model and insourcing more tasks, British Gas adopting more open source and commodity technology, and Microsoft implementing a two-tier ERP model.

In this volume, many of those strategies have gone mainstream. So, you see names like Plex, Rimini Street, Workday, Salesforce at many of the customers. In addition, now we see a wide variety of new strategies we had hinted at in Section 0.

Here is a sampling:

- Ring-fencing ECC with many of SAP's own cloud properties as with SuccessFactors at Terumo BCT and components of C/4 at Pregis.
- Two-tier deployments with SAP ByD in the subsidiaries.
- Migration from ECC to S/4 on-premise at Johnsonville Sausage.

- New implementations in the S/4 Public Cloud at a restaurant chain.
- Trying out relatively new on-premise, but impactful SAP functionality like IBP at Louisiana-Pacific.
- Trying out Leonardo ML pilot projects as at Costco and Queensland OSR.
- Developing new ISV functionality on SCP like Vertex with their indirect tax app
- Moving to new licensing and hosting models like Bombardier with IBM.

We also saw blends from this growing toolbox of strategies. So, we are seeing companies migrate to newer SAP products and simultaneously shifting to TPM vendors like Rimini Street for support of legacy SAP products. GEBHARDT has been implementing a variety of SAP cloud products around its ECC on-prem implementation. Additionally it has developed a customer portal and set of predictive maintenance services using Leonardo IoT and new AIN capabilities.

Given this wide proliferation of products and strategies in SAP World, my firm, Deal Architect, recommends (and often facilitates for clients) an intense offsite meeting to help customers take a fresh look at the changing market. That should cover and assess the fit of many of the strategies above, while also evaluating internal and external talent and fit with emerging technology trends.

Of course, some customers will scoff even at the mention of reengaging with SAP. SAP has not done itself many favors. It has committed several unforced errors, as we will see in the next section.

Section IV
Unforced Errors

CHAPTER 9

Not a Boy Scout

⟿

"Purpose" has become a big buzzword in corporate hallways, and especially at tech vendors such as Google, Facebook, Apple and others that have come under increased scrutiny for a variety of privacy, diversity and other issues. *Forbes* runs an annual "Just 100" list honoring socially conscious companies.[54] Nine out of the top 10 in the 2018 list are in the technology sector.

Benioff, CEO of Salesforce, has been particularly active on a number of social issues, including diversity and homelessness in San Francisco. His stance certainly helps in recruiting those Millennials who are picking career paths based on "purpose." Corporate buyers are much less comfortable with such public posturing. Indeed, Forrester Research cautioned, "As brands try to engage the tribal, outrage-driven social arena, how do they pick and choose sides? What is authentic?"

---

[54] https://www.forbes.com/just-companies/#17a57af52bf0

John Donahoe, former CEO of eBay and now CEO of ServiceNow, defines corporate "purpose" as revolving around questions such as: *Why should people want to work here? Why do we exist? Why would customers want to do business with us?*

SAP answers the first question pretty effectively. It was the only company in the world to qualify on all five country lists of the annual Glassdoor Employees' Choice Best Places to Work 2018.[55] SAP made the list in the U.S., UK, Canada, France and Germany — where it received a first-place win. "Unlike other awards, there is no self-nomination or application process; instead, it's entirely based on the feedback employees have voluntarily and anonymously shared on Glassdoor. To determine the winners of the awards, Glassdoor evaluates all company reviews shared by employees over the past year."

As for *Why do we exist?*, here's what SAP's website says:

> "Our promise is to innovate to help our customers run at their best. SAP is committed to helping every customer become a best-run business. We engineer solutions to fuel innovation, foster equality, and spread opportunity across borders and cultures. Together, with our customers and partners, we can transform industries, grow economies, lift up societies, and sustain our environment."[56]

But SAP's answer to Donahoe's third question — *Why would customers want to do business with us?* — is not always that clear.

---

[55] https://news.sap.com/2018/12/sap-best-place-to-work-glassdoor-employees-choice-lists/?source=social-Global-BrandGlobalSocial-FBPAGE-Holidays_Features-SAPStory_Branding-LifeatSAP-ST5_Work_Future_of_Tech&campaigncode=CRM-YD18-SOC-GBSM

[56] https://www.sap.com/corporate/en/vision-purpose.html

In the first volume of *SAP Nation*, I pointed out SAP liked to benchmark itself against Oracle and claim to be a "cleaner" company. That's not exactly a high watermark. Oracle is a litigious company, and if you parse court reports you can see the company does not qualify for many "most admired company" awards. Still, SAP used to behave like it was on higher moral ground — even though in 2007 Oracle sued SAP for copyright infringement. The case was settled in 2014, with SAP paying Oracle a sum of US$359 million.

Since that book came out in 2014, SAP has found itself in the middle of at least three prominent incidents leading to court cases and government investigations — which have hardly boosted its desire to be seen as a "purpose-driven" brand.

Indirect Access (IA)

In the software industry, audits often cause unnecessary friction with customers. Most vendor executives, when you catch them in a relaxed state, will acknowledge that only a very tiny percent of corporate customers actually "cheat." Usually, the issue is poor interpretation of legalese fine print. More often than not, audits generate opportunistic revenue for a vendor region or industry sector that needs to make its numbers for the quarter or year. With very high software margins, there is usually little sympathy for software vendor pleas that they are the aggrieved party.

The sad fact is audits boomerang against vendors who initiate them: Several CIOs and procurement folks tell users to freeze that vendor's footprint. Most of these are loyal customers who would gladly pay more for new functionality but resent what Brian Sommer of TechVentive — a frequent collaborator with me on advisory projects who is originally from the oil patch in Texas — calls "shale-fracking their customers' wallets." He says a number of software vendors have been bad actors, for the following reasons:

- Litigating against their own customers.

- Over-auditing their customers and charging usurious penalties for any out-of-compliance infraction, no matter how immaterial.

- Blackmailing current customers into signing deals for unwanted newer products just to make audit issues go away.

- Making customers buy new licenses or subscriptions for applications that customers have dutifully paid maintenance fees on for decades.

- Jacking up subscription renewal pricing materially once they believe the customer is "locked into" the solution and can't easily switch to another vendor.

As Sommer sums it up: "Customers want their ERP vendors to be leaders, not leeches."

One of the most toxic contractual terms in vendor world is that of IA, where users exchange information with SAP software in dialog or prompt mode. The issue is not with licensed users who access the software using its UX, but rather with those in surround-systems that have been custom-built or licensed from other vendors. SAP wants to also be compensated for those users accessing data in the SAP system. In the on-premise world, licensing was mostly named-user-based. In the new world of sensors and machine-to-machine data exchanges, such legacy on-premise metrics reflect a time warp.

SAP could have proactively gone to customers and said that in light of the new digital scenarios — where cloud applications that ring-fence SAP, bots, IOT devices and machines are accessing SAP applications much more than humans are — the user-based pricing model designed in the 1980s needed to be retired. Indeed, going forward, with S/4, it makes sense to offer customers what SAP calls its "Digital Access Model."[57] Instead, it also looked backward, and started invoking IA claims on contracts signed in a galaxy far, far away.

That has led to heartburn among SAP customers. I have heard the anger in my consulting with clients for years. Some of their plaints: "It's OUR data, not owned by the SAP system!" "SAP was invited to bid for the surround software, lost it fair and square, and still wants to be compensated." "This is a time bomb — we are getting hit after years of paying SAP maintenance. If we had known this up front, we likely would not have implemented SAP." And there were also plenty of unpublishable rants.

Customers thought IA was very unfair, but some would grudgingly agree the greed was not confined to SAP. Other enterprise vendors had their own sneaky practices, as Sommer pointed out. But to a person, they would "punish" SAP by not inviting them to future business for a couple of years. I am convinced for every dollar SAP collected in IA, it was precluded from bidding on five bucks in new business.

---

[57] https://news.sap.com/2019/01/digital-access-model-hasso-plattner-founders-award-finalist-profile/

Shaun Snapp at Brightwork Research & Analysis explained the evolution of the IA concept. He is an analyst, not an attorney, so the terms are his way of simplifying the concept:

> "The first IA, and the general definition, was essentially a form of cheating on the part of the customer. If the application was charged on the basis of a user license, a customer could circumvent user licenses by developing a front end that would allow them to access the functionality but without paying a user license. SAP came up with what I call Type II IA. If you connect any commercial, non-SAP system to SAP, either its database or an application, then that falls under indirect access liability. And so because it is universal, it's just a question of whether SAP wants to enforce a claim against the customer. Maybe in the past 10 years, SAP began changing the IA clauses in contracts or making it more prominent in their contracts. The issue is that the person reading the contract did not know what SAP's version of indirect access is, and they did not realize their liability. Therefore, it's a bit of a booby trap that was put into these contracts.
>
> SAP's enforcement appears to be completely arbitrary. It's based upon intimidating the account and extracting from the account, particularly from accounts that are not doing what the rep wants. I mean, if we think about it in the hypothetical sense, SAP could then bring a claim against every one of its customers. It could say, 'You owe us IA on everything that you connected to our applications.' Of course, they're not going to do that because that would end their ability to gain future business.

It's a concept where everyone could charge everybody for IA, including the customer who should be able to charge SAP for IA because SAP is connecting to their legacy systems. I mean, that sounds a bit ridiculous but, if you extend the logic, that's how you eventually can arrive at that type of conclusion."

A UK court ruled in favor of SAP against a customer, Diageo, in early 2017. The amount SAP claimed seemed to fit the "time bomb" scenario described above. According to the text of the judgment, the beverage company and SAP had begun their software license and maintenance agreement in 2004, and came into dispute after Diageo deployed two new third-party systems in 2012. Far more quietly, SAP settled its US$600 million software licensing dispute with Anheuser-Busch, the U.S. subsidiary of its beverage conglomerate AB InBev, on a similar IA matter.

IA used to be an irritation for individual SAP customers. Many would cave in and buy some of SAP's new products and then just leave it on the shelf. SAP, in turn, could report to Wall Street how well its newer products — cloud and in-memory — were selling. But these two high-profile cases turned the matter into a full blown PR crisis across the customer base.

As David Blake, UpperEdge CEO, wrote:

"SAP is no longer nipping at its customers' heels on the issue of Indirect Access and instead is shocking some of its loyal customers by going for the jugular. Through our customers, we have observed SAP uses Indirect Access violations as an excuse for predatorily squeezing fees from their customers, and worse, seizing the opportunity to reduce flexibility and promote an anti-competitive environment."[58]

SAP CEO McDermott acknowledged the problem in his keynote at Sapphire Now in May 2017. All of SAP should have rallied around his promise of a solution. Months later, there had been only dribbles of information about it. In SAP's defense, user groups like ASUG and DSAG were reporting intense discussions with SAP on the topic. In April 2018, SAP finally announced a new framework. Three items were of note in the announcement:

a) A move away (at the customer's choice) from user-based licensing to that based on document counts.

b) An organizational realignment that separated license sales departments and procedures from auditing and compliance groups and procedures.

c) Mechanisms for license exchanges and contract conversions to move to the new construct.

I quite liked the fact that the initiative was branded Project Trust. You can snicker when a corporation uses terms like "intimacy," but it reflects some humility that SAP felt the need to regain the trust of its customers. The licensing metrics were more aligned with a world in which surround-systems, machines and sensors — more than humans — interact with

---

[58] https://upperedge.com/sap/sap-and-indirect-access-is-sap-taking-advantage-of-its-customers/

core ERP processes. The friction over users having to pay SAP for accessing their own data stored in SAP's tables was being acknowledged. By moving to document-based compensation, SAP was agreeing to get paid for "work" if and when its software actually performed some task — calculations, validations, etc.

I also liked the organizational shift where audit initiation would be done outside of sales. So, the hope and expectation was that audits would more likely be driven by actual breaches of compliance rather than by revenue quota drivers. Additionally, I liked the initial validation they have had from polling several of the global user groups and many customers — they told me they estimated they had talked to 200 — across a wide section of industries and countries.

I told them I still had a number of reservations:

- For a project that was meant to simplify pricing, most customers would have to go through a rigorous analysis of their likely document count exposure. It sounded intrusive. The matrix of nine document types (sales, time management, material, etc.), some priced on a line item basis, would not be appealing to many customers. (Think, for example, of a customer in the CPG sector with each user processing thousands of orders, each with hundreds of line items.)

- In the 10 months since McDermott announced they would look at the issue, I would have liked to have seen more rationalization of industry-specific pricing — e.g., based on meters in the utility sector — and to have seen that across processes which touch both on-premise and cloud SAP offerings. I told them if they wanted customers to open up old contracts, some two decades old, they should be prepared to revisit all kinds of terms, not just the ones they chose as their focus.

- While the new compliance group would initiate any reviews, business resolution would still be done in the field. I told them I wanted to see how strong the Chinese wall was between the two groups.

- In addition to "trust," I wished this team had also targeted "realism." Over the last two decades, value in enterprise software has been shifting from transaction processing to intelligence and analytics. I told them I was not sure the exchange/conversion values SAP proposed (to move from user to document-based pricing) reflected the fact that on-premise ERP functionality pricing has steadily declined, especially in the face of the growing cloud computing alternatives. In a world where machines are doing more of the work at the front end of so many processes, improving quality of data, etc., why should you continue to pay for (often duplicative) work done by an ERP system at the back end of that process, at the same compensation rates they were paid for at an earlier time and place?

- For customers who choose to stay with current contracts based on user counts or more recent order counts, there did not appear to be much protection from IA reviews. SAP said it would not seek back maintenance, but there could still be license exposure.

- My final point was that customers did not surround SAP just for the fun of it. In the 1990s, when SAP took off, CIOs controlled most of the technology budget in organizations. Today, VPs of Products, CMOs, Owners of Industrial Assets and other C-level executives have their own technology budgets. They want functionality or cloud flavors SAP can not offer. Many invited SAP to compete for their business for surround functionality, and SAP could not win. ECC had not evolved much, and S/4 is only gradually replicating ECC (and small amounts of industry) functionality, and these are mostly in on-premise deployments. Putting customers through lots of rethinking from user to document counts would make a lot more sense if SAP could offer a much bigger function point footprint.

Snapp's reaction was more critical:

"They came up with a new plan that was supposed to make everything better, but the new plan was very complicated. It ends up with SAP having even more ability to see what would be going on inside of a customer. Not everything, but they're checking transactions, so they would know all the purchase orders or sales orders, and they would charge on the basis of that. They would know how many are being processed, right? It's a very invasive scheme that SAP came up with, and when I analyzed SAP's documentation I predicted it would not work, even while SAP resources were roundly praising the change. It was obvious it would not work because it is too invasive and too high in maintenance."

Blake at UpperEdge even broached the idea of SAP being exposed to claims of unfair restraint on competition:

> "With the public disclosure of the Diageo and Anheuser-Busch lawsuits, competitors are becoming aware of SAP's Indirect Access rules and the impact it can have on their businesses. Therefore, we believe it is only a matter of time before competitors start to scrutinize sales opportunities they lost to SAP, where the customer already had SAP solutions installed but went through a competitive bid process to address other workflows, and look to see if the decision to select SAP was influenced by SAP's Indirect Access licensing rules."

(Interestingly, as we discuss below, Teradata is also using the anticompetitive theme in a lawsuit it has filed against SAP on a separate matter.)

Jon Reed at *diginomica* was more measured about SAP's IA proposal:

> "I get the sense sometimes that SAP feels they are a bit singled out on this issue, given they are hardly the only vendors that have auditing complaints from customers. I believe that's the wrong attitude.
>
> This winning approach would be an iron resolve to become an industry leader in how large-scale enterprise projects are priced. The document pricing model then becomes a bridge to further pricing innovation that is, to be sure, incredibly hard work, but is also inseparable from any transformation that so-called intelligent/cloud

enterprises should deliver. Add real-time license monitoring. When that becomes state of the art, there should
be no more audits. You always know where you stand."

A few months later, Reed's *diginomica* colleague, Howlett,
reported from the UK & Ireland User Group Connect event in
November 2018 that "talk in the halls was not especially positive,
with the view among those I asked that SAP has made glacial
progress in helping/resolving the IA issue."

In an interview with me, Howlett said he had told SAP
executives: "Suck it up. Tell Wall Street. Get rid of it. It's a one-
hit-wonder. You'll be back. It will be fine. Your customers will
love you for it .... You're going to have to, or it's death by a
thousand cuts."

IA exposed a darker side of SAP. They resented customers
going with alternative surround-systems. IA came across as
punitive and pouty in that sense. Their document-based "solution" showed an unwillingness to accept that ERP systems were
doing much less valuable "work" for customers than they did
in the past. Machines, sensors, bots are monitoring for event
triggers and capturing data, validating it, massaging it and
doing many of the tasks ERP systems used to do in the past.
Worse, by annoying customers with threats of IA, SAP was
being frozen out of new opportunities in which its growing
stable of products would be competitive.

Years from now, analysts will be arguing whether IA was
more hurtful to the SAP brand than its callous attempt to raise
maintenance rates in the midst of the last, deep recession. Back
then, it delayed the move after complaints from a large number
of customers.

Teradata

In June 2018, Teradata, a provider of database and analytics-related products and services, filed a lawsuit against SAP claiming, among other things:

> "SAP could not have so quickly developed and marketed HANA in the first place without its theft of Teradata's trade secrets. Now, using the fruits of that theft and its position in ERP Applications, SAP is attempting to foreclose Teradata from supplying EDAW solutions to many of the largest corporations in the world."[59]

Having been an expert witness on a few software industry court cases, this was my immediate reaction:

> "I am not sure what to make of this. Usually, you hear murmurs in the industry about some impending action but this appears to come out of left field … Not saying one side has more merit than the other, but it will mean looking at a lot of documentation to say who developed what and when before the other did."

Teradata has asked for a jury trail, which raises additional questions:

> "I want to see how Teradata attorneys can succinctly explain arcane optimization algorithms to a jury. Also how they refute SAP's considerable prior art when it comes to analytics — their three-tier architecture in

---

[59] https://www.corevist.com/wp-content/uploads/2018/06/TeradataSuit-1.pdf

R/3 which allowed it to support multiple databases and understand how users access certain fields more than others, Business Warehouse going back to 1997, its Business Objects acquisition in 2007 and its Sybase acquisition in 2010 and many other elements. In *The New Polymath*, in 2010, I had written about work at the Hasso Plattner Institute in Pottsdam which I believe was the genesis for what became HANA."

The case will likely meander through the legal system for a while, but John Belden at UpperEdge commented on short-term issues for SAP and its customers:

"While it does not seem likely that the judge will grant a temporary injunction to prevent the use of SAP HANA due to the impact of clients currently using the code, SAP will need to deal with the immediate fallout of the lawsuit. Specifically, SAP will need to:

1. Put in place a PR and communications strategy to address three important constituencies:

Current users of the SAP HANA BW database that are now currently at risk of having to dispose of their existing software. Potential future SAP customers who will have a legitimate reason to delay upgrades until the issues associated with product tying are resolved. Investors who now have reason to doubt SAP's growth strategies and profit projections and concerns regarding potential damages associated with the lawsuit.

2. Ready a legal team and allocate internal capacity in preparation for discovery. Given the gut punch delivered by Oracle in 2014, SAP will likely not hold anything back in putting in place a top-tier legal team. UpperEdge expects SAP to technically challenge the statute of limitations on trade secret claims, which is three years in California. They will also need to reserve internal capacity in preparation to comply for what will likely be some broad discovery requests made by Teradata.

3. Consider an alternate S/4 product roadmap. SAP will need to internally put on the table a roadmap for S/4 that allows customers more flexibility going forward with the data warehousing and database products. It is much more likely that customers will feel emboldened by the Teradata lawsuit to press for this flexibility."[60]

Sommer of TechVentive wrote:

"Potential customers of S/4 applications or custom HANA apps may seek indemnification from SAP for infringement claims by Teradata. Prospects may want more than the usual indemnification language found in a software agreement or the language that their procurement department insists is added to a contract. Indemnification may also need to cover the costs a customer might incur if

---

[60] https://upperedge.com/sap/teradata-sues-sap-implications-for-sap-and-its-customers/

it must replace HANA with Teradata products or pay a license to Teradata. In some rare cases, customer might want to peruse their own worded contracts to ensure they have included indemnification rights."[61]

As with the prior Oracle lawsuit against SAP, a jury trial could bring reputational damage.

A *MarketWatch* article described a courtroom scene in the Oracle trial:

"But SAP's counsel could not wipe away the image conjured up by the testimony, as the former TomorrowNow developer Ritchie also described employees discussing the legality of what they were doing, and worrying about their own personal liability, at what sounded like a truly sleazy operation."[62]

The article said SAP "executives must have spent their second day in U.S. federal court squirming in their seats."

Corruption

"As a global company with a commitment to integrity and compliance, the past three months have been humbling for us," said Adaire Fox-Martin, member of the Executive Board of SAP SE, in a statement on October 26, 2017.

"The allegations of wrongdoing in our South African business have had a profound impact on our employees, customers

---

[61] https://diginomica.com/2018/08/09/teradata-v-sap-what-it-means-to-customers-and-prospects/

[62] https://www.marketwatch.com/story/oracles-goal-in-trial-make-sap-look-corrupt-2010-11-04

and partners, and on the South African public — and we apologize wholeheartedly for this."[63]

She was referring to what Reuters described as 'German software maker SAP found compliance breaches and "indications of misconduct' in $50 million of public sector deals in South Africa involving the Guptas, friends of former president Jacob Zuma accused of corruption."[64]

A couple of years earlier, SAP had another corruption incident in Panama:

> "The SEC said [SAP employee Vicente] Garcia helped arrange SAP's sale of software licenses at an 82 percent discount to a Panamanian partner, which used the savings to create a 'slush fund' for bribes.
>
> A Mexican subsidiary of SAP then falsely recorded the slush fund as legitimate discounts on its books, which were later consolidated into SAP's own financial statements, the SEC said."[65]

Stanford Law School[66] and Sullivan and Cromwell LLP keep track of U.S. SEC and DOJ enforcement actions under the Foreign Corrupt Practices Act that was enacted in 1977. The record shows that in the four decades through 2017, there were 562 actions filed between the two agencies, with sanctions in excess of US$18 billion. Clearly, corruption continues to be big business in global settings.

---

[63] https://news.sap.com/2017/10/sap-provides-update-on-ongoing-investigation-into-its-south-africa-business/

[64] https://www.reuters.com/article/us-sap-safrica/germanys-sap-admits-misconduct-in-south-africa-gupta-deals-idUSKCN1GK19M

[65] https://www.reuters.com/article/us-sap-se-sec-idUSKCN0VA3HW

[66] http://fcpa.stanford.edu/statistics-analytics.html?tab=2

The South Africa incident had embroiled several other big brand companies:

"McKinsey and KPMG, which have also been accused of exerting undue influence in the awarding of government contracts, responded by making changes: KPMG replaced its management in South Africa and McKinsey offered to pay back $81 million it earned in 2016 from business it carried out for Eskom."[67]

So, SAP is not alone, and this is not the first or last time a global company like SAP will be exposed to such temptations or have its internal controls fail.

However, it is bemusing because SAP can be sanctimonious from time to time. For a while, SAP used to hype its efforts around sustainability. I wrote in 2011, "But while its tools help companies report carbon data, to my knowledge none of its functionality has helped any customer reduce that carbon. For an enterprise-wide vendor like SAP with access to the shop floor, to the data center, to the logistics supply chain, that is a huge opportunity it needs to step up and take advantage of."

SAP CFO Luka Mucic has been quoted as saying, "SAP considers the ethical use of data a core value. We want to create software that enables the intelligent enterprise and actually improves people's lives." McDermott similarly likes to say that SAP wants to "help this world run better and improve people's lives."[68]

---

[67] https://www.handelsblatt.com/today/companies/corruption-cloud-sap-embroiled-in-south-african-corruption-allegations/23580766.html?ticket=ST-593589-ewBPCJ5IunJUO4EGEVVZ-ap1

[68] https://www.forbes.com/sites/sap/2018/06/01/sap-ceo-bill-mcdermott-tech-has-to-be-for-good-and-for-all/#1354b35e7147

Less words, more demonstrable customer outcome. Nobody expects SAP to be a squeaky-clean Boy Scout. As an observer commented like Google, SAP may want to consider its own "Don't be evil" and "Don't be creepy" mottos.

CHAPTER 10

Fool Me Twice,
Shame on Me

⤳

An Italian proverb goes, "When a man deceives me once, it is his fault; when twice, it is mine." U.S. President George W. Bush famously botched the phrase in one of his speeches: "There's an old saying in Tennessee — I know it's in Texas, probably in Tennessee — that says, fool me once, shame on — shame on you. Fool me — you can't get fooled again."[69]

The reality is that SAP is getting a second chance as it rolls out cloud versions of its on-premise solutions. Has it learned from the first wave experience of ERP projects? Let's look at three areas where it should be doing better:

---

[69] https://georgewbush-whitehouse.archives.gov/news/releases/2002/09/20020917-7.html

Working with Service Providers

Five years ago in the first volume of *SAP Nation* I described the show floor at Sapphire Now in Orlando, FL:

> "The technology exhibitors gladly spend millions each year on the event. They rent booths as large as 2,000 square feet. The signage, up to 22 feet tall, is a burst of colors, shapes and sizes. Furnishing the booths is expensive, but chicken feed compared to the cost of flying and accommodating hundreds of their staff. SAP gives them 50 to 60 conference badges as part of their sponsorship, but many exhibitors share the badges to ensure more of their employees are available to host guests in the booths and hospitality suites, or to mingle with customers during the keynotes and breaks. They pay extra for shuttle buses, escalator clings, bottled water, hot coffee cup sleeves and other "swag" branded with their logos. It is good return for their investment. SAP says "87 percent of exhibitors surveyed in 2013 reported that they were either extremely or very successful in reaching their objectives."

In 2018, Sommer of TechVentive, himself a former Accenture partner, walked around the Sapphire Now booths with his camera and noted:

> "I must have missed the memo that announced that ERP as a concept is gone and has been replaced with a 'journey.' When I think of a journey or a trip, I think it helps to have a destination in mind before setting off

on this adventure. So, what's the destination that the integrators et al. see ahead for SAP customers?

It turns out that while there's no unanimity in the destination per se, they all seem to think that customers:

- Will need lots of external help getting there.
- Aren't prepared to handle the scale of the journey by themselves.
- Need to think about highly transformative efforts that will dwarf prior projects.

It was interesting that for such material, complex, fuzzy projects that are being hyped, the partner messaging would suggest — for the most part — that the move to S/4 should go fast. How can something so transformative, so disruptive be so easy to accomplish?

I think the answer is that many firms are really only selling a bunch of lift-and-shift services. Some want to move your on-premise S/4 to a cloud — preferably their own cloud, not necessarily SAP's public cloud.

These lift-and-shift projects are *NOT* transformations. In fact, as one gleeful integrator told me on the flight to Orlando, they are selling a technical platform upgrade to get the customer's systems ready to someday support more advanced, digital capabilities.

That kind of project has little economic value. The incremental cost to upgrade and eliminate a lot of technical debt will be great, while the incremental benefits may be negligible. It might be great business for systems integrators, but I suspect many executive committees and boards of directors will not approve such expensive, low-value-added projects.

I suspect a number of the outsourcers and integrators are hoping that this is the second coming of ERP. They're hoping that SAP customers will move in droves to the S/4 solution as this will reenergize their SAP practices."

Josh Greenbaum of Enterprise Applications Consulting put it in more humorous, Shakespearean terms:

> *"But there's still this one issue that bedevils us all*
>
> *It's customer success, and we're dropping the ball*
>
> *Our partners — the big ones — are making the sales*
>
> *But once the deal's closed, mediocrity prevails.*
>
> *The cloud doesn't change that age-old story:*
>
> *Inexperience leads to results quite gory.*
>
> *Projects still fail at an alarming rate.*
>
> *And in the cloud, that really mucks up our fate.*
>
> *You can't get renewals when customers aren't happy*
>
> *And too many projects are looking quite crappy.*
>
> *We know as execs this problem is real,*
>
> *But changing our culture has little appeal.*
>
> *When it's worked for so long and we've made all that money*
>
> *Despite results that are truly not funny."*[70]

---

[70] https://www.linkedin.com/pulse/week-before-fkom-midwinters-night-dream-saps-2019-verse-greenbaum

In volume one of *SAP Nation*, I had an entire chapter on spectacular failures around SAP products. The parade continues, with recent stories like these:

- "Disruptive discount grocery brand Lidl has made an uncharacteristic misfire, shelving a seven year project to introduce SAP to its business. The attempts wasted an estimated €500 million, with Lidl now looking to revive its old system."[71]
- "Haribo is a German candy manufacturer that manufactures gummy bears and other candies. In late 2018, they began going live with SAP and quickly began experiencing supply chain disruptions. This ultimately affected sales, causing revenue to decrease after go-live."[72]
- "IT consultancy Wipro has paid National Grid US$75m to settle a lawsuit over a botched SAP implementation that cost the utility firm hundreds of millions to fix."[73]

In earlier parts of this book, we highlighted how many customers are using smaller, lesser known SIs and outsourcers for their S/4, SuccessFactors, Leonardo and newer SAP projects. Many were burned by massive overruns and project failures in their first wave of ERP projects, often associated with the larger SIs, and are being cautious this time around.

But in other ways, things have regressed, not improved. SAP now brags it has 18,000 partners. That's way too many. It

---

[71] https://www.consultancy.uk/news/18243/lidl-cancels-sap-introduction-having-sunk-500-million-into-it
[72] https://www.thirdstage-consulting.com/lessons-from-the-sap-transformation-problems-at-haribo/
[73] https://www.theregister.co.uk/2018/08/06/botched_sap_implementation_national_grid_wipro_settlement_75m/

would do better for itself and its smaller partners by ruthlessly culling that number.

SAP also continues to be enamored with its bigger SI partners. You can understand their view that such partners are a channel or at least an access path to influential client executives. But the continued lack of certification or controls? SAP's brand suffered considerably from the overruns and failures in the first wave of ERP.

The issue is actually less about SAP, and more about the slow evolution of SIs and outsourcers. At this stage, with two decades of cloud computing experience, the ecosystem should be teeming with "born in the cloud" SIs who were raised with Google, Amazon, Salesforce and Workday technologies plus Agile methods.

In the SAP world, there is little automation in service delivery, and still way too much consultant travel. In the 1990s at Gartner, I had pointed out that for many customers the consultant travel budget by itself exceeded the cost of SAP software. That is still depressingly true at too many SAP customers.

Darwin Deano, SAP CTO at Deloitte Consulting, responded to a question I asked at an event:

> "We're 20,000 people. It's not going to completely change overnight. But I can assure you that every SAP project is benefiting from things like automation and other new ways of working. We're not going to be making our revenue from what we did 10 years ago."

Wipro has an offering called QuMiC for what it calls a "reliable migration" to Oracle cloud applications.

My question is why is it taking so long? There should already be much more remote delivery, use of automation in data conversion and testing, and use of machine learning in parameter configuration. I would also like to see proactive commitment to multitenancy and public clouds.

And given multiyear contracts, a commitment to continuous improvement. How about delivering even a fraction of the efficiencies shown by Amazon Web Services? Thomas Vachon, Principal Cloud Architect for Harvard University Information Technology, catalogued AWS's pricing trajectory, and summarized it as follows:

"AWS has publicly reduced its pricing across various services 62 or 65 times, depending on who you ask or what metric you utilize. With these changes, it becomes hard to understand historical pricing trends for AWS other than they make it cheaper as their internal modeling allows."[74]

I have not met a single person in the software and services sector who does not take pride in Gordon Moore's Law and the price/performance curve technology supposedly moves on. In contrast, I have not met a single executive in those sectors who will not argue that it does not apply to them. They want you to believe it only applies to Intel chips.

Oh really? Productivity and efficiency can apply everywhere. Go see Six Sigma and CMM Level 5 shops. Many of SAP's Indian outsourcing partners earned their stripes with

---

[74] https://www.stayclassyinternet.com/articles/investigating-AWS-pricing-over-time/

those price and quality metrics. They seem to have forgotten how to do the same around SAP.

AWS has delivered all those price cuts in the last decade. And look how fast it has grown during that time. So here's the moral from that story: If you move down Gordon Moore's curve, you will also move more quickly past Geoffrey Moore's chasm.[75] SAP needs to push its service partners down that price/performance curve.

In fairness, it is not just Deloitte. Mueller, CIO at Pregis (introduced in Ch. 3), is ex- Deloitte, E&Y and Cap Gemini, and he said most large firms are "able to pull together digital teams and more agency type things for the sexier stuff, but they're not able to compete with the niche players as well for the smaller and middle market. They're obviously big where they have the relationships in the Fortune 100 …. But the model is still based on bringing in a staff of green beans and a couple of people pulling projects together, with a couple of senior managers and partners selling it."

Jarret Pazahanick is an SAP and SuccessFactors Consultant and SAP "Mentors Alumnus" who has been a member of the SAP partner ecosystem for over 20 years. He provided additional insights from the field around some of SAP's newer products:

> "One of the things I was excited about when I moved into the cloud consulting world after SAP's acquisition of SuccessFactors was the opportunity of a 'new world' for customers. My assumption was that SAP planned to fix

---

[75] https://www.amazon.com/Crossing-Chasm-3rd-Disruptive-Mainstream-ebook/dp/B00DB3D81G/ref=sr_1_1?crid=36R8Z2V9OZIID&keywords=crossing+the+chasm+by+geoffrey+moore&qid=1548025938&sprefix=crossing+%2Caps%2C198&sr=8-1

their bloated and out-of-control partner ecosystem and clean up many of the sins of the past which are well outlined in the *SAP Nation* books. The expectation was that any cloud-consulting partners that SAP selected would understand that the delivery model was different than on-premise. At a minimum, consulting partners should come to market with an agile implementation approach, small consulting teams, remote consulting, shorter engagements and operate in a customer-friendly way that has not always been present in the SAP ecosystem.

Unfortunately, that is not what I am seeing on the ground. What I have observed working on projects and talking with customers is the same runaway partner ecosystem model of the past. All too often I find that SAP sells the software and walks away thinking, 'We've done our piece.' They do not fully grasp that with the cloud model customers are renting the software and can more easily go elsewhere to other strong competitors in the marketplace such as Workday and Salesforce. com. SAP's approved partners are an extension of their product and play a big role in customer satisfaction, yet they've done little differently to improve their partner ecosystem.

With cloud-based technologies such as SuccessFactors and S/4 Cloud, SAP has the ability to monitor every partner. They can view every consultant that has access to their customer system, they can monitor projects, and they can have well-established and reviewed checkpoints and provide expert quality assurance — all of which play a big role in customers' success. When you look at a partner ecosystem that's growing at a rapid pace of

2,000 new partners a year, it becomes very difficult to manage and police that volume — and ultimately, it is the customer that suffers. SAP doesn't truly realize how bloated their partner ecosystem is, how it's impacting their customers' satisfaction and hurting future sales. Happy, live and referenceable customers are the best salespeople that they could possibly have.

Partners play a critical role in successful implementations, getting customers live, and ensuring happy and referenceable customers. It's very difficult for customers who are only implementing software every 10 to 15 years to have the in-house expertise to do these complex implementations on their own, and so partners are a key component. Customers don't realize the risk they bear — and the marketplace is littered with high-profile public and private failures. There is a great old poker quote, 'Look around the table and find the sucker, and if you don't see the sucker, you're it.' When dealing with most vendor and partner sales organizations, the customer can easily turn into the sucker if they aren't aware of how important their software and partner decisions are. If they don't engage with an independent, trusted advisor that has their best interests at heart, they risk failure. Since SAP is not providing adequate oversight and controls, smart customers spend a lot of time, effort and due diligence on software selection to make sure they find the right software and partner for their organization. This involves deep research and vetting of their consulting partner, as well as every consultant that joins the project. In addition, they assign their best and brightest team members to the project.

I've seen little change in projects over the past 20 years. I was recently on a large SAP S/4 project with over 100 consultants, from one of the large well-known consulting partners, in what turned out to be a three-year implementation and a consulting model straight out of the 20th century. This is a real disconnect from what I heard from SAP's CEO Bill McDermott on a Wall Street quarterly Q&A. He talked about the speed of getting customers live on SAP S/4 HANA was now 'in terms of weeks.' Industry insiders have joked that he meant '156 weeks.'

Albert Einstein said, 'The definition of insanity is doing the same things over and over again but expecting different results.' Sadly, even with a perfect opportunity for SAP to move their partner model into the 21st century in a way that would help customers, they have decided to keep with the status quo, much to the delight of their partners (a.k.a. SAP's external sales organization)."

B2B peer review sites like G2 Crowd have grown in popularity since the first volume of *SAP Nation*. G2 Crowd claims more than 600,000 validated user reviews on a variety of technology products and services. Its categories include SAP products like Concur and SAP ByD resellers. As of early January 2019, however, there were nearly 5,000 reviews on AWS, compared to only one on Accenture's SAP practice. Clearly, there is inconsistent coverage across service providers.

One new site called Raven Intel is more specifically focused on service providers who implement SAP and other enterprise software. The site gathers and publishes reviews of enterprise cloud HR software implementations and consulting services.

Its founder, Bonnie Tinder, told me in an interview, "SAP SuccessFactors projects account for roughly 30% of Raven's data, covering all major regions of the world, North America, EMEA, APJ, Latin America and South Asia, with over 20 industries, from advertising and business services to manufacturing and utilities. That represents approximately 260 cloud HCM module installations, from Core HCM to Talent and Learning."

The site is relatively new and, for now, is focused only on HCM projects, but it is a start. The data shows solid project scoping is a precursor to projects being delivered on time and on budget. Of the SAP SuccessFactors projects reviewed by Raven, 70% were scoped properly, but where customers cited multiple change orders (needs not covered during the pre-sales process), customers were three times more likely to rate their implementation experience negatively. According to one SAP SuccessFactors customer, "Make sure that you are absolutely crystal clear on timelines for change orders — i.e., when something's going into preview vs. production. We had a few snafus in that area that were very frustrating." Raven also found one of the biggest contributors to project dissatisfaction was significant team member changes. One customer related having lost count of the number of project leads from the consultant side, which did not bode well for an overall satisfactory project.

Peer reviews can only go so far. Service procurement disciplines have traditionally been weak. As I wrote at Gartner in the 1990s, buyers spend six months evaluating software, but only six days deciding on the implementation service provider — and then they spend six times as much on services. Since then, buyers have become much more vigilant about implementation project procurement. I saw that during interviews for this book. Customers are judiciously using SAP resources for newer S/4 releases and Leonardo functionality. They are using boutiques with specific skillsets. Most customers still don't do as good a job with post-live private cloud or application management procurement. We are seeing three- to five-year SaaS contract renewals follow a similar pattern, and turn contentious.

My firm, Deal Architect, has helped numerous companies run RFPs to select SIs, evaluate hosting/private cloud providers and take them on due diligence trips to India and East Europe as they evaluated offshore centers. In general, these are "life events," not services most companies procure on a regular basis and deserve way more attention that they get.

In the 1990s, service partners used to promise benefits from "reengineering" business processes and also suggest their "industry prints" would help fill the many gaps in R/3 functionality across industries. Neither promise came true. Many of those services firms, often in newer iterations, are dusting off those previous campaigns. Only this time they promise benefits with the more contemporary buzz phrase "digital transformations" around the more modern S/4.

There is an additional risk this time around. Many SAP partners are proposing private cloud or on-prem deployment of S/4 (and possibly C/4 going forward). Seriously, if you are doing S/4 in a private cloud with SAP GUI, how different is that from the thousands of ECC projects you claim to have done, and why do you deserve a premium?

Additionally, the on-prem or private cloud model threatens to continue the previous cycle of expensive, on-premise ECC implementations with their hosting, upgrades and application management costs. It will also complicate SAP's efforts to obtain sufficient data in the cloud across customers to train its machines to deliver in ML scenarios.

Pazahanick pointed out SAP did not recruit "born in the cloud" service providers even as its cloud properties have grown in importance. In the next wave, SAP will need to recruit partners steeped in knowledge of open-source tools and ML skillsets as it pitches its platform and Leonardo to a growing base of customers. Although Wall Street will not like it, SAP should consider expanding its own services capabilities around the new products. Helping the migration of its 400,000+ strong customer base to its newer solutions should be one of its highest priorities.

While we wait for SAP to reshape its services ecosystem, customers should be stepping up their own due diligence. They would do well to put a "Fool me twice" reminder on the calendar when they are negotiating a major services contract.

Industry Solutions

C/4 is seeing a lot of attention and investment at SAP. As we saw in Ch. 4, Atzberger, President of the unit, is bringing a lot of energy to this renewed focus. In an analyst briefing in December 2018, he had a slide which showed the CX market being the "biggest addressable market in technology." You can pardon Atzberger's bit of bombast as he showed the CX market bigger than the market for SAP's other promising products: S/4, Leonardo, SCP, etc.

What struck me was that there was no mention of vertical markets on that slide. By some estimates, just the fintech (banking and brokerage) sector addressable market is by itself bigger than CX. Then you have the many industries SAP does business with. Its site[76] says, "45 of the 50 top utilities com-

---

[76] https://www.sap.com/industries.html

panies in the world run SAP solutions" and "18 of the top 20 global apparel and footwear retailers run SAP solutions." But which solutions? Most of these industry extensions have not seen the in-memory, cloud and machine learning innovations SAP has been bringing to its horizontal applications like CX and SuccessFactors. They are still in client/server architectures in on-premise settings.

Functionally, they often fail to reflect the many changes these industries have seen. Supply chains are being redefined with modern distribution centers and last-mile delivery options. Utilities are focused on net metering and predictive maintenance. Insurance companies are being challenged to rethink business models in line with growing data about the events they cover. Banking is being reshaped by a swarm of fintech vendors. Every process in every industry is being reimagined with automation — drones, AI, ML, autonomous vehicles, kiosks and RPA. There is no industry whose operational books of record have not been reshaped.

This time, SAP's vertical trajectory is similar to what it had in place around R/3 in the 1990s. Industry solutions started arriving years after customers could have used them, given their Y2K challenges.

The good news for SAP (though not its customers) is that its competition — Oracle, Infor, Workday, Salesforce, etc. — offers even less when it comes to operational books of record for most industries. As we saw in Ch. 6, the bad news is that when customers try to do major transformations, they are faced with the prospect of modernizing only their financials, HCM or CRM functionality and not any of their industry-specific processes. They are forced to live with hybrid architectures with attendant master data, security model and UI incompatibilities.

I turned to Jim Holincheck, former Workday, Gartner and Accenture executive (and a colleague of mine at a start-up), and asked him why there is relatively low investment in verticals. His reply:

"There's plenty of competing priorities. As a software company, you can look at multiple dimensions in terms of how you grow the business. So, verticals are part of that equation. Completing your horizontal product set is one of the best opportunities to leverage your existing customer base and be able to upsell that set of customers. So, at Workday, this resulted in investments like Workday Recruiting, Workday Learning and similar solutions. The financial modules and Workday planning were other priorities in terms of what that built.

Another dimension that comes into play is geography. Every geography that you take on requires investment not just from a product perspective, but also from a service and support perspective. Product, sales and services all have to be aligned. In our experience, I found that sales often wanted to push into new countries that get them increased opportunity to sell within regions. The same products that they already know would be easier to sell.

Another dimension is around the customer size. We had a lot of discussions about that in the early days at Workday. You could say we were really targeted at the sort of midsize to large organizations, and then went upmarket to the largest, most complex organizations in the world. This is still a typical path that vendors follow, but there's a lot of opportunity in the midsize market. Being able to take the same set of products and make investments in terms of sales and services, make them easier to sell and easier to consume, also becomes a priority.

For Workday verticals, there was an early push into higher education. That was an area that [co-founder] Dave Duffield was passionate about. Our experience was that it's a really big investment to build what I call an operational system of record for a vertical. I think it's a quandary that many vendors find themselves in: 'Do we play the long game?' Do you create that operational system of record or do you play where you can get instant leverage and get a faster return on that investment. I don't think Workday is unique in that regard. If you look at other vendors who have a lot of revenue coming from horizontal solutions, I think they make the same types of choices.

As a new vendor, I agree with the premise that one way to differentiate is to focus on specific verticals and not play against the horizontal providers. I'm surprised more haven't tried to do that. Maybe it's a VC type of mentality. The horizontal addressable market tends to be pretty large because it touches the potential of so many organizations. With verticals you're limited in terms of the set of customers that are going to buy it.

I think we will see newer models emerge for vertical functionality, and I'll use higher education as an example. At one point, when Workday came along and put the stake in the ground to develop the student solution, there was an open source movement in higher education where a number of the universities got together. 'Hey. We've got all this intellectual capital. We all have similar needs, so let's come together and create that kind of solution.'

An alternative is a group of commercial customers who decide together to go to a vendor, saying, 'If you build this, we'll be your early adopters, we'll be your design partners and we'll pay for this.' That's probably a lot more compelling and attention-grabbing for a vendor.

You have SIs which also brought some of that domain knowledge in addition to the software vendor. If you go back to the verticalization of SAP in the last wave, SIs were a large part of that development."

Holincheck did not mention another option available to SAP, Oracle and other on-premise vendors. They already have a rich base of customers across industries. They could easily convene design partners from this population to develop the next-gen vertical software. In fact, applying my second definition of "technical debt" in Ch. 8, they should have already been using billions in maintenance fees they received for their industry solutions to keeping vertical extensions current.

Of course, corporations have options of their own, including developing their own technology businesses. While Amazon gets lots of attention for the growth of its AWS cloud infrastructure, think how big its commerce and fulfillment technology units would be if it sold those as separate services? In its annual shareholder letter, Amazon reported:

"In 2017, for the first time in our history, more than half of the units sold on Amazon worldwide were from our third-party sellers, including small and medium-sized businesses (SMBs). Over 300,000 U.S.-based SMBs started selling on Amazon in 2017, and Fulfillment by Amazon shipped billions of items for SMBs worldwide."[77]

Or take JP Morgan Chase, which employs nearly 50,000 people in technology — more than 31,000 in development and engineering jobs, and more than 2,500 in digital technology.[78] JPM is increasingly delivering solutions to customers, including via Athena:

> "At the heart of the world's biggest investment bank is an all-seeing program that allows its traders and salespeople to value trillions of dollars in stocks, bonds and currencies …. Now, J.P. Morgan is letting clients access the trading program — named Athena after the Greek goddess of wisdom — to run analytics on their own investments."[79]

Amazon, JPM and Berkshire Hathaway are starting a healthcare company.[80] Guess what their initial focus is expected to be? "Technology solutions." When it comes to industry functionality, expect technology buyers to increasingly become technology vendors.

---

[77] https://www.sec.gov/Archives/edgar/data/1018724/000119312518121161/d456916dex991.htm

[78] https://www.bankrate.com/banking/jpm-big-banks-spend-billions-on-tech-but-theyre-still-laggards/

[79] https://www.cnbc.com/2018/11/05/jp-morgan-selling-trading-software-in-glimpse-of-wall-streets-future.html

[80] https://qz.com/1192693/amazon-jp-morgan-and-berkshire-hathaway-are-starting-a-healthcare-company/

I gleaned another perspective on verticals from Ganesh Bell, who is now President at Uptake, but previously had spent time at SAP and GE:

"Look at utilities, the rail industry, oil and gas or chemicals. SAP is in many of these industries and doing really well. There's a physical model of the coal-fired power plants, wind turbines, solar panels and the grid. The physical network is in dichotomy with the utility economic model which is moving beyond electrons. They are offering new energy services and don't just move electrons around. The gap between the economic and physical models is one of massive value creation opportunities and requires people to go deeper into those industries.

For the last several decades our systems have been optimized for humans entering data. We need to look at all these industries and think about the deep vertical algorithms that we have to deliver. Machines have been generating data for decades and nobody's been listening. Now we have robots, drones and even augmented humans that will be generating data. So, if you just think about that shift that's going on, we believe that we're moving from a model of automating business processes to automating decisions. That's a big shift from the old school of IT enterprise apps model where doing horizontal with a little bit of verticalization was enough. To do this correctly now, you need to have deep verticalization.

When I look at this, I see the need for a newer architecture to transform those industries. We believe that architecture has to be cloud-native technology, across multiple clouds. It's got to be intelligent at the edge, and it has to be born in the era of machine learning. In many industries, industrial machines generate terabytes of data a day, more data than most end users put on the consumer internet in a whole year, and more data than most enterprise app systems ingest or even store.

At Uptake, we're focused on deep industry outcomes. We go further in trying to understand the annual energy production of a wind turbine, the cost of uptime and are you improving the heat rate in a gas turbine. That requires deep understanding of the industry. That's where we're starting from. We're starting from the outcomes and building back the stack.

I am grateful for my time at SAP. Learned a lot. It's a fantastic company. Companies that buy SAP, I believe are making good decisions on the IT side. It's always been challenging to bring the OT (Operational Technology) side along. We finally have a way to generate value out of OT that has not been there before. I believe the architecture I described is true both on the IT and the OT side. However, we're so focused on that intersection of IT and OT, we're not going to do ERP or just financials.

For us it's not about understanding the financials, it's understanding the value of the outcomes for our customers and helping them make money. This can be the cost of downtime, cost of improving productivity of assets and the people we're focused on. The asset may be a wind turbine, but the setting is a wind farm. The people are field service workers, asset managers, plant managers and field technicians. We're trying to optimize their work. We're also trying to optimize, not just their labor cost, but because of predictive maintenance and service, their parts and inventory.

Several decades ago, ERP was the killer app. We kind of think of our killer app as asset performance management, and service optimization around the app is our suite of software, if you will, to help operators optimize their business.

SAP did a fairly good job with verticalizing their suites, with relatively simple business processes. Going deeper into verticals is a harder problem and requires domain expertise. For example, when we talk about renewable energy, or rail, we have people who actually have been the head of operations in those industries. Our head of energy was the former President and Chief Innovation Officer of Exelon, the largest utility in North America. When he engages with our customers he knows the precise challenges. If you remember SAP with HANA, you had to buy an analytical stack independent of your ERP, CRM, or supply chain app because analytics weren't baked in, or built in, to these apps. With Uptake, it's truly ML/AI analytics. Because of the volume of data being generated, you're able to do predictive maintenance, but you need to understand the asset, the operations and the fault codes.

We acquired Asset Performance Technologies last year. When we talk about verticalization that means we can go in and say we understand the 800 critical assets that run these industries. We understand the 57,000 ways they are going to break. That means 57,000 ways I can stop it from breaking, and I can then recommend actual predictive maintenance strategies. It's hard to do that with legacy architecture. It's also hard to do when your business model is built on simple extensions of verticals on your horizontal.

SAP and Salesforce have trained customers, in a fairly obvious way on how to buy ERP, and how to buy CRM. I think we are in the very early days of teaching customers how to buy solutions like ours.

Every industry has unique outcomes. If it's energy production, or if it's velocity in rail, those things translate to dollars. And these are KPIs that many executives in these industries actually get compensated on. We can quantify a value, and it ends up being pretty large because these are multimillion-dollar assets.

For example, the potential value generated by an average large wind farm is US$3.3 million per year. So, when you go to a large wind farm operator with thousands of turbines, it has massive value. In the rail industry, the potential value generation per locomotive per year is around US$180,000 and there's thousands of locomotives that can be connected to our cloud. The other thing we're learning is that we had been focused narrowly on just the value we're creating around productivity, reliability and uptime of those assets. There is the visibility we're providing across a company's assets that helps our customers to conduct better capital allocation across their company, which in itself is worth millions of dollars.

In most cases, our customers are learning about outcomes. Here's an interesting thing in software. When you buy a CRM system, there's no guarantee your sales team's going to perform well. If you buy ERP software, there is no guarantee your business is going to run well. Whereas there's a direct line and a correlation to buying Uptake and customers saving or making money. That path has not existed before in ERP or CRM."

The difference between IT and OT comes through clearly when you hear SAP, Oracle or IBM executives talk. For example, Peter Maier, President, Industries Organization, SAP, said in an interview:

"In the oil and gas industry, SAP Road Maps enables our customers to become an intelligent enterprise. We help them with an intelligent suite where we basically have better user experience and voice recognition to speak with the system. We combine it with all the data — the master data and the data management and finally new innovations are created. SAP Leonardo innovations like machine learning, Artificial Intelligence, blockchain are relevant in an industry context. We help determine what machine learning means in procurement for the oil industry, blockchain in transportation for the oil industry, and AI in the predictive maintenance context for the oil industry."[81]

There's plenty of contemporary technology talk in what Maier said, but the customer conversation is increasingly moving to operational metrics and outcomes.

---

[81] http://bwcio.businessworld.in/article/SAP-Road-Maps-Enables-Customers-To-Become-Intelligent-Enterprises-Peter-Maier-President-Industries-Organization-SAP-/20-12-2018-165424/

I received some perspective from Sharma (introduced in Ch. 2) on why companies like SAP and its peers don't look beyond IT:

> "They focus on the CIO. When you go talk to the CIO, you're going to hear mostly about IT problems or you're going to hear about processes that the business has already implemented that need to be now automated. At best, you're going to have a company like Mulesoft or Mercato going in and saying, 'We can automate your IT processes. We'll apply some intelligence to it.'
>
> What you don't have is discovery of the business problem, per se. There's a start-up called Drishti. A friend of mine is a CTO there. They attach a camera to the work desk of a quality assurance person in a factory. It ensures that when you buy a Black & Decker drill, it has been tested. Or when you're buying a vacuum cleaner, it's been turned on and off. It is essentially putting eyes in the factory and replacing the manager.
>
> SAP started out trying to transform manufacturing companies by automating processes. If asked today, 'What does automating a factory mean?' I think they would find out that the answer is very different.
>
> It's now less about tracking an entry in a database or ordering inventory and more about the reality that factories now have eyes and arms. We call them robots. And factories have legs. We call them automated bots that move boxes around.
>
> If you spend all your time talking to people who wonder if their systems can run on 30% less compute capacity, you will get some innovation and transformation. You

will get a Nutanix and Rubrik who will cut your costs in half. But those companies won't help you completely rethink what a factory should look like."

Sharma then talked about on an even bigger vertical than Bell had referenced — that of healthcare:

"One of my companies called Suki has a way for doctors to talk aloud to take notes when working with patients, without having to use a 30-year-old interface from Epic for their electronic health records or handwriting those notes. But there are other companies that are saying, 'No, we don't need that patient-doctor interface.' Ping An Good Doctor is a service in China that takes care of basic needs of a customer who may not have access to a doctor. From a regulatory perspective, we are kind of limited in this country so I expect those things to emerge in Southeast Asia, India and China.

Another area is what I would call programming the DNA and the biome. Both your gut bacteria and genetics are now programmable. It is now recognized that it's very likely that people with software skills, or those with joint degrees in computer science and medicine or bioinformatics are going to try and start companies looking to find new drug targets and new cures for diseases using computational methods.

Then the third area, which I find fascinating, is what you would call digital therapeutics. Every disease will have an app. I'm of the firm belief that in 10 years it'll be very natural for all of us to go to an app store. The moment you find out that you have a disease, whether it's acute or chronic, you will be prescribed an app, approved by the FDA. We have seen some early signs of that already. Livongo Health has focused on diabetes for the last couple of years. The new FDA administrator has been actually a boon to this way of thinking because he is accelerating their approval process.

Literally, you will get a prescription. Your insurance company will pay for it. The doctor will monitor it and say, 'For six months to a year you'll be on this app. You'll use it. Then if you get cured, you're done.' I think that's very exciting and that's just for type II diabetes.

There's a company that's just entered an FDA trial to essentially 'cure' back pain by using an app. I think we will find that few businesses will fix some of these things through day-to-day, small changes. In the past, we never had an effective mechanism to deliver or monitor this and, frankly, get paid."

Markets don't wait forever. And this is where SAP may be miscalculating by not modernizing its applications in the many industries that have funded so much of its growth in the last couple of decades.

System Sprawl

Tim Cook, CEO of Apple, likes to talk about ruthlessly managing product sprawl. He told *FastCompany* in 2018:

"In the scheme of things versus our revenue, we're doing very few things. I mean, you could put every product we're making on this table, to put it in perspective. I doubt anybody that is anywhere near our revenue could say that."[82]

He is following in the footsteps of Steve Jobs, who returned to Apple in 1997 and drastically trimmed its product line. He told developers at Apple's Worldwide Developer Conference in 1997 that focus:

> "... means saying no to the hundred other good ideas that there are. You have to pick carefully. I'm actually as proud of the things we haven't done as the things I have done. Innovation is saying no to 1,000 things."[83]

Indeed, when Jobs passed away in 2011, the Apple website offered only 15 products.

In contrast, while working on this book, I got so many repeated reminders from my team on the explosion of products and acronyms in SAP world that we decided to include a list of just some of the acronyms in the section called "Do you speak SAPese?" For context, SAP is only about a tenth of Apple's size in revenues.

Owen Pettiford had a humorous blog post depicting the many cloud flavors available to run S/4:

> "One analogy that I like is that of the Mobile Phone:
>
> **Public Cloud** — This would be how my Mum consumes her SmartPhone, she comes to me and tells me what

---

[82] https://www.fastcompany.com/40525409/why-apple-is-the-worlds-most-innovative-company
[83] https://www.imore.com/saying-no-1000-things

she wants, I set it up and she uses it. When she wants something difficult, I tell her that the phone can't do that.

Private Cloud — This is a bit like how I use my SmartPhone, I have loads of apps and accessories but all of them have come from the phone's app store and are supported by the phone's manufacturer.

On Premise — With HANA — This is like my daughter's SmartPhone which she has hacked to mean that she has access to the guts of the phone, writes her own apps and downloads stuff from un-official websites — all at her risk.

On Premise — Without HANA — This is like not running a SmartPhone and saying "why do I need to do anything but phone, text?"[84]

Pettiford could have additionally color coded his phones green, brown or blue in line with the greenfield, brownfield and other colors we saw in Ch. 6.

AWS, Azure and Google have big booths at most SAP events. In Asia, the Alibaba cloud is gaining steam. Many customers are choosing to deploy on SAP's own data centers. Many of SAP's outsourcing partners deliver private cloud proposals with their own hosting partners. The matrix of on-prem/private/public single/multitenant deployments continues to morph.

For the past several years, HANA is usually front and center at TechEd, SAP's developer event. Yet, SAP's own cloud acquisitions like SuccessFactors have been slow to move to HANA.

---

[84] https://blogs.sap.com/2015/02/04/understanding-sap-private-cloud-public-cloud-and-on-premise-important-for-s4hana-roadmap/

S/4 today only covers a small part of the enterprise; most SAP customers continue to live with Oracle, SQL Server, Sybase and DB2 in surround applications. In that sense, it is still an open database world.

In Ch. 4, we saw the proliferation in UX. Listening to Maricel Cabahug, you see expectations change dramatically as you move within an enterprise. And yet, you step back and see that many customers migrating to S/4 are asking for the old keyboard-and-mouse-driven SAP GUI interface that SAP has been maligned for in the past! It makes the user transition easier, they say.

Two ways to look at it: Either all that choice is good for customers or, conversely, you can be horrified at the management nightmare that comes from that much choice. Contrast this to Workday's Power of One (introduced in Ch. 7):

> "Workday Co-Founders Aneel Bhusri and Dave Duffield conceived the Power of One when they started Workday to eliminate some major issues they identified in the world of legacy enterprise applications. In that world, a vendor's software development organization, partner ecosystem, and customer base is split among supporting different versions of applications and database platforms, with different customizations and maintenance schedules. This approach doesn't empower a community, it drains it. Vendors and their partners have to split their resources among too many things. Customers have entirely different experiences from one another, which hinders communication, collaboration, and ultimately, innovation."[85]

---

[85] https://blogs.workday.com/defining-the-power-of-one/

It was not surprising to hear Sacré of Sanofi (featured in Chs. 3 and 7) say he was impressed when Workday told him "no," whereas SuccessFactors was happy to say "yes" to developing bespoke functionality for them. Now, you could argue Workday is narrow in geographic and industry coverage. But SAP has shown little discipline in saying "no" — other than to be hostile towards Oracle's database and its infrastructure cloud.

Can SAP manage that much heterogeneity? How much are its customers willing to tolerate in complexity? When you read the challenges SAP itself has had just integrating its acquisitions in the last few years, you have to wonder about its customers who do not have anywhere near the 25,000 R&D resources that SAP can rely on.

I asked *diginomica's* Howlett about this, and he replied:

> "SAP's going through a genuine pivot. Do they have the right talent for it? Personally, I doubt it. They are transactional and this is not that. It comes down to delivery. There are too many old farts still in that business, if I'm perfectly frank with you."

But then he reminded me,

> "You've said for many, many years that, at the end of the day, big though it may be, SAP actually only accounts for a fraction of the entire IT landscape. When you start to look at what that landscape looks like, it's a hell of a lot more complex than SAP with its own versions."

Howlett is certainly right when you compare to similar sprawl at Oracle, IBM and other technology vendors. At the risk of invoking a stereotype, you expect more tidiness from a German company. In German language, there are two words, *Putzfimmel* and *Kehrwoche*[86], that we don't have in English, but roughly refer to what we would call neatniks.

In *SAP Nation 2.0*, I asked:

> "When you layer in SAP's product portfolio on top of its customers' application portfolios and the 13,000 partners it claims, a different six-letter word that also starts with 'S' comes to mind: Sprawl.
>
> SAP's runaway success in the '90s came about because its R/3 product dramatically reduced enterprise sprawl. Can history repeat itself? Will S/4 replace today's sprawl, this time caused by SAP itself?"

The answer so far is "no." If anything, the sprawl has grown significantly. On the one hand, SAP tells customers to decommission customizations in ECC as a way to pay for migration to S/4. On the other hand, it encourages them to build extensions missing in its industry cloud offerings using its SCP. The mixed messages keep adding to the sprawl.

Coester (introduced in Ch. 5) echoed the sentiments of many long-time practitioners as they balance the pros and cons of their favorite technology vendor:

> "In my view, SAP's single biggest misstep was trying to force HANA onto an unwilling user base. Watch the backlash; it's coming. I predict SAP will be forced

[86] https://blogs.transparent.com/german/the-german-culture-of-cleanliness-putzfimmel-and-kehrwoche/

to open the DB platform up eventually or give HANA away for free.

On the upside, we see new blood and new thinking onstage. SAP admits they have lost touch with the customer and wishes to reconnect. Simplification of such a gigantic product landscape takes time, money and incredible executive willpower. For SAP to succeed going forward it will have to change its solutions and make them easier to deploy and run.

In summary, I would say despite the challenges that SAP is a materially changed business and I am the most upbeat as I have been in 15 years about them as a solution provider."

So, SAP has to overcome the "unforced errors" we have discussed in the last two chapters. But let's not get overly pessimistic. Competitors like Oracle and Salesforce have delivered stinging, but not fatal, blows. SAP has 400,000+ customers across every industry and geography. That is an incredibly formidable asset for it to leverage. Let's look at its opportunities in the next section.

SECTION V

Manifest Destiny?

CHAPTER 11

X's and O's

∿→

Jeff Bezos, who has led Amazon through an amazing phase of growth over two decades, has been quoted as saying, "Friends congratulate me after a quarterly-earnings announcement and say, 'Good job, great quarter,' and I'll say, 'Thank you, but that quarter was baked three years ago.' I'm working on a quarter that'll happen in 2021 right now."[87]

Similarly, the SAP management team plans ahead, but where is it headed over the next few years? SAP has a tendency to concentrate on its peers. It often forgets it is the leading enterprise application vendor. Its closest rival, Oracle, is even more distracted by infrastructure and platform markets.

I reached out to *diginomica's* Howlett and asked him what he thought of SAP's prospects. He framed his thoughts around SAP's recent Qualtrics acquisition. At US$8 billion and 20 times

---

[87] https://www.forbes.com/sites/randalllane/2018/08/30/bezos-unbound-exclusive-interview-with-the-amazon-founder-on-what-he-plans-to-conquer-next/#583fa3df647b

revenues, the price has raised plenty of eyebrows. SAP, on the other hand, says it allows for blending Quatrics's X (experience) data with the O (operational) data that SAP systems have in spades.

Howlett opined:

"The Qualtrics acquisition absolutely fascinates me. Everybody who has commented has said one of two things: A) The price is ridiculous; I actually don't care about that. B) The survey functionality; I don't care about that either. That's just the entry point into being able to understand what SAP is really about here. If they can execute on all four of the vectors that Qualtrics claims to have ownership in — brand, employee, customer and product — then this will be a fundamentally different SAP. What they're basically trying to say is that if they can have better, more immediate touchpoints into those four areas, then they can manage the business in a completely different way. That is absolutely and completely different to anything that we've seen before.

Fundamentally, it means you have to start with the employee. You can't start anywhere else. Because, if they don't do that piece, then the whole "not invented here" syndrome that has bedeviled SAP for the last 30 to 40 years will never go away, and people moving on from ABAP will never, ever happen. That's the critical point as far as I'm concerned.

The customer side naturally follows because, as I've said for many, many years, the customer relationship management, as originally conceived, never came to pass. If you do the employee piece first, then that becomes the mirror image for what you need to do with customers. In other words, you treat your employees and your customers as equals on the same playing field.

Now, when you go to product, what does that mean? A part of the Qualtrics story centers around the notion of "product." Does that mean Qualtrics provides the entry point to better understanding which products work, which don't and whether products can be usefully turned into services? I don't yet understand whether they're going to deliver on that in new and novel ways compared to what is already available from existing product testing and service innovation. Of greater concern is knowing how that might operate at, say, a Mercedes-Benz or BMW where the SAP relationship has traditionally been focused on B2B and manufacturing operations rather than processes that in this context appear to be more closely associated with B2C. Is SAP really saying, 'We're going to change or help you change not only the B2B relationship inside the supply chain but also extend this into the B2B2C environment'? If the latter, then this will require an act of faith by customers and close attention to process details, infused with extensive collaboration between parties. If my interpretation is correct and SAP pulls it off, then it will represent a leapfrogging of process improvement that is absent today. We should also recognize this as an aspirational future state that goes well beyond incremental improvement from the application of improvements to the discrete and siloed process paths that characterize today's operations.

When you talk to me, at a high level, about where are they going, it's not a question of where are they going;

it's more of a question of whether they can go. That's the big question I have for them in 2019."

Tilting the Bell Curve

SAP would benefit from a different sort of X's and O's — the kind football coaches use to game plan. And SAP *customers* would benefit from yet another kind of X's and O's — as in a more friendly, "lovey-dovey" SAP: XOXOX.

Perhaps, SAP could start becoming a first mover with its customer base, and at the same time start thinking on a bigger scale. There are plenty of other markets where SAP might adopt a fast follower approach after missing out on the first wave of opportunity.

Let's first discuss the first mover option.

Some say the Bystander group is playing "blink" with SAP. They are betting that SAP will back down on its "end of support dates."

Mueller of *Constellation* said, referring to ECC and moves to S/4:

"The next two or three years will show if SAP can create the value proposition. We'll see how much customers push back. SAP could say, 'We listened to our customers and we will give you another two or three years (beyond 2025), but you have to pay not 18%, but 21% or 25% or maybe even 30% in annual maintenance.'

However, the writing has been on the wall and for years now. It should have been clear to every CIO that the innovation is happening on the S/4 side. Do you want to be in 2030, 11 years from now, with an ERP system that cannot run machine learning, which doesn't have a good IoT story and so on?"

Or as Wright of Accuride and Howlett of *diginomica* have pointed out, it's tough enough today to recruit younger talent to an ECC and ABAP shop. Can you imagine what it will be like in 2025 or 2030?

Mueller continued:

"The question is, can SAP show TCO advantages and functional equivalency to encourage customers to migrate to their newer products? Will SAP generate enough value in other areas, like Leonardo, to justify the cost of re-implementing because they should not port all the customizations in ECC?

The other question is, what's the competition going to do? Is Oracle going to get its act together? If I have to re-implement anyway and the Oracle Fusion offering is significantly more mature than what SAP can deliver, that would be interesting to watch."

SAP cannot manage what Oracle or other competitors will do. It can, however, tilt the bell curve of its customer base. In Chs. 5–8, we classified the customer base into Risk-Takers, Modernizers, Diversifiers and Bystanders, with the last group being the most populous.

What if SAP could turbocharge customer conversations so the Risk-Takers and Modernizers help convert the Bystanders? What if it can turn the tide among the Diversifiers so more of them return to SAP products? In Ch. 8 we highlighted a wide range of strategies customers have been trying out. All kinds of good things could come from such a tilt both for customers and SAP. Next, SAP could entice similar Diversifiers and Bystanders in Oracle, Infor, Unit4 and other customer bases. Many of them have been waiting for next-gen applications for even longer than SAP customers.

In Chapter 4, Grassl of SAP had spoken about driving awareness in developers, engaging them, and focusing on their product adoption as he competes for technology talent for his customer base. His approach is a good model for the rest of SAP — every aspect of the business, be it pricing or be it partnering, should be focused on tilting this bell curve.

Tilting the Bell Curve

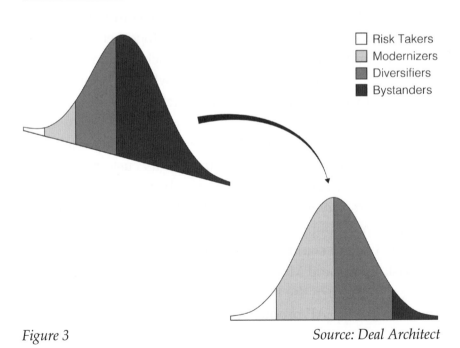

Figure 3

Source: Deal Architect

It will take, however, plenty of steps, as we describe below:

Once Again Make Applications Job #1

SAP has the biggest "business applications" laboratory — across business process, geography and industry. However, every few years SAP gets bored with applications and dabbles in platform and infrastructure areas. It seeks out partners and acquisitions to grow its applications' reach when a better approach would be to partner with its customers. It is sitting on the mother lode of business process and enterprise application innovation and that's where they need to put their focus. Fahey of Louisiana-Pacific described one such example around IBP in Chapter 3.

The industry desperately needs a business application leader. After two decades, when you look at the global and industry landscape of applications, only about 20% is available in the public cloud. Most application vendors are investing heavily in platforms. In a way, it's abdication. A good analogy would come from the food sector. You go to a restaurant you really like and the chef says we have changed our business model. We are only serving semi-cooked meals now. Enjoy the meal at home. Or come on in, but be aware we are now offering grills. You bring your own ingredients and cook your own. That's similar to what SaaS vendors are doing with their emphasis on platforms when they are being paid to deliver "cooked meals" in the form of applications.

Build a Waze-Like Navigation Tool

Over the course of writing this book, I felt like I was peeling an onion. In Ch. 10, we discussed the sprawl of products, protocols, deployment models and partners. Even SAP struggles to explain what it has in its portfolio. As I have heard from a number of customers and prospects, they need help navigating — they need roadmaps, product details, access to other customers and references. They want answers relevant for their industry, geography and business process. And it goes beyond customers. Most analysts I run around with have siloed views of SAP and its partners. Partners struggle to keep up with the diversity. SAP needs a Waze-like navigation application. Of course, it cannot just be an app. It needs an organizational unit to help people connect the dots. This is an area in which user groups like ASUG may be able to help SAP.

The Suite — for the Win!

Of course, just providing people with maps would only highlight how disconnected the SAP empire is. You would see some major highways, and easily see where more connectors are needed to secondary highways and local roads. Mueller of *Constellation* said: "It will be also interesting to see what SAP is going to do with what I call 'the five sisters': Ariba, Hybris, Fieldglass, Concur and SuccessFactors. Because they're being re-platformed on HANA right now, they will be on SCP, PaaS-wise. They're going to use the SAP analytics tools. It's how are they going to play together with S/4, and that is something SAP has not addressed yet."

SAP is starting similar integration with the growing components of C/4. The overlap between multiple SAP applications and the lack of integration between industry functionality and S/4 is glaring, as Coetser noted in Ch. 5. On the other hand, if you had a good map, you would also see a number of undocumented paths across the customer base. These are the side roads, tricks and traps that customers share with each other at events.

Sommer of Techventive provided an example:

> "Just look at the innovation in a process like recruiting. There are big data feeds to source candidates, recruitment marketing and candidate relationship marketing solutions, video interviewing with AI-powered candidate assessments, etc. The process can be very different, but it takes work by a vendor to deliver this reimagined process. This same reinvention is required for every business process."

Such reinvention is indeed happening at SAP, as Sven Denecken described around the procurement process in Ch. 4 — going from digital to intelligent to automated to autonomous — but it is not consistently represented to the outside world.

SAP salespeople like to say, "The suite always wins." SAP needs to invest in making a number of disconnected pieces look and act like suites. Yes, it is a monumental task, but SAP also has an army of over 25,000 developers.

Speak a Different Economic Language

In Ch. 10, Bell of Uptake talked about a new way of selling — one focused on customer outcomes, not TCO or ROI. Even if that is too far a bridge, Sommer challenges SAP to think differently in the current economic model: "While I know there would be substantial backlash to this — from Wall Street for sure — I think SAP needs to get to the point where they EARN a customer's business every single month. That means getting rid of long-term subscriptions, not charging for software until after the customer is in production, having reasonable renewable subscription pricing, a commitment to ever lower pricing (a la Amazon AWS), etc."

As we discussed in Chapter 9 in the section around IA, value in enterprise software has been moving away from transaction processing to analytics, intelligence and machine learning. Automation in the form of sensors and wearables is performing edits and validations ERP and CRM software used to do in the past. Their pricing needs to reflect that shrunk role. Finally, SAP is starting to talk open source in SCP, and as it evolves its developer ecosystem. This brings even higher expectations of very different economics.

Customers joke that SAP stands for "Send Another Payment". SAP has to transition from treating its customer base as a Bank with a Line of Credit to that of an Innovation Bank. If it can deliver creative solutions for their specifications, customers will gladly pay for them.

Polish the Brand

For over a decade, SAP has branded itself with its "Run Better" and "Run Simple" campaigns. Indeed, in 2018, in a marketing survey, it was named the most valuable German brand and ranked even higher than BMW and Mercedes-Benz.[88] The enduring image, however, of SAP in the enterprise technology world is that of its ERP products, and there, expensive ones. Between the unforced errors like IA (which we discussed in detail in Ch. 9) and the persistence of 35-year-old technologies like ABAP in the customer base, you could argue that SAP actually has a brand challenge. Wright of Accuride, Hortovanyi and

---

[88] https://www.research-live.com/article/news/sap-most-valuable-german-brand-in-2018-ranking/id/5033672

others have pointed out that ECC and ABAP are not attractive to young technology talent. As Dennett discussed in Ch. 4, it also has to become better respected in open source and ML circles. Mueller of SAP talks about expanding its image way beyond ERP. All these factors point to a need to rethink the branding.

Take Control of the Ecosystem

Projects around SAP should ideally be repeatable, predictable and delivered virtually. Long-term contracts should follow continuous improvement cost curves. If AWS can deliver 60+ price cuts over a decade, SAP's partners can deliver at least a handful.

Sommer of TechVentive recommends: "Partners should be delivering multitenant versions of SAP's software and not recommending single-tenant products that enable the partner to sell maintenance services over the life of the software. The focus should be on the customer, not the partner's income stream. Driving value for customers should be paramount. Driving revenue for the partners is not the correct outcome."

To add nuance to that point: Driving revenues for SIs should not be the goal, but clearly should be for ISVs on the App Center. The enterprise world has not seen vibrant platforms like the Apple iOS store or the Amazon Fulfillment engine. SAP should aim to deliver that in the enterprise world.

Additionally, in Ch. 10 we discussed how 18,000 partners is way too many. That number needs to be ruthlessly culled. It also needs to reflect shifts in SAP's product portfolio which call for more cloud, open source and ML capabilities.

A number of SAP customers described in Ch. 6 its automation including Simplification Lists and inspection of custom modifications as they migrated to S/4. No reason SAP cannot expect similar automation from its SI partners. In the last two decades, they have implemented millions of ERP, CRM and other implementations and upgrades. That knowledge base could be used to train machines and bring more AI to bear on projects.

Short- and Longer-Term Opportunities

In Ch. 1, we described the Louisiana Purchase. It was a major risk for President Jefferson but it doubled the real estate of the young United States. What if the population had just yawned and clung to the Atlantic Coast and not moved to the new territories? That's a good analogy to what SAP faces. It has new real estate in the form of S/4, Leonardo, SCP, HANA and its cloud properties, and yet the majority of its 400,000 customers are clinging to the "coast" of legacy products. Helping them migrate is SAP's major short-term opportunity.

Lewis and Clark then opened the country's eyes to real estate way past the new boundaries created by the Louisiana Purchase. Successive presidents arranged to grow the country's real estate all the way to the Pacific. That's the even bigger, second opportunity — for SAP to become a fast follower in many markets it missed out during the last two decades. We cover the opportunities in the next, and last, unit.

CHAPTER 12

From Sea to Shining Sea

⌁➤

In a presentation to analysts in December 2018, SAP's Atzberger excitedly called the CX business segment he leads "the largest addressable market in technology." Atzberger's addressable market estimate of US$30 billion a year is nothing to sneeze at (in a later presentation he expanded it to US$100 billion a year and included "platform and integration to operational systems"), but he was primarily looking at competitors like Salesforce, Microsoft and Adobe. If you expand your horizon you would see the CX market is at least 5X, if not 10X, as big. In the last two decades, digital advertising has gone from near zero to over US$200 billion a year. Google, Facebook and increasingly Amazon are the big beneficiaries of this shift in marketing dollars. Around them are digital agencies. Accenture Interactive has aggressively acquired digital agencies and is now the biggest agency in the world.

In Atzberger's defense, at that point, he could not discuss the Qualtrics acquisition pending its closure. However, it is safe to assume he was pleased that his CEO McDermott had made one of the biggest investments in the company's history to bolster the company's CX portfolio. McDermott did discuss the investment in an interview:

> "Qualtrics has a market potential of more than $40 billion …. At Qualtrics, we had to strike really fast and resolutely. We recognized the great potential of the company when the founders spoke of going public. The IPO was oversubscribed by a factor of 13. On the capital markets, goodwill would immediately have shot up to 10 or even 12 billion dollars. It was like when Facebook bought Instagram for a billion dollars. The picture platform had 13 employees and zero turnover. Today, their value as part of the Facebook universe is more than $100 billion."[89]

In Ch. 11, we looked at how SAP could become a first mover with its huge incumbent customer base. At the same time, SAP could be thinking much bigger. There are plenty of other markets where SAP could adopt a fast follower approach after missing out on the first wave of opportunity.

Take infrastructure as a service. Most tech executives will tell you software and hardware are like oil and water. Oracle's limited success with Sun and its cloud infrastructure does not help change their perspective. Microsoft has been a shining exception. Indeed, *The Wall Street Journal* wrote, "Microsoft Corp. tried through the years to compete in a range of buzzy

---

[89] https://news.sap.com/2018/12/manager-magazin-sap-ceo-bill-mcdermott-manager-year/

consumer businesses, but it was Chief Executive Satya Nadella's focus on selling humdrum yet fast-growing computing services to companies that allowed it to reclaim the title of world's most valuable company."[90] Could SAP, if it decided to invest more heavily in cloud data centers, lead a grudging EU into the world of cloud infrastructure? As Mueller of *Constellation* pointed out in Ch. 8, U.S. cloud vendors have not built much in the way of cloud infrastructure in mainland Europe. If any tech company can lead European customers, it would be SAP.

Or take the world of the Industrial Internet and Industrie 4.0. In Ch. 2 we discussed GE's "Power of 1%": 1% in fuel savings in aviation and utilities, 1% productivity improvement in healthcare, 1% reduction in oil and gas cap-ex. In just five sectors combined — rail, aviation, healthcare, power and oil and gas — GE had projected US$276 billion in efficiencies over 15 years."[91] These were only in sectors GE was interested in, where it sold turbines and MRI scanners. There is a far bigger market around connecting other assets, listening to them, delivering predictive maintenance and other tangible benefits.

Or take verticals. Just take one sector — fintech. According to Deloitte, "264 companies have received a total of US$7.71 billion in investment since 1998. Contrast that with China, where only seven payment fintechs are found, but these are backed by US$6.92 billion in funding. Similar patterns are seen in deposits and lending, investment management, personal insurance, and real estate leasing/purchase and sale."[92] After leading its peers

---

[90] https://www.wsj.com/articles/how-microsoft-quietly-became-the-worlds-most-valuable-company-1543665600?mod=e2fb

[91] http://gelookahead.economist.com/infograph/industrial-internet-the-power-of-1-2/

[92] https://www2.deloitte.com/de/de/pages/financial-services/articles/the-next-phase-of-fintech-evolution.html

to industry solutions in the early 2000s, can SAP do so again with so much turmoil in so many verticals?

Or take smart products. Fanelli, introduced in Ch. 4, recruiting ISVs for the SAP AppCenter said she regrets that a decade ago SAP did not target R&D executives who are helping build smart products. She is, in essence, agreeing with what we pointed out in Ch. 2 — SAP and other enterprise vendors missed out on that design, engineering and contract manufacturing market. SAP can always aim for this the second time around.

In Ch.3 Fahey of Louisiana-Pacific talked about the community of customers SAP had put together across industries and countries. SAP can do that easily across so many unmet enterprise application markets. It has the reach and the domain knowledge few other vendors can match.

On Its Own? Or with Someone Bigger?

I belong to a group called the *Enterprise Irregulars* (EI), a moniker inspired by Sherlock Holmes' ragtag team of young intelligence agents on Baker Street. We named ourselves the *Irregulars* to contrast with the Main Street analysts like Gartner and Forrester, even though many of us came from such firms. These days, EIs contribute to research at *Constellation, diginomica* and *ZDNet.* Some of us are entrepreneurs, others investors and technology executives, and still others are technology advisers and serial authors.

While our published work gets syndicated to the EI site, a far more consequential part of the membership is a private chat room where we debate a wide variety of enterprise topics. Most of this is harmless speculation, and we call each other nasty names as we disagree, which is often.

After Thomas Kurian moved from Oracle to become CEO of Google Cloud, one of the threads in the EI chat was around acquisitions he could potentially explore. One of the targets discussed was SAP.

My initial reaction was, "Seriously?" Then I thought about it. A few years ago, you would have said "no way," but with Apple, Google and Microsoft sitting on over US$500 billion in cash between them … who knows? Dr. Plattner is not getting any younger, so he might welcome an "exit."

At the risk of repeating ourselves, SAP would bring one of the widest, most sophisticated and loyal application customer bases in the world — spread across countries, industries, business processes and sizes of enterprises. There are many duplicate products in the SAP portfolio that an acquirer could spin off to lower the investment exposure, or in response to regulator objections.

So, in the spirit of harmless speculation, I asked what about Amazon? Or Microsoft? They have had more success in the IT side of enterprises than Google has, and they would potentially be able to leverage SAP more effectively.

Of course, the EU would have a say if a U.S. company tried to acquire SAP. Influential German customers and GDPR regulators would take a stand if a U.S. cloud company was the bidder.

However, my biggest concern about such a scenario is personal orthodoxy. For me, tech M&A hardly ever benefits customers. Integrations tend to be messy and lengthy. Throughout this book, we have pointed out the challenges SAP, Oracle and Microsoft have had as they integrated their own acquisitions.

So, I hope the "SAP as part of another entity" scenario gets only a cursory look. I much prefer a scenario where SAP executes on the first mover/fast follower blend we have described earlier.

If anything, I would like SAP to find a different inspiration from Google and more specifically from X, the idea incubator of Google's parent, Alphabet.

Astro Teller, Captain of Moonshots at X (seriously, that is his name, title and company name), said in an interview with *The Wall Street Journal*:

> "Nine years ago, if you had written down a list of the problems that Google was trying to solve in the world, transportation wouldn't have been one of them. In fact, connectivity, what Loon is working on, wouldn't have been one of them. Health care wouldn't have been one of them. Other than internally, cybersecurity wouldn't have been one of them. Those are all things where we said, 'There's something important here that's worth working on whether or not Google is focused on this.' Google doesn't need us to solve Google's problems."[93]

But to be able to do so, SAP needs its own version of a Manifest Destiny Call.

Manifest Destiny?

In the start of the book, we shared that in his inaugural address in 1801, U.S. President Thomas Jefferson had talked about a nation "with room enough for our descendants to the hundredth and thousandth generation." A couple of years later, Jefferson instructed Lewis and Clark as they began their pioneering

---

[93] https://www.wsj.com/articles/astro-teller-captain-of-moonshots-at-alphabets-x-is-on-a-roll-1540310778

westward trek: "Those who come after us will fill up the canvas we begin ...."

Jefferson was an optimist and helped fire up a country's imagination for a massive westward expansion.

SAP needs a similar call to action.

Enslin of SAP told me in an interview: "I learned from Bill [McDermott] really how to be bold, how to be brave, how to take on things that are much, much bigger than you, and to just keep stretching for it."

McDermott, himself, after announcing the large Qualtrics acquisition, said, "Very few people are aware of the implications of courageous decisions. Especially not if they're hit unexpectedly .... Looking back in a few years, SAP will have reached a whole new level with the Qualtrics deal. We dream and fulfill dreams. That's the wow factor that distinguishes an average company from a great company."

I am sure some readers feel I am pushing SAP to dream too big. Well, let me remind them my *New Florence* blog covers a wide range of STEM disciplines, not just infotech, but also cleantech, healthtech and countless other areas of innovation. The markets I have cataloged here are largely infotech. Compared to that range of dreams that Teller has been dreaming for Google above, what qualifies for "big thinking" in enterprise IT is still somewhat mundane.

Of course, SAP is not the only vendor who sees this second wave opportunity. Dave Vellante of SiliconANGLE Media paraphrased IBM CEO Ginni Rometty's message at her Think conference in February 2019.

"Chapter two is about the hard stuff. It's about scaling AI and creating hybrid clouds. It's about bringing the cloud operating model to all those mission-critical apps and enabling customers to manage data, workloads, and apps and move them between multiple clouds. This is a trillion dollar opportunity and IBM intends to be #1."

Throughout this book, we have seen glimpses of a very different enterprise application market of the future. In Ch. 2, Sharma had described a new generation of startups being funded in Silicon Valley. We saw Lee invest in over 150 AI startups in China. Vembu of Zoho described how much easier it has become to develop new enterprise class apps. SAP is encouraging more ISVs to develop apps on SCP. It is encouraging developer communities around the world. There are plenty of mentions of Python, PyTorch and Kubernetes throughout the book.

In India and elsewhere, big outsourcers like TCS are going after vertical niches. IBM with Watson, Accenture with SynOps, Uptake, C3 and others are increasingly defining apps that are more machine than human-centric. Oracle, Salesforce, Workday, Microsoft, Apple, Google and Amazon are not sitting still. How will SAP navigate around this much bigger net of coopetition?

McDermott has a best selling book titled "Winners Dream". On Facebook, he periodically posts inspirational quotes such as "My parents gave me permission to dream big. Do the same for those around you".

So, how bold can SAP's and McDermott's dreams be? Are they ready to issue the Manifest Destiny clarion call to go from "sea to shining sea"?

The continent of enterprise computing is waiting to be tamed.

EPILOGUE

Fences and Migrations

∿→

You don't have to be a *National Geographic* pho-
tographer to be fascinated with migrations. Wildebeest in the
Serengeti, salmon swimming upstream, flocks of birds headed
to warmer places all make us stop in wonder.

Personally, I have additional interest in two unique sets of
migrations.

I have a fascination for the history of human migrations
during the U.S. westward expansion in the 1800s. I research
arcane topics like: How did the pioneers on their wagon trails
eventually settle on oxen as their beast of burden? How many
different routes did the 49ers take on the Gold Rush to California?
What was life like for the Chinese workers who blasted through
the Sierras to build the transcontinental railroad? What about
the Eastern European farmers who arrived to turn our prairie

into the granary of the world? So much pain and suffering, and yet it resulted in enormous human progress.

My other passion is a professional hazard: I like to assist on corporate system migrations. Over three decades at PwC, Gartner and now Deal Architect, I have helped countless clients migrate systems to Mainframe, AS/400, client/server and cloud destinations. I have traveled with them to Boulder to evaluate data centers and to Bangalore and Budapest to help find them talent to support their systems. As you heard from many SAP customers, there was much pain and suffering in the migration, yet look how far we have come.

"Good fences make good neighbors," wrote Robert Frost. But they don't hold back determined migrations. Or a flying Peter Pan. I still need to bug Dr. Plattner to tell me his Peter Pan story. I am curious if it has anything to do with his story about Tom Sawyer's fence.

I hope this book has given you some ideas as you ponder your own SAP journey. If you need a friendly phone call, introductions, help with facilitating a strategy offsite or some other advisory support, we are always here to help. Call us at 813-884-4908 or drop us a line at vm@dealarchitect.com or via LinkedIn at https://www.linkedin.com/in/vinniemirchandani/.

Index

~~>

Steiner, Matthias, 109–110, 112–113
Strativa, Inc., 281
Streibich, Karl-Heinz, 41, 171
SuccessFactors (part of SAP), 6, 53,
    85–86, 128, 152, 155, 158, 178–179,
    219, 240–243, 253, 275, 287, 315,
    318–319, 322, 339, 341, 354
Strativa, Inc., 281
Suki AI, 336
Sullivan and Cromwell LLP, 308
Sun Microsystems, Inc (part of
    Oracle), 30, 38, 50, 360
Support Revolution, 25
Swete, Stan, 53
Sybase, Inc. (part of SAP), 305, 340
Systems Union (part of Infor), 27

Tata Consultancy Services (TCS),
    40, 215, 312, 366
TechVentive Inc., 293, 306, 355, 357
Teller, Astro, 364–365
Tencent Holdings Ltd., 37, 39
Teradata Corp., 302, 304–307
ter Kulve, Peter, 231
Terumo BCT, Inc., 5, 6, 287
Tesla, Inc., 31, 107
Tinder, Bonnie, 322
TomTom, N.V., 32
Trane, Inc., 32
Tufts University, 94
Twilio, Inc., 31
Tzitzon, Nick, 113–115, 272

Under Armour, Inc., 5, 233–234
Uber Technologies, Inc, 31, 90
Unilever plc, 5, 231–232
Unit4 N.V., 275, 279, 352
UpperEdge, LLC 297, 302, 305–306
United Parcel Service, Inc., 42, 95
Uptake Technologies, Inc., 36,
    47–48, 330–334, 355, 366
Ultimate Software Group, Inc., 25
Urman, Yael, 260–262

Vachon, Thomas, 317
Vellante, Dave, 365–366
Velocity Technology Solutions, 223
Vembu, Sridhar, 46–48, 229, 366
Vertex, Inc., 7, 119, 288
Vijayasankar, Vijay, 94–95
Virtustream (part of Dell
    Technologies), 186

Wailgum, Thomas, viii
Wainewright, Phil, 86–87
Walgreens Boots Alliance, Inc., 32
The Wall Street Journal, 360, 364
Waterval, Huub, 169–170
Waterwatch Cooperative, 5,
    165–167
Wells Fargo & Co., 86
WhatsApp Inc., 31
Whirlpool Corp., 32
White, Topher, 74
Wingenter, Dr. Torsten, 70–71, 73